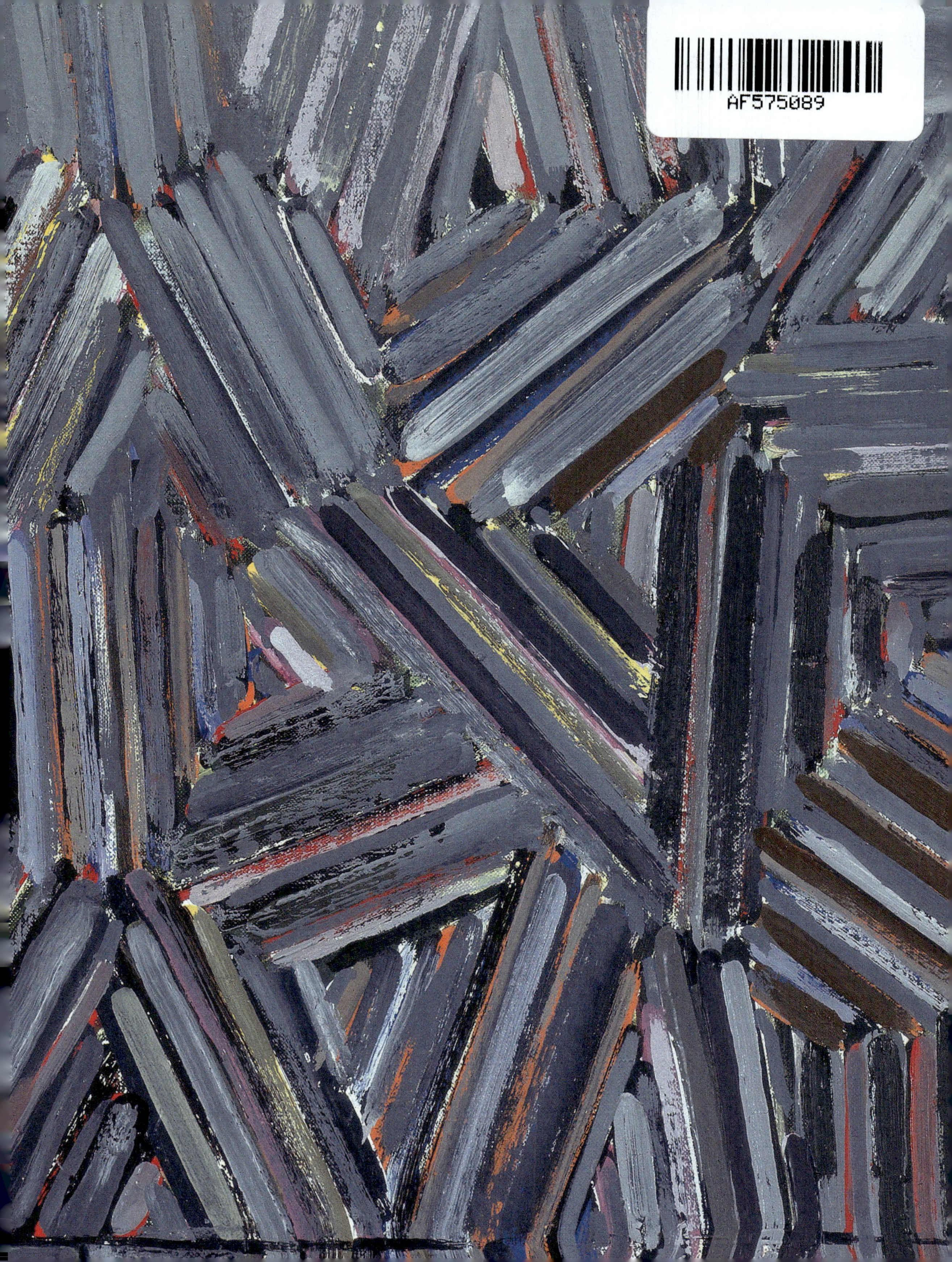

A Thing Among Things

The Art of Jasper Johns

JOHN
YAU

A Thing Among Things

The Art of Jasper Johns

JOHN YAU

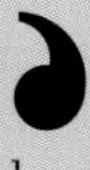

d·a·p

Distributed Art Publishers, Inc.
New York

Contents

Acknowledgments

Initially, I planned to write an essay in response to the negative reviews of Jasper Johns's exhibition "Catenary" at Matthew Marks Gallery, New York (May 7–June 25, 2005). I knew in advance that the essay would appear in the *American Poetry Review*, because its editor Arthur Vogelsang had been offering to publish my essays on art for two years. Arthur made no restrictions as to length or subject matter, which was a rare and wonderful opportunity. The essay ended up being around sixty pages, and was published over two issues. At some point, while working on the essay, I realized that I wanted to write a book, but had no idea as to who might be interested in publishing it. I gave copies of the articles to my friends, including Jeremy Sigler and Cory Reynolds, and it was Cory who brought them to the attention of Sharon Gallagher, executive director of D.A.P./Distributed Art Publishers. From the moment Sharon, Cory, and I talked, and Sharon decided to publish a book based on the two articles and a book on Johns that I had published in 1995, *The United States of Jasper Johns*, I knew that I wanted to start fresh, and not just cobble together what I had already published. It took longer than I expected to finish the book, which is often the case with writers, and everyone at D.A.P. was patient and never pressured me, which is not always the case with publishers. Susan F. Rossen, whose passion for clarity was bracing and refreshing, edited the manuscript. Todd Bradway oversaw the design and production, as well as obtained the reproductions, and did a lot more that I am not aware of. The care that each of these people showed, and the amount of love and time they put into the book, were more than I ever expected, and I can never thank them enough.

I would like to especially thank Tom Micchelli, who was the first person to read the entire manuscript, make edits, and offer suggestions. I would also like to thank Sarah Taggart, administrative assistant to Jasper Johns, who has been responding graciously to my requests for more than twenty years. Many thanks to the individuals who helped me with the research for this book: Julia Haywood, Suzanne McClelland, Craig Olson, Haley Mellin, and Liz Riviere. I am grateful to Eve Aschheim for patiently listening to me talk about some idea I had about Johns at any hour of the day or night.

Ever since I first wrote about Jasper Johns's art in the mid-1980s, he has neither tried to direct me nor commented on my reading of his work. He has patiently answered each technical question, and often gone to great lengths to explain something to me that I just didn't get. I would like to thank him for giving me the freedom to go my own way. There have been a lot of false starts, missteps, and long detours, but I would like to think that they have all been instructive.

I dedicate this book to John Ashbery and David Kermani because they were there at the very beginning, and helped me to start writing about art.

for John Ashbery and David Kermani

Introduction

I.

As nearly everyone interested in modern art knows,
Jasper Johns's early work paved the way for
the stylistic dominance of both Pop Art and Minimalism.

Johns is credited with almost single-handedly reintroducing the image into painting's two-dimensional format, and with reconciling its flatness with things seen in the world. His use of pre-existing objects such as flags and targets launched the now-ubiquitous neo-Dada predilection for emptiness and ready-mades. One consequence of this groundbreaking work having been made so early in his career is that many writers now have the luxury of pitting the older artist against his younger self. Invariably, they declare the winner to be the Johns who impacted the course of art with his first exhibition at the Leo Castelli Gallery, New York, in 1958.

There are two obvious reasons why this comparison is meaningless. First, it is akin to asking someone who has changed history to do so again, and then expressing disappointment when he does not. This becomes more problematic when that history is based on a paradigm that Johns never subscribed to, but that many of his early champions claimed was the single most important issue in painting: the iteration of its two-dimensional surface. These observers saw his Flags as flat things that underscored painting's flatness, while introducing image and reference into the realm of abstraction. However, once Johns had made his mark with an instantly recognizable statement, a number of critics began to resent the apparent difficulty of his subsequent output, particularly after Andy Warhol appeared on the scene in the early 1960s. Thus, Johns has come to be regarded as the increasingly obscure poet, while Warhol has been accepted as the populist with his finger on America's collective pulse. This simplistic viewpoint is central to two markedly divergent interpretations of Johns's work, which represents the bifurcation of American art after Abstract Expressionism. One asserts that Johns pointed art in a reductive direction marked by a necessary historical progression toward its virtual disappearance, while the other holds that he engineered a populist revolution that shifted art from an elitist position to an egalitarian one, clearing the path for the rise of Warhol. At the center of both is the belief in "the death of painting," either because this resolved all the formal issues inherent to the medium or because its dependence on the handmade was supplanted by mechanical processes and images derived from the mass media.

Rather than explicating the meaning of Johns's paintings and sculptures, each of these opposing viewpoints plugs his art into an overarching view of art history; one emphasizes opticality, painting's two-dimensional surface, and progress, while the other focuses on mechanical means, the elimination of craft, and the democratization of subject matter. Thus, the second reason it is wrong to compare Johns's later production with what preceded it is that many of the young critics who championed his early work were influenced by aspects of Clement Greenberg's formalist theorizing, particularly his emphasis on flatness and the credo that the ultimate goal of modernism was to achieve a state of pure non-objectivity, where art could only be about art. This narrative may have seemed right for Johns's use of flat things such as the American flag, and, with some minor adjustments and refinements, it may have continued to seem right for his crosshatch paintings of 1972–81. But ultimately this reading limits what art can be about, as it condemns or ignores paintings that do not comply with formalism's mandates or with other critical agendas. Consequently, it is wrong to negatively compare Johns's earlier and later work using formalism's very narrow understanding of what is permissible in painting.

One result of these paradigms of progress is that Johns's exquisitely painted, two-dimensional icons and his tactile surfaces are regarded as pivotal links between the Abstract Expressionists' expressive personal brushwork and Warhol's use of mechanical means such as silkscreen. Adapting Karl Marx's manifesto of historical progress and the rise of the worker, various theorists have posited that Warhol's seemingly anti-elitist aesthetic has been the destination of art ever since the nineteenth-century French artist Gustave Courbet's harsh, innovative realism demolished Neoclassical and Romantic ideals. By the time of Warhol's death in 1987, Johns had gone from being the precursor of populism to becoming its anathema. While granting that he had successfully resolved a theoretical stumbling block by reconciling formal flatness and everyday reality, critics complained that he had not been able to go on. In their view, by relying on mechanical means, Warhol had not only made further advances in painting while exploding its acceptable range of subject matter, but also, in a delicious irony, parodied and mimicked painting, clearly signaling that it was dead. In this scenario, Johns was relegated to a stepping-stone in an eschatological history that climaxed in the triumph of the mechanical, the use of off-the-rack images, and the obsolescence of the hand.

Starting in the late 1950s and continuing through the 1960s, Johns's *Flag* (fig. I: 1) became the linchpin in an elaborate argument about how to address Jackson Pollock's legacy, which included breaking with the Western tradition of painting as a window, as well as achieving a state of pure abstraction in which paint, freed from the burden of description, finally became paint. As Johns's champions saw it, *Flag* was both a flag and not a flag. Tactile surface *cum* solid object, it was not a window onto another space. Conflating image and format, *Flag* was a flat thing that many considered both brilliantly mocking and exceptionally efficient, a view that helped establish the take on Johns as a precise and icy ironist. While Johns's early paintings did open up, for his contemporaries, numerous ways—including those of Pop Art and Minimalism—out of what was widely regarded as a stylistic stalemate, they should not necessarily be read in terms of what they led to.

The critical consensus held that a successful radical painting conformed to the following rules: all allusions to reality had to be banished, drawing in paint was no longer necessary, paint had become paint, and the painting had to reify flatness. Greenberg's followers reasoned that Johns had shifted attention away from painting as a surface to painting as a thing, albeit a flat thing, and that allusions to actual things were permissible as long as they were two-dimensional and did not, as in Johns's work, reference the reality from which they derived. Both Johns's art and the way it was read laid the groundwork for the use of comic strips by Roy Lichtenstein, stripes by Frank Stella, and photographs by Warhol, as well as the reception of those uses. The difference between Johns and those he influenced is that they developed styles, while he eschewed them. The historical record of the past forty-odd years suggests that style, which is easily categorizable and therefore effortlessly assimilated into the critical orthodoxy, is more prized than meaning.

The shift of critical approval from Johns to Warhol occurred for a number of reasons. One was the latter's immense popularity with a wider public. This caused consternation among some critics, while delighting those for whom Warhol's increasing notoriety signaled the end of elitism. By transferring subject matter from consumer items and Hollywood icons to fine art, Warhol unintentionally promoted the view of Johns as an elitist, a throwback to an earlier era. In addition, Warhol's use of silkscreen and his effective removal of the hand from painting, combined with his mimicry of it, were seen as advances over Johns's hand-brushed encaustic. Historically and narratively, Johns existed somewhere between Pollock and Warhol: postwar art's missing link. By the late 1970s,

fig. Intro.: 1 **Frank Stella** *JILL* 1959
Enamel on canvas 90 3/8 x 78 3/4 in. (229.5 x 200 cm)
Albright-Knox Gallery, Buffalo

when many historians and theorists deemed art about art a dead end and declared that art's purpose now was to embody institutional critique, the negative judgments of Johns had become more deeply entrenched and more numerous.

At the same time, formalist critics who saw Warhol as the enemy squeezed painting into a cul-de-sac and then were quick to conclude that it had died, particularly after reaching its supposed apotheosis in Stella's "black" paintings (see fig. Intro.: 1) or in Helen Frankenthaler's color-field abstractions. Stella and Frankenthaler had arrived at an optical state in different ways. In employing a housepainter's brush to apply black commercial paint to an unsized canvas, Stella offered both the formalists and those with Marxist leanings a brilliant solution: he was the self-appointed worker who made high-minded abstractions that embodied both opticality and an impersonal way of applying pigment. He did what was necessary to satisfy different critical views of what was the right thing to do in the wake of Pollock's poured abstractions. Stella's use of housepainters' tools and materials proved that the withering away of craft was a fait accompli, a torch that would be taken up with a vengeance by Warhol when he stopped painting and began using mechanical processes. This shift was seen as another step in the historical progression toward painting's inevitable demise.

Because of his central influence on both Stella and Warhol, it seems to me that how we read Johns's oeuvre is likely to influence how we think about painting. If painting is indeed dead, then the long-accepted readings of Johns will be able to withstand an alternative reading, particularly if it does not challenge the very basis of the formalist ones that were first applied to his work and that persist in one form or another. However, if the formalists' approaches to Johns's art were wrong from the very beginning, which I believe they were, then it might also be likely that the assertion that painting is dead was wrong as well. Clearly, I am proposing that, from the start, Johns was not focused either on flatness or on the iteration of painting's two-dimensional surface, and that the issues he was addressing had nothing to do with a formalist agenda. In addition, as the artist's work of the past fifty-plus years bears out, the formal issues that he chose to address are impossible for him to definitively resolve; they remain open because they confront the reality that life both precedes our arrival and presumably continues after our departure.

II.

The view that Johns is a remote and hermetic artist began to crystallize over four decades ago, in the early 1960s, when he undertook an intense dialogue with the work and thinking of Marcel Duchamp, an artist who continues to provoke controversy and misunderstanding.

A decade later, in 1973, focusing on painting's surface, Stephen Koch contributed to an early model of Johns's project to which many still subscribe:

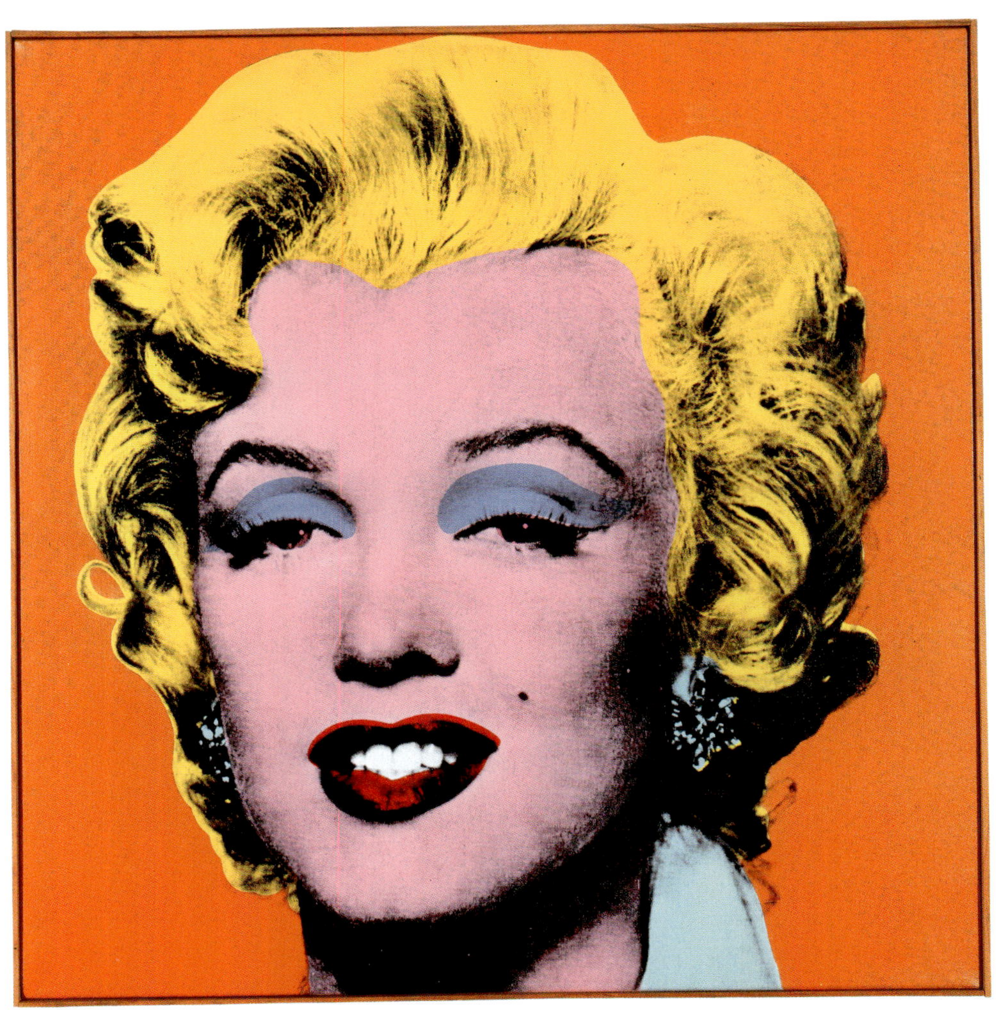

fig. Intro.: 2 **Andy Warhol** *SHOT ORANGE MARILYN* 1964
Synthetic polymer paint and silkscreen ink on canvas 40 x 40 in. (101.6 x 101.6 cm)

> These young Americans followed Duchamp's chilly lead down two parallel paths. The first begins in Duchamp's arch obscurantism, the part of his work that culminated in the *Large Glass* in the Philadelphia Museum. That obscurantism led to the hermetic style, to an abstracted and cryptic surface in which the visual struggle, the "push-pull," was an unresolved struggle over the disclosure of meaning itself. The result at its best produced a sumptuous surface on which meaning was significantly refused. Duchamp Path Number One led to Jasper Johns.[1]

Koch described the other possibility as follows:

> The Second Path—a parallel one—moves from Duchamp's wise-guy wit, from the mustached *Mona Lisa* and from his bottle rack and urinal as sculpture, through the opposite of hermeticism. It passes through absolute legibility. Here the picture surface discloses its meaning instantly. But it is the afterglow of the instant that matters here. For Path Number Two leads to a special region where cynicism and naivety cannot be distinguished, where populism and romantic decadence merge. That is, it leads to Warhol. Depending on which path you prefer, Warhol is possibly Duchamp's greatest pupil. He is surely Duchamp's most influential pupil.[2]

Koch's view articulates an attitude about Johns and Warhol that dominates nearly all discussions of their work. It is easy to see why. In 1964, for example, Johns completed *Watchman* and *According to What* (figs. VI: 1, 2), which Kirk Varnedoe characterized as disjunctive assemblages.[3] In that same year, Warhol finished the silkscreen paintings *Sixteen Jackies* and *Shot Orange Marilyn* (fig. Intro.: 2). Johns's work demands—and rewards—close attention; it is further enhanced by one's knowledge of art history, while Warhol's portraits of celebrities decidedly do not.

In the configuration that Koch set up, and that many observers are content to follow and elaborate upon, lurks the tired old debate of opacity and difficulty versus transparency and legibility. While Koch applied the test of "absolute legibility" only to Warhol, he could easily have done so to Stella, who famously dismissed critical discourse on his early work with "What you see is what you see."[4] Thus, two seemingly very different and even oppositional artists, one who was central to Pop Art and the other who was key to Minimalism, are linked by the fact that their work "discloses its meaning instantly." Johns, however, even at this relatively very early stage in his career, had departed from this art-world standard, but critics found it necessary to shoehorn his work into the formalist camp that valorizes the literal over all else.

As Koch put it, Johns creates a "sumptuous surface on which meaning [is] significantly refused." This suggests that Johns has emptied meaning out of his art, and that its emptiness is what distinguishes it from Warhol's. Johns, of course, complicates this by incorporating images of real things (a flag, a map) into his work. But never mind about that. To follow the formalist argument, which is different from Koch's, Johns uses things to comment upon painting's essential flatness. In other words, what you see is not what you think you see. It is this gap between seeing and knowing that has caused all sorts of misreadings of Johns's art, particularly in regard to its relationship to his personal life.

If we understand Johns's paintings as commentaries on painting's formal identity, we are apt to regard him as a brilliant, witty, somewhat brittle artist involved in an esoteric, even academic enterprise. Is it any surprise, therefore, that many critics see the difficulty (or the reputed meaninglessness) of Johns's post-1960s production as a calculated affront to the anti-elitist stance of American culture and, by extension, American art? The public understandably prefers art that is transparent, easy to get. Johns's Flags and Targets are a prelude to Warhol's imagery, or so the mantra goes. The former's formalist use of the commonplace led to the latter's use of such popular icons as Elvis, Marilyn, and Jackie, while Johns's preference for encaustic was seen as old-fashioned and Warhol's employment of mechanical processes was regarded as cutting-edge. And while Johns's *Flag* may have been a brilliant solution to the problems of painting's identity, the artist's later work does nothing nearly as innovative, at least in formalist terms. For one thing, it does not have to; once a problem has been solved, it is absurd to solve it again. It would seem that, for Johns, there was nowhere to go but downhill.

The increasingly negative views of Johns's oeuvre since the early 1980s are all too predictable. Not only has he disappointed popular expectations by moving on, rather than repeating a signature style into perpetuity, but he has also become the poster boy for an obsolete form of formalist criticism, whether it truly explicates his work or not. Nowadays, once we "get" that Johns has transposed into his work Pablo Picasso's *Woman in Straw Hat* (fig. X: 2) or a fevered figure from Matthias Grünewald's *Isenheim Altarpiece* (c. 1512–16), we do not bother to look deeper. Those tapped into Greenbergian criticism will know there is no "why," and the uninitiated will shrug at the prospect of a "why" they assume will be too obscure to be useful in any meaningful way. It follows then that we can learn nothing about ourselves or about life from looking at Johns's paintings. This dead-end is, of course, formalism's legacy.

If one accepts this reading of Johns's art, one is likely to reach one of two conclusions: that his game is fun and stimulating, or that he is an intellectual elitist whose work has no relevance in an art world of instantly ascertainable meaning. As this debate circles itself like a ghost chasing its shadow, I cannot help but wonder whether there might not be another way to see Johns's oeuvre, which is the point of this book. But first I must raise some questions, the answers to which will help form the basis of my argument.

The primary questions are these: What if it is possible to identify a singular, touchstone vision in Johns's work, to which he has habitually returned throughout his career? What if this vision is not hermetic, but derived from daily life? Might it not be regarded as a key to Johns's art? Can it be claimed that the very different sets of themes, techniques, materials, and subjects that he has utilized within a given period—a map of the continental United States, a coffee can crammed with dirty brushes, a bathtub with a painting by Picasso taped above it, or a Catenary titled *Near the Lagoon* (fig. XI: 6)—all resonate with that central idea? Would it then be possible to conclude that, while the visual facts keep changing, seemingly without preplanning or even an internal logic, the basic core of the perception preoccupying Johns remains consistent and nameable? Would not this conflation of a recurring vision with radically different styles and methods suggest that, while his art might be difficult, it is not deliberately closed? Might it not also evoke the possibility that the artist is compelled to work the way he does in order to deepen his insights into this pursuit? Finally, what, if anything, does this vision have to offer?

By now it is obvious that I am proposing that a significant number of Johns's works are directly connected to, as well as revealing of, a concern that has absorbed him from the outset. I believe that the power of this project has enabled him to take a preformed thing (a visual ready-made), be it a map or a motif from Picasso, and not only "make it new" but also make it work in a different way than it was originally intended. I aim to establish that John's reuse of previously explored motifs (a semicircle, for example) is not, as many have argued, a self-referential form of quotation, but a deepening of the thing's meaning. In effect, the artist moved away from flags and maps and located new things or actions, did so within a specific, highly defined context that has inflected them with meaning, and determined their placement according to a single, generative vision. In order for Johns to feel satisfied with his work, he must seamlessly and efficiently integrate his things into an exacting visual order determined by what he calls "necessity." In contrast to those who accuse him of being hermetic, I propose that the increasing visual complexity of Johns's art is the result of his gaining a further, more powerful understanding of his primary fixation: What does it mean to be a thing caught in, and carried along by, time?

In order to transform his insights into art, Johns has had to resolve two formal problems. One is that the materials he uses (encaustic, Sculp-metal, bronze, oil paint) must enable him to register and reconstruct his perception, which, as he understands it, consists of two interlocking modes, "looking" and "spying" (see Chapter Six). The other is that this dualistic perception must be articulated within a figure/ground situation in order to embody his materialist understanding of reality, which is that he is a thing among things, weighted by gravity and dragged forward by time. And yet, despite the current of consciousness of time and mortality running through his work, I do not regard his project as being morbidly fixated or sense that his art exudes despair. At this point, I think it useful to consider what the artist himself has said about his choice of subjects and motifs. During a 1998–99 conversation with Richard S. Field, Johns stated, "I think that most art which begins to make a statement fails to make a statement because the methods used are too schematic or artificial. I think that one wants from a painting a sense of life. The final suggestion, the final statement, has to be not a deliberate statement, but a helpless statement. It has to be what you cannot avoid saying, not what you set out to say."[5] Here Johns amplified something he had said to Michael Crichton in the mid-1970s: "I wanted to know what was helpless in my behavior—how I would behave out of necessity."[6] Both "helpless" and "necessity" suggest that Johns's preoccupations lie not in social behavior, but in what is fundamental to all human beings: sleeping and dreaming, consumption and excretion, involuntary thoughts and memories, aging. These are actions over which we have little or no control. For all of Johns's dazzling intellect and technical virtuosity, it is the bodily realm of his existence that he has anchored in his art. It is a necessary (to use Johns's word) part of the equation.

Johns's comments to Field hardly sound like those of someone who is deliberately remote, obfuscating, or retreating. A detached artist is unlikely to state that what "one wants from painting {is} a sense of life." But can Johns's long-held commitment to the "helpless statement" be formally and philosophically reconciled with his belief that a painting must convey "a sense of life"? And more important, does Johns's work convey what exactly this sense of life is? These are among the questions I try to address in this book.

INTRODUCTION
NOTES

1. Stephen Koch, ***Stargazer: The Life, World, and Films of Andy Warhol*** (New York/London: Marion Boyars, 1973; repr. 1985, 1991), p. v.

2. Ibid.

3. Kirk Varnedoe, *Jasper Johns: A Retrospective*, exh. cat., with an essay by Roberta Bernstein (New York: Museum of Modern Art, 1996), p. 223.

4. Interview by Bruce Glaser with Frank Stella and Donald Judd, broadcast by WBAI-FM, New York, Feb. 1964; published as "Questions to Stella and Judd," ed. Lucy R. Lippard, *ARTNews* 65, 5 (Sept. 1966), pp. 55–61. Stella: "My painting is based on the fact that only what can be seen there is there. All I want anyone to get out of my paintings and all I ever get out of them is the fact that you can see the whole idea without any confusion. What you see is what you see."

5. *www.yale.edu.opa28.n17story4.html*

6. Quoted in Michael Crichton, *Jasper Johns*, exh. cat. (New York: Harry N. Abrams, in association with the Whitney Museum of American Art, 1977), p. 27.

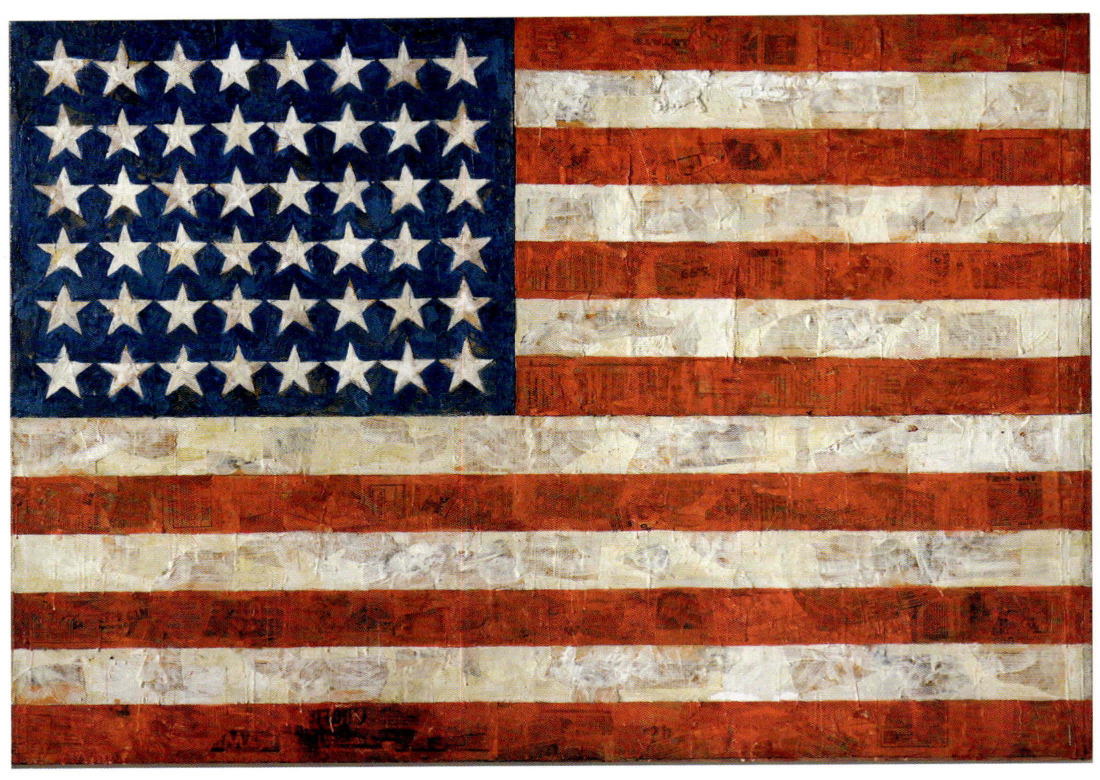

fig. I: 1 **Jasper Johns** *FLAG* 1954–55
Encaustic, oil, and collage on fabric mounted on plywood (three panels)
42 1/4 x 60 5/8 in. (107.3 x 154 cm)
The Museum of Modern Art, New York. Gift of Philip Johnson in honor of Alfred H. Barr Jr.

Chapter 1

I.

Jasper Johns has said
on numerous occasions
that the inspiration for *Flag* (fig. I: 1)
was a dream in which
he saw himself
painting an American flag.

To think of *Flag* as a literal response to a dream that the artist re-created in waking life does not contest the formalist tenet that painting should be about painting, and the restating of its flat surface. While this reading has been widely embraced, it is wrong on several counts.

For Clement Greenberg and other formalist theorists and critics writing in the mid-twentieth century, painting's highest goal is a self-reflexive one: it is about its essential identity as a two-dimensional plane. In the year that Johns finished *Flag*, he also completed *White Flag* (1955), *Green Target* (fig. I: 2), and *Figure 5* (fig. I: 3). All but *Flag* are monochromatic. Largely made of encaustic, which was then a little-used medium, they synthesize the surface with commonplace objects, entities so familiar (flags, targets, stenciled numerals and letters) that some observers christened them with the Duchampian term "ready-mades."[1] Critics deduced that the ready-mades Johns chose were two-dimensional and therefore synonymous with the picture plane. According to this viewpoint, *Flag* is about nothing but itself, since a flag, like a painting, is basically a flat piece of pigment-covered cloth; Johns had done the unexpected, conflating the two into one. Tacitly acknowledging Greenberg's theorizing about painting's two-dimensionality, as well as opening painting up to familiar images, the work was embraced by many who, while influenced by Greenberg, wanted to establish themselves as independent thinkers.

In 1956, less than two years before Johns's first, groundbreaking exhibition in 1958 at the Leo Castelli Gallery, New York, Jackson Pollock died in a car accident. According to Greenberg and others, Pollock's work had been in decline throughout the 1950s, and Willem de Kooning's *Women* paintings constituted a definite retreat from abstraction.[2] Many felt that painting had reached an impasse, and neither artists nor critics seemed to know what should happen next. In this context, Johns appeared to be just the right artist for a younger, emerging generation of formalist-minded critics to champion and for his peers to emulate. It is not difficult to understand why these young writers embraced Johns's work. Here was someone in his twenties living in New York and making hybrid paintings of flags, targets, numbers, and letters that were unlike anything else being done at the time. His art seemed to have nothing to do with Abstract Expressionism and its slashing, emotive brushwork. Rather, it appeared to be a near-perfect fit for the pre-existing formalist paradigms of these writers. And so they forced it into an account that promoted their own critical stance while catapulting Johns to stardom, even as they ignored his deepest preoccupations and the focus of his project: common experience.

II.

All of the readings of Johns's groundbreaking early work that I have briefly mentioned arise from the seminal genesis of *Flag*, in which, as stated above, the artist purportedly set out to re-create a flat object seen in a dream.

His objective in making *Flag*, however, was not to reconstruct the flag, but something far more elusive, which was to reconstruct the dream itself. This assertion necessarily leads to a re-evaluation of Johns's definition of seeing, which includes dreaming. Rather than

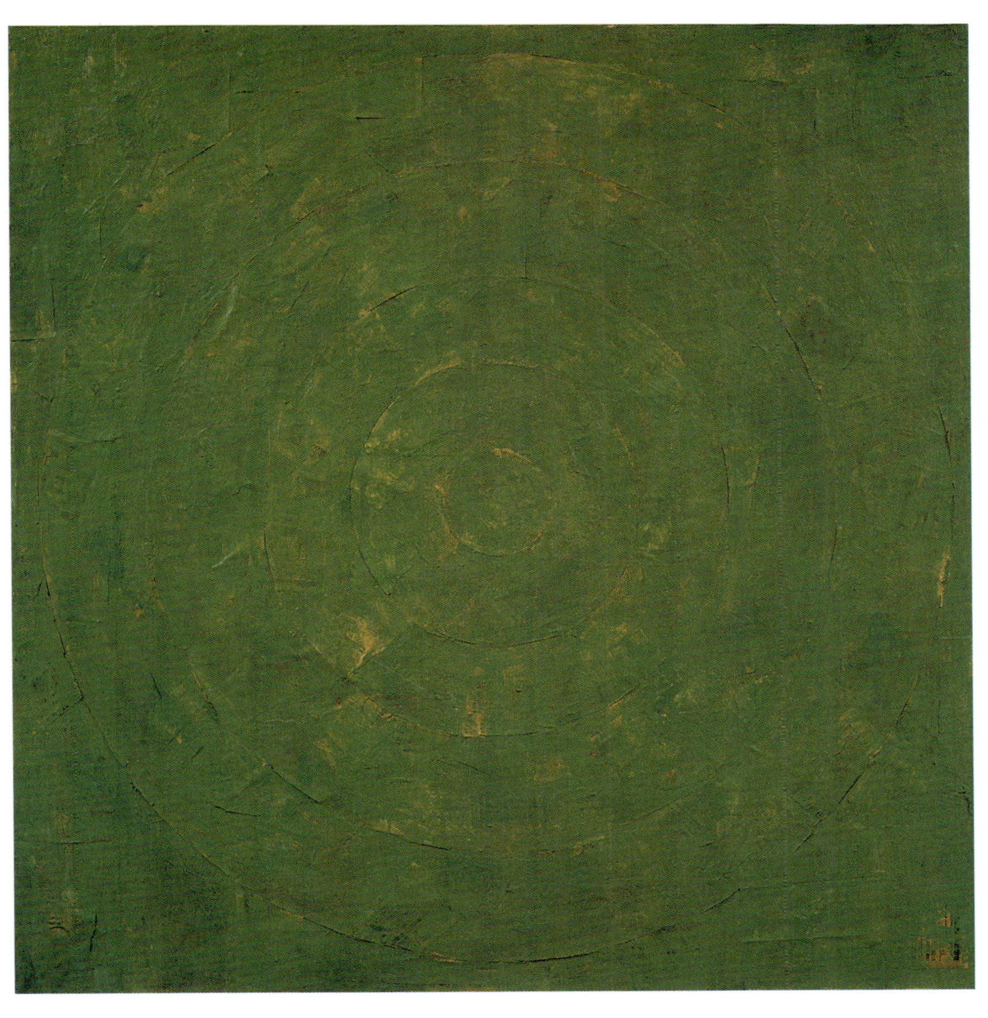

Jasper Johns *GREEN TARGET* 1955 fig. I: 2
Encaustic on newspaper and cloth over canvas 60 x 60 in. (152.4 x 152.4 cm)
The Museum of Modern Art, New York. Richard S. Zeisler Fund

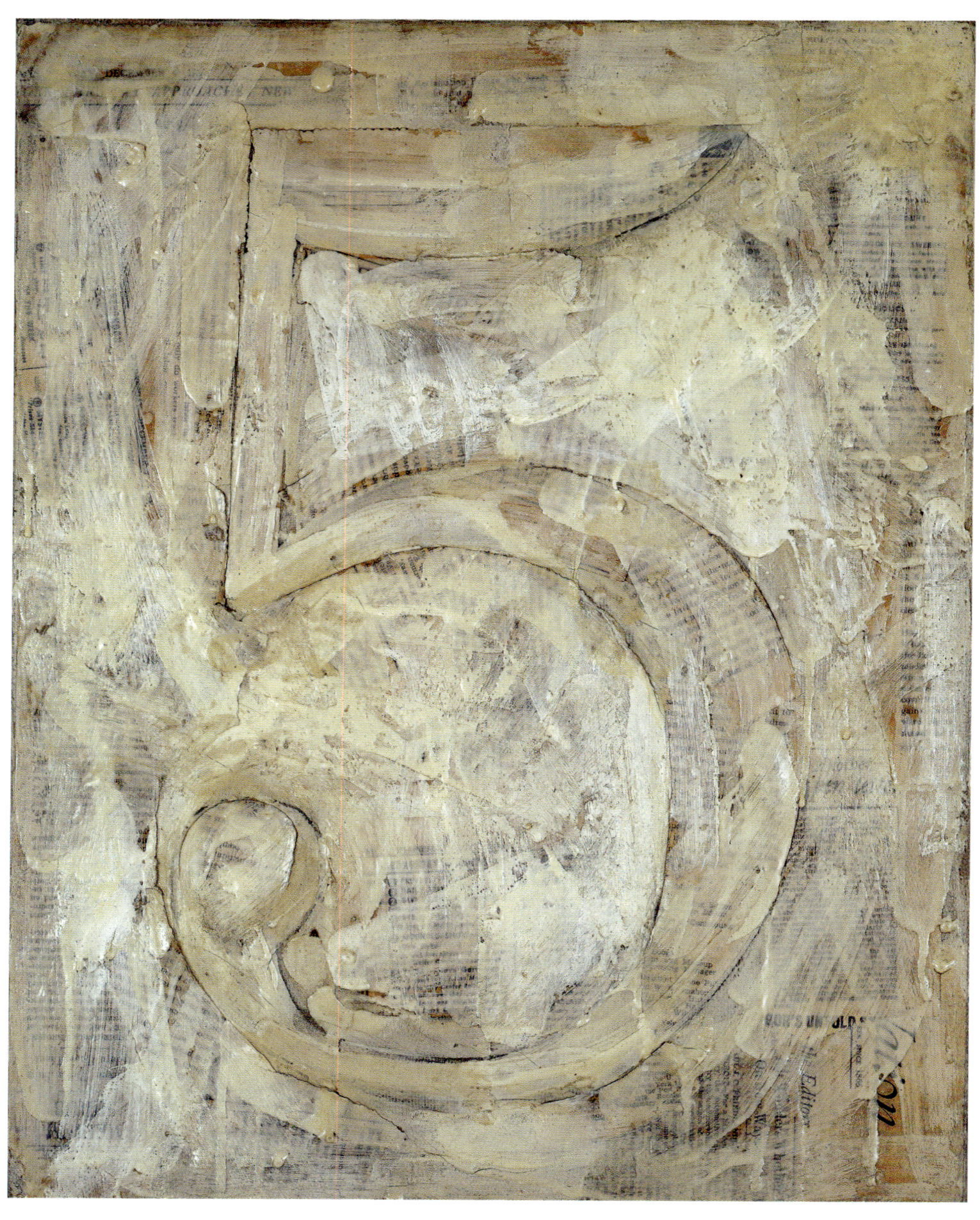

fig. I: 3 **Jasper Johns** *FIGURE 5* 1955
Encaustic and collage on canvas 17 1/2 x 14 in. (44.5 x 35.6 cm)
Collection the artist

manipulating the ocular conventions governing realism and abstraction, his goal was to reconstruct the mental perceptions basic to all dreams, not his particular dream about the flag. Had he confined himself to interpreting this one dream, he most likely would have utilized a psychoanalytic model explicating the meanings of dream symbols. In effect, he would have been making a deliberate statement rather than a helpless one.

Flag is simultaneously the culmination and the beginning of an unwavering, career-long investigation of those experiences over which an individual has little or no control—sleeping and dreaming, our feeling the effects of gravity, our need for food and drink, and our entrapment in and vulnerability to time. Johns's work is distinguished from that of others by his connection of sight, which in *Timaeus* Plato connected to human intelligence or the mind, with those senses associated with the material body, which the philosopher believed to be the home of what he saw as the other, less gifted modes of apprehension. In so doing, the artist rejected an age-old hierarchy, which privileged vision above the other senses; he also defined a material realm of shared experience, even if its specific manifestations, such as dreams, isolate us from one another. In addition, by bringing the different senses and modes of apprehension into closer proximity, Johns began his career by openly rejecting the theory that the goal of painting was to culminate in a state of pure opticality.

Johns's alignment of sight with the other senses, particularly touch and the awareness of gravity, is crucial to the understanding of his work. In fact, he does something far more radical; he also joins the ocular with the textual. By connecting, as he did in *Flag*, these two, at times antagonistic, modes of comprehension without favoring either, the artist subverted the visual convention that has dominated Western art beginning with the Greeks. In fact, the ocular is thought to be intrinsic to the Christian tradition, while the textual is considered to be a cornerstone of the Hebraic tradition. The irony, of course, is that the critics who embraced *Flag* honored the optical above all else. Ultimately, Johns's early champions recognized his innovations on their own terms, rather than on the far larger and more challenging ones his art marked out.

Johns's juxtaposition of the ocular and textual modes within a single work should be framed by his abiding preoccupation with the figure/ground (or subject/background) relationship. This can be defined as when there is a primary or positive shape, the figure, which is noticeably separated from the surrounding ground, or negative shape. Traditionally, the figure is the dominant element of the dynamic. In reconstructing a dream, Johns recognized that the "seeing" that occurs in dreams subverts all the accepted views of figure/ground. Where does the dreamer end and the dream begin? Does the figure inhabit a dream (landscape) or does the dream inhabit the dreamer? Or, as *Flag* seems to ask, are dreamer (figure) and dream (ground) both distinct and inseparable? This vision of indivisibility is one key to understanding the foundation of Johns's art; it is also vital to his approach to figure/ ground. At very different points in his career, he has incorporated motifs in which figure and ground are indivisible, as in the map of the continental United States, with its landmass as the figure and oceans as ground.

For Johns seeing is not a matter of isolating one thing from all the rest, but of acknowledging and processing simultaneity. In *Flag*, for example, we both see a flag and read the collaged fragments just below the encaustic surface. Each demands a different kind of engagement. The artist's concept of simultaneity dissolved the traditional figure/ground relationship and replaced it with a new philosophical paradigm. In 1959 Johns cited "Leonardo's idea ('Therefore, O painter, do not surround your bodies with lines...') that the boundary of a body is neither a part of the enclosed body nor a part of the surrounding atmosphere." In the same statement, he also wrote, "Generally, I am opposed to painting which is concerned with conceptions of simplicity. Everything looks busy to me."[3] (It would seem that Johns was already implicitly critical of the reductive approach of Frank Stella and the literalism of Andy Warhol before these artists became known.) For Johns there is no boundary between figure and ground, because nothing separates us from reality. In addition, it is the busyness of reality, which includes dreams, that he seeks to preserve in his art. Consequently, his comprehension of simultaneity led him to construct intensely compressed, layered works, sometimes with objects attached or inserted, and to paint two bronze sculptures. In each of them, both entitled *Painted Bronze* and dating to 1960 (figs. III: 4, 5), Johns successfully challenged the traditional understanding of figure/ground in an articulation of the relationship between them that is consistent with his vision of reality.

By painting *Flag* from a dream, Johns both defined and kept true to his project, which was premised on a kind of self-interrogation: "I had a wish to determine what I was. I had the feeling I could do anything.... But if I could do anything I wanted to do, then what I wanted to do was find out what I did that other people didn't, what it was that other people weren't.... It was not a matter of joining a group effort, but of isolating myself from any group. I wanted to know what was helpless in my behavior—how I would behave out of necessity."[4] While Johns's observations suggest that he is both elitist and hermetic, it is useful to remember that the dream underscored his isolation from others, as well as suggested that this state was common to others. In the flag, particularly the canton, where the white, five-pointed stars are arranged on a blue field, Johns recognized that his isolation was a widespread condition. Each star (or dreamer) is part of the blue night sky (a larger, common reality), while isolated from all other stars (or dreams).

Johns repeatedly uses the word "what" rather than the expected "who." This choice underscores his determination to delve beneath the dominion of appearances, where who we are is paramount, in order to discover what is "helpless in [his] behavior," the passive and involuntary conditions that compose shared experience. He wants to define the essential nature of his material being and not to assert his social identity or hide behind it. For while we have not had the same dream of a flag that he had, we too have dreams. Basic to Johns's use of the word "what" is the constantly changing matter of which we are made, and that, more than anything else, connects us. Johns equates helpless behavior with the physical basis of our existence, something we cannot escape. We are all at the mercy of time, which is ruthless. Being able to see, even with our mind's eye as we do in a dream, does not save us.

In order to re-enact a dream and be true to its reality, it is very likely that Johns asked: What does it mean to remember a dream? The Chinese philosopher Chuang Tzu (c. 399–295 B.C.) put it most succinctly:

> Once, I, Chuang Tzu, dreamed I was a butterfly and was happy as a butterfly. I was conscious that I was quite pleased with myself, but I did not know that I was Tzu Suddenly I awoke, and there was I, visibly Tzu. I do not know whether it was Tzu dreaming that he was a butterfly or the butterfly dreaming that he was Tzu. Between Tzu and the butterfly there must be some distinction. (But one may be the other.) This is called the transformation of things.[5]

Anticipating Johns's materialist understanding of reality, and his inseparability from it, Chuang Tzu spoke about himself and the butterfly as if they were things, material objects, which are interchangeable. Understood in terms of painting, one could ask which is the figure and which is the ground. The philosopher and the butterfly are bonded and transposable.

Like Chuang Tzu, Johns finds the meaning of reality in apparent contradictions, and in an awareness that the sense of sight is not to be fully trusted. If appearance and reality —the butterfly and Tzu—can seem identical, how does one decide what is true? During the course of working on *Flag*, it seems that the artist soon understood that a dream, whatever its actual content, is by its very nature (subjectivity experienced by an individual) the diametric opposite of the collective history symbolized by the flag. By undertaking the painting, Johns most likely recognized from the outset that he had to look at the American flag with fresh eyes in order to express its origin as a dream. And that, in order to stay true to his experience, he had to make the flag reveal the unavoidable state of separateness inherent in dreaming, and to communicate the extensive nature of our remoteness from one another. Johns had had a dream, a common occurrence. It was not something that had singled him out. The effort to be objective about a subjective experience required that he remain detached, observant, and analytic—a method of observation that we associate with science.

The ambivalent and shifting relationship between mind and body is reinforced while recalling a dream. For when the reality of a dream is intense enough to seep into waking life, we might well ask, what is the connection between our minds and bodies when we are dreaming? Which self has had the dream, the waking or the sleeping self? What is the dynamic between these selves when, as we all know, the dreaming self is quite capable of committing acts that would horrify the waking self? It is in the specifics of Johns's reconstruction of his dream that the meaning of *Flag* resides.

If we choose to accept that Johns literally transposed a thing seen in a dream to the realm of painting, then we must acknowledge that the work is simultaneously autobiographical and rooted in the belief in a unified "I," an authorial being who inhabits a stable world in which change is predictable and reality is rational. We might also conclude that Johns's interest in the flag is ironic, but, at the same time, purely formal; it confines its attention to a flag, a flat object whose design is made up of red and white horizontal stripes and a blue square, or canton, containing a set number of white stars. In addition, if we are convinced that *Flag* is a painting about painting, then we are likely to believe that the dream also helped the artist solve an aesthetic issue identified, for the most part, by Greenberg and like-minded thinkers. But if we do not buy that *Flag* is necessarily rooted in either a unified "I," where the waking and the dreaming self are both fixed and the same, or that it is a comment on painting's irreducible nature, then we must try to see what Johns was striving to achieve while assembling it.

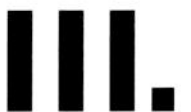

The outward goal Johns initially set was plain enough; the painting should resemble an American flag circa 1954.

He cut a bedsheet into three different-size rectangles, each corresponding to one section of the flag: its canton (blue square with white stars), an adjacent rectangle corresponding to the upper seven stripes (four red and three white), and a third rectangle comprising the lower six stripes (three red and three white) running the entire length of the flag. He planned to complete each section separately and then join them when the oil paint had dried.

Johns most likely believed that separating the sheet into three sections would allow him to more effectively focus on the problems raised by juxtaposing one clearly delineated area of color against another. However, as he subsequently made clear in two distinct places in the painting, he must have recognized that, by first separating and then rejoining the sheet, he was paralleling the process of remembering his dream. To reconstruct a dream after it no longer exists, the dreamer must grasp at separate, often elusive, parts and consciously piece them together. In Johns's case, he reunited the United States or, to put it another way, he physically repeated both the act of remembering a dream and what the flag symbolizes: the uniting of separate states. He did not make the flag synonymous with a two-dimensional surface, as so many have argued; rather, he made the construction of the painting synonymous with remembering a dream.

Johns might have chosen a bedsheet because it was the largest piece of blank cloth he had on hand. As far as we know about his early production (in 1954 he destroyed all the works in his studio), he made small, boxlike objects before he worked on *Flag*, and might not have had or perhaps could not even afford to have a large piece of canvas available. Painting on canvas was not yet part of his practice, and to spend money on this support was likely to have been extremely difficult for someone with few resources. While the act of using one's bedsheet suggests the urgency with which Johns approached his subject, it is also very likely that he was aware that he was beginning with the very site of dreams, possibly even the one he was using when he dreamed about the flag. In order to turn the bedsheet into the subject of his dream, he had to cut it up and put it back together, actions that echo both the act of remembering and that of analytic thinking.

The other insight that Johns must have had about using a sheet concerns the nature of dreaming. In a single, brilliant stroke, he transformed painting's traditional figure/ground relationship into a metaphor for the dreamer and the dream. If the dreamer is the

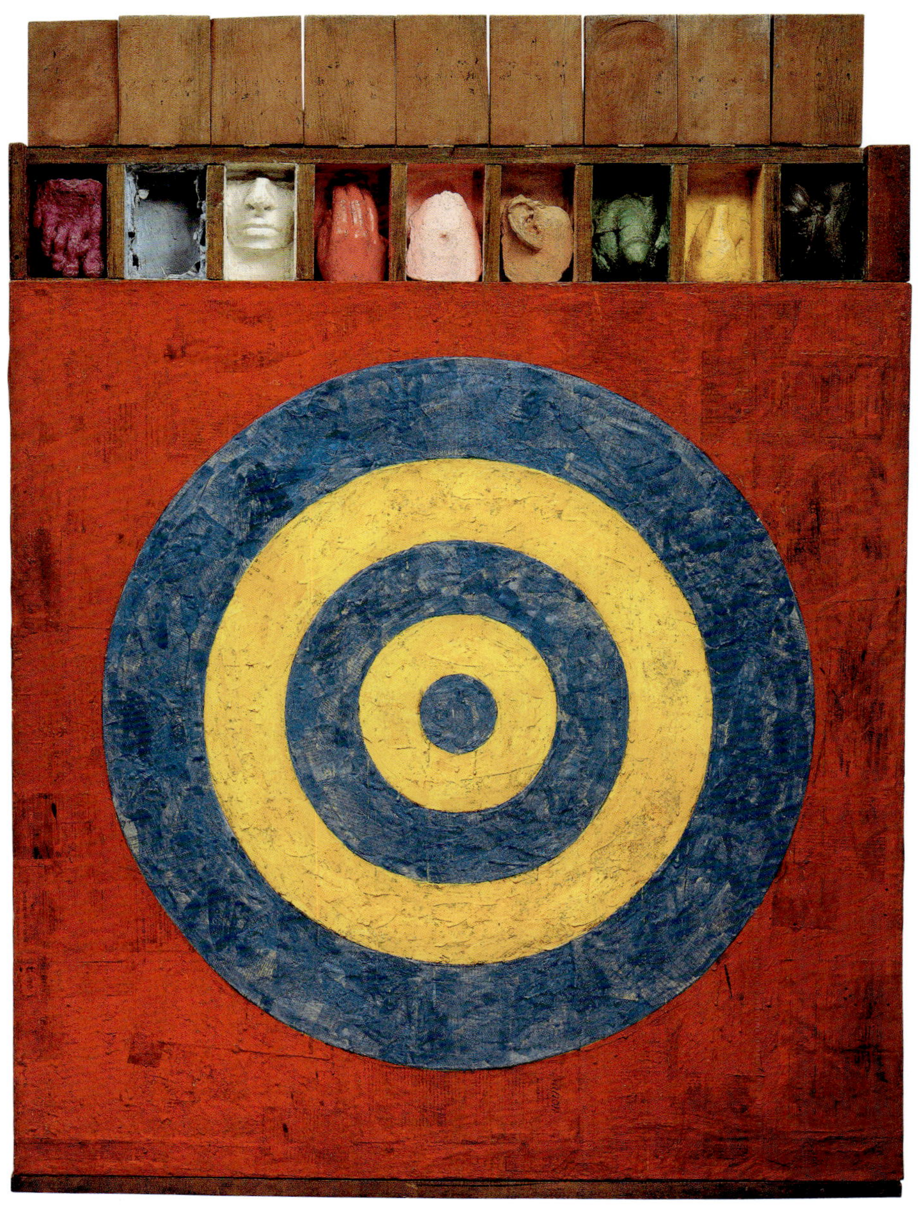

Jasper Johns *TARGET WITH PLASTER CASTS* 1955 fig. I: 4
Encaustic and collage on canvas with objects 51 x 44 x 3 1/2 in. (129.5 x 111.8 x 8.8 cm)
Collection David Geffen, Los Angeles

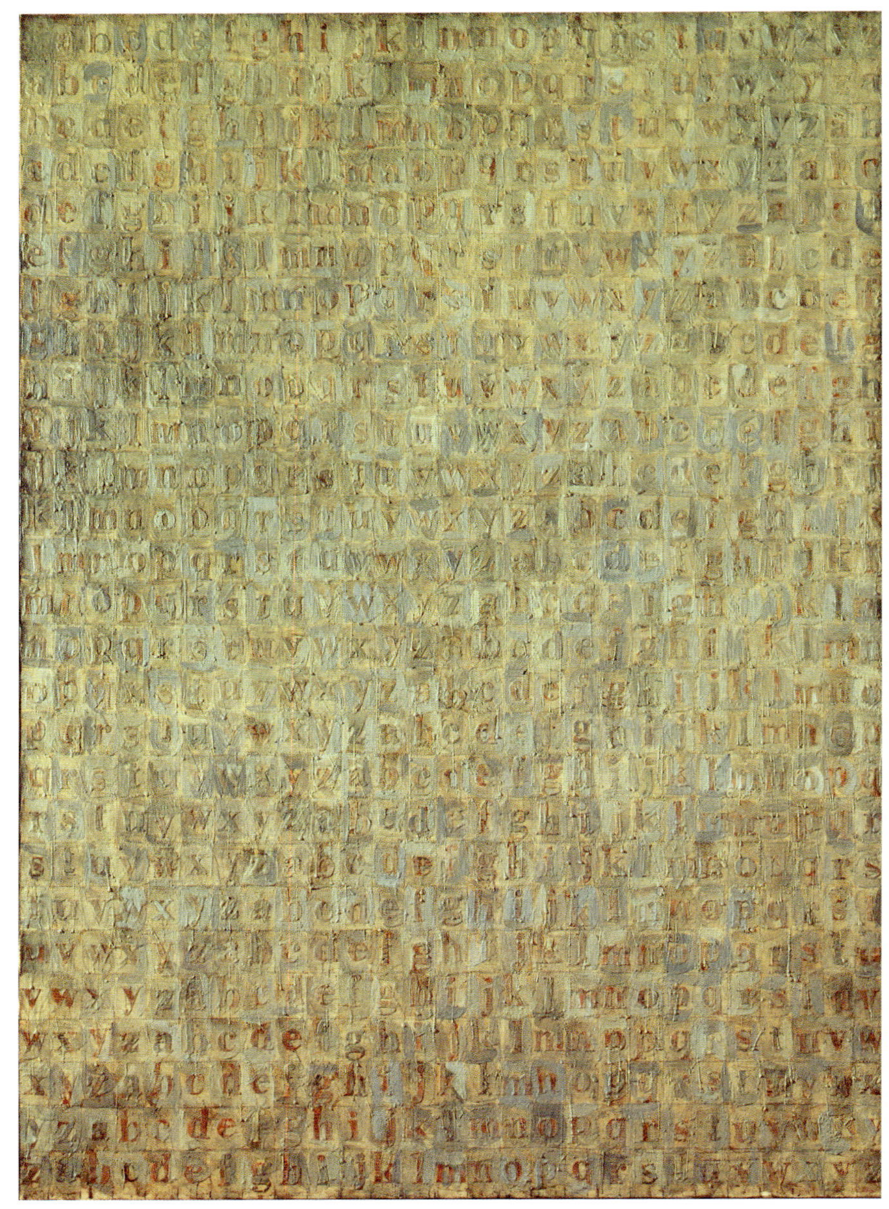

fig. I: 5 **Jasper Johns** *GRAY ALPHABETS* 1956
Beeswax and oil on newspaper and paper on canvas 66 1/8 x 48 3/4 in. (168 x 123.8 cm)
The Menil Collection, Houston

figure and the dream is the ground, he probably asked himself, what is the actual ground of a dream? One answer is the body; a dream is an experience that occurs in the interior rather than the exterior world. In *Flag* the dream is the flag, which Johns rendered synonymous with the sheet (the site of dreams) and the newspaper (evidence of both daily life and time). In *Flag* figure, ground, time, and day-to-day existence are indivisible. If Johns had depicted himself working on a painting of a flag, he would have removed the dream from its site and transposed it into a conventional narrative. This would have diluted the dream's power, a primary experience that he wanted to reconstruct.

In *Flag* a physical thing and the rectangular picture plane are one and the same because any standard ground would have turned the experience into an anecdote, a moment recollected in tranquillity, which is exactly the opposite of what Johns was after. By making the dream a palpable object with no ground, while simultaneously bonding image and sheet, Johns held on to his dream experience in the present tense. Meanwhile, the newspaper collage locates the dream in time because dreams are not timeless. The present tense is the sine qua non of Johns's work, the condition it inhabits and defines, even as it anticipates the future and/or looks back at the past. This understanding of the power of the present tense—the full-frontal immediacy of experience—is what further connects Johns to Pollock, and to the latter's subversion of painting as window, a tradition that had held since the Renaissance.

Johns linked many of his central preoccupations in *Flag*: the helpless body, the proximity of sight and the other senses, the act of seeing as acknowledgment of simultaneity, the ambivalent figure/ground relationship, and the recognition that we are at the mercy of time. For Johns, as many of his subsequent paintings and sculptures make evident, figure and ground are at once distinct and inextricably bound together. Neither an abstract plane nor a plane for abstraction, the ground is the artist's analogue for reality, in which we are caught and can never fully escape.

Green Target (fig. I: 2) can be understood as Johns's take on the phenomenological paradox that it is impossible to grasp, through sight or any of our other senses, our own bodies in their entirety. The work itself is a collage of cutout newspaper and cloth, all painted the same green. As with *Flag*, figure and ground are inseparable because the body exists in isolation from itself and others; it inhabits both a common, pre-existing world and a specific one that cannot be fully understood. *Target with Plaster Casts* (fig. I: 4) stresses the fragmentary, disconnected nature of sensory experience through the differently colored body parts encased in wooden cubbyholes, an empty compartment, and a cast that is unrecognizable. In *Target with Four Faces* (1955), each visage possesses a nose, mouth, and cheeks, but no eyes—which emphasizes our inability to see or experience our physical selves totally. In all three of these Targets, Johns conflated the visual and tactile, sight and recognition.

The letters in *Gray Alphabets* (fig. I: 5) and the numerals in *Gray Numbers* (1958) conflate the ocular, textual, and physical without privileging any one of them. Contrary to those who believe *Flag* is about painting's flatness, and that Johns's choice of motifs—the target, the alphabet, and numbers—represents his commitment to formalist pursuits, I would advance that *Flag* and these subsequent paintings are actually the first manifestations of the artist's preoccupation with the body's existence in time and space, with those states that are inherent and unavoidable, and with the fact that isolation is the innate condition of existence. He realized that, in his art, he had to address the figure/ground relationship in ways that clarified these concerns.

IV.

While working on *Flag*,
Johns switched from enamel to encaustic
because he got tired of waiting
for the oil pigments to dry.

He also found it difficult to keep colors from bleeding into one another. Having previously experimented with encaustic in a small sculptural object, *Star* (1954; Menil Collection, Houston), which he made for a friend, Johns realized that the medium's properties could help him resolve the compositional problems posed by the design of the flag. The slow, deliberate way *Flag* came into existence suggests that the meaning of the painting was not immediately apparent to Johns upon awakening, but that he arrived at it during the course of working on the picture. Once he had these insights, he built upon them, and has continued to do so ever since.

Encaustic is simply beeswax. It comes in a solid form, which must be heated slowly until it melts into a watery state. This allows one to mix pigment into it until it achieves the desired saturation. As soon as the liquid encaustic is removed from the heat and brushed onto or soaked into a strip of cloth or newsprint, it begins to harden. Because it hardens almost instantly into a solid layer, unlike oil paint, which dries from the outside in, the artist can overlay discrete coats rather quickly. After the painting is complete, the surface of the encaustic must be heated again, or "burned in," with a hot iron; this seals the painting. In this last step, the temperature must be just right, or the wax will loosen and drip.

Encaustic can also be used as a preservative to seal ephemeral, collaged materials like paper, protecting them from humidity and light. Although Johns used encaustic before he painted *Flag*, it was not until the first *Map* (1960) and *Water Freezes* (1961) that he began to identify the medium's two states—solid and liquid—as the poles of reality, which are structure and dissolution. In the largely white *Figure 5*, the numeral's silhouette is barely distinguishable from the field of encaustic drips and brushstrokes, some of which are aligned with the collaged figure's physical edge, while others are brushed over the form. Here, Johns explored the inseparability of figure and ground, as well as tacitly acknowledging that the combination of the number 5 and encaustic mirrors the symbiotic states of form and chaos. In later works, Johns elucidated this vision more explicitly.

Johns used encaustic in an unconventional manner in *Flag*. He dipped pieces of newspaper and cloth in hot wax and applied them to a surface that he had already painted with enamel. Like puzzle pieces, these fragments define, as well as correspond to, the borders of the canton and stripes. The collage elements of the stripes are lined up in rows, with some more flush with the edge between red and white than others; each star is cut out and covered, in part or in whole, in white encaustic. Johns was not painting the image of a flag but constructing an object, and in this regard *Flag* is similar to *Star* and other previous works. He was not yet a painter in the traditional sense, but, through rather original means, he was making a thing that was both a painting and a flag, and not a painting or a flag.

Flag is a conservator's nightmare—a fragile ensemble of bedsheet, enamel, newspaper, and encaustic, all mounted on plywood. In the early 1990s, when I mentioned to Johns the instability of this combination and the problems of preserving the painting, he replied, "Yes, it's falling apart, just like me." Johns's reluctance to discard *Flag* during its problematic early stages conveys a lot about both his tenacity and about what the work meant to him. Rather than accept *Flag*'s failure and ditch it, the artist chose to keep working on the site where the dream might have occurred.

Two distinct visual passages make apparent that *Flag* is about the nature of dreams. Placed in the third white strip from the top, a little above and to the right of the composition's center, and visible only if we move close to the surface, is a collage fragment, covered by encaustic, with the words "Pipe Dream" (fig. I: 6b). Because it is both prominently located and correctly oriented (many of the other collage pieces lie on their sides), the phrase comments on an affinity between an American flag and a painting: both are "pipe dreams." In the case of the flag, the primary metonymic symbol of the United States, the pipe dream is the shared experience and ideals of those who founded and built the country. The painting, however, presents a different story: the dream was an isolated and isolating experience whose solitariness comes across both calmly and forcefully.

There is another meaningful collage element: the words "United States," made of embossed white letters, peek through the blue encaustic on the right-hand side of the star in the lower-left-hand corner of the canton (fig. I: 6c).[6] Tracing a circle's circumference, the letters curl out from the star's right side, like a trail of cosmic dust. The deliberate placement of the phrase "United States" next to the star should obviate any belief that the location of the words "Pipe Dream" was serendipitous. "United States" names Johns's vision of his relationship to reality, particularly as exemplified by the dream. He was united with the dream, and yet also distinct from it. The stars in the canton are inseparable from their surroundings. The symbiotic relationship of figure and ground, particularly the effect of the second on the first, has been one of Johns's central concerns since *Flag*. In addition to uniting the states of dreaming and waking in order to make *Flag*, Johns's placement of the phrase "United States" in the canton's blue field (or night sky) is the first indication of his attentiveness to the literal meaning of words.

Despite the autobiographical source of *Flag*, Johns's art has never been about who he is, and it is unlikely that he is interested in hiding something about himself in it. This is not to deny that he embeds literal, iconographic, or metaphoric things in his paintings, sculptures, and works on paper. The reason he does so proceeds from his materialist

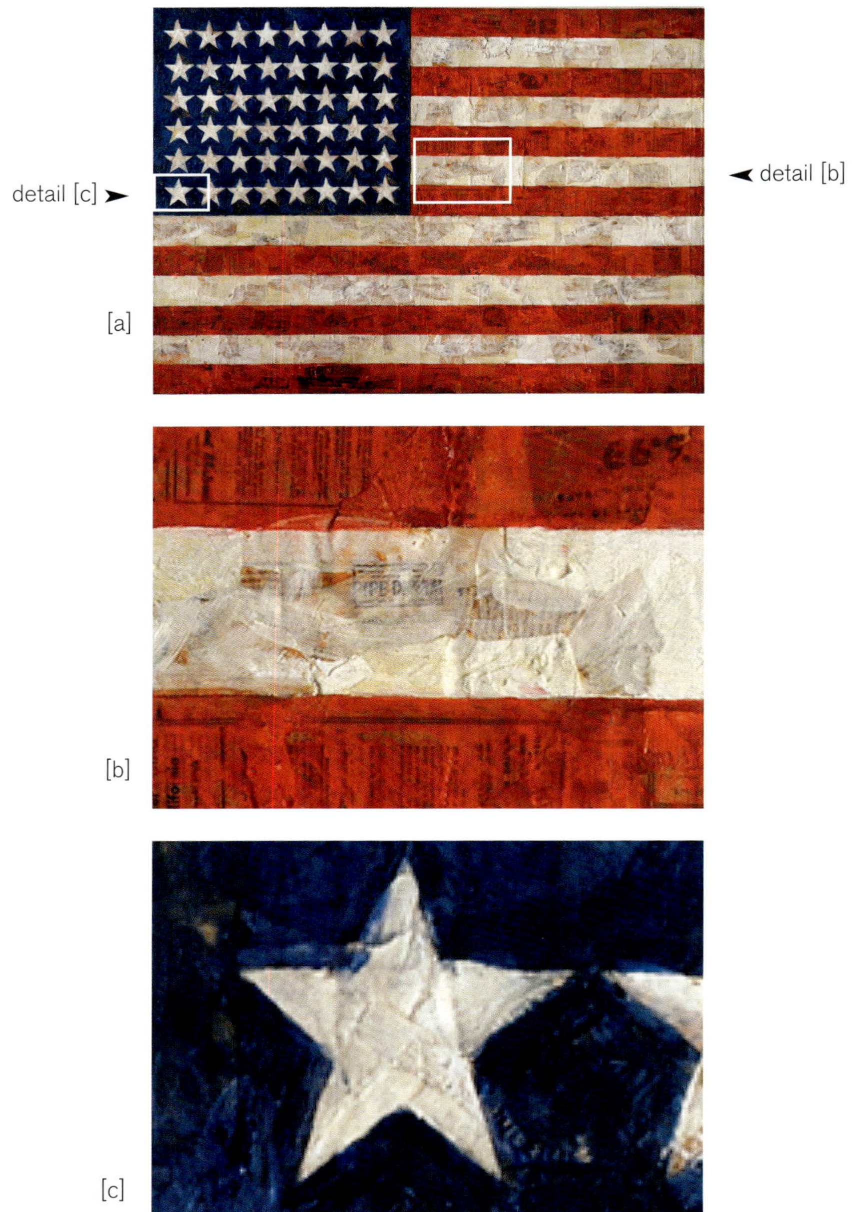

fig. I: 6a-c **Jasper Johns** *FLAG* [a] and two details [b, c] 1954–55
See fig. I-1.

vision, which he expresses through his innovative use of both the figure/ground relationship and simultaneity, which, in Johns's work, means that reality cannot be taken in all at once. *Flag above White with Collage* (1955), for example, features a flag and a strip of black-and-white photographs near the flag's right edge, peering through red and white encaustic stripes. Formally speaking, Johns distinguishes himself from other artists of his generation because he does not align himself with the modern ocular tradition—the manifestation of formalism dating back to Cubism, which in its earliest stages was a vehicle for speculating upon the existence of the fourth dimension. He focuses on what it means to live in time, rather than on the possibility of transcending our material state.

V.

On the level of appearance,
Flag obviously resembles an American flag
from the mid-1950s;
its blue rectangle contains forty-eight stars,
and there are thirteen alternating
red and white stripes.

What strikes me is the degree to which the painting is both similar to and different from its real-life counterpart.[7] *Flag* is not a flawless copy of the flag, but a flaglike object that the artist constructed. The painting requires long and determined attention, coupled with a willingness to scrutinize it without judgment, until its full nature becomes apparent. Once the familiarities begin to drop away, what one sees is a layered, tactile object made of colors, words, and images, a busy and complexly engaging thing.

As mentioned above, the flag's stars are discrete shapes made of pieces of paper, covered or partially covered by white encaustic, that together form a larger pattern. Formally, each star is a unique, hand-cut silhouette. Typically, a silhouette is a flat, monochromatic image whose edges define both the limitations of its existence and its isolation from the world, an isolation that is material and actual rather than introspective. Johns's stars, however, are inseparable from the night that surrounds them. As unique facts—no two are exactly alike—the stars embody our inevitable solitariness, as well as visually echo the condition of dreaming. Asleep, and possibly dreaming, each of us travels through the night alone, like a friendless star. Our dreams, however startling, do not bring us proof of the miraculous. In its insistence on its own separateness, as opposed to its referent's symbolism of collective aspirations, Johns's *Flag* reveals the propaganda associated with any flag, which is that it affords the individual citizen a sense of protection from the passage of time. Even if we disagree with it in its totality, it is a fiction in which we choose to believe.

Johns is not satisfied with feeling that he can paint anything. For him the idea of artistic freedom is an illusion, as deceptive as the solace offered by a flag. At best the individual is a deeply fissured "united states" of the five senses and the intellect, the body and the mind. *Flag*'s collaged printed and photographic materials, surface tactility, colors, familiar subject, and three joined sections all demonstrate the division of our senses and the changing relationship between body and mind. The painting compels us to assume different vantage points, to step back to take in the whole and to step forward to examine every detail. Each view is only partial. Using one sense and then another, we are unable to experience *Flag* in its entirety.

The shifting relationship between the senses renders our comprehension of reality problematic, especially when we refuse to search for sanctuary in a belief system that seeks to counter the inevitable toll taken by time, as Johns seems to have been doing throughout his life. We exist in time, and eventually we surrender to it. This is the vision of existence that is central to Johns's project: it is the perception in which he dwells, and from which he has never pulled back. He wants to keep looking at both the reality he inhabits and the one he knows is approaching. Despite the termination that awaits him, he wishes to focus on the present and all that it can disclose. Coinciding with his sensitivity to creation's indifference is his deepening exploration of his own helpless behavior and growing awareness of the proximity of chaos.

Another way to consider Johns's early work is to see the *Flags* as being concerned with the connection between the isolated individual and a social realm that valorizes identity, the *Targets* as expressing the partialness of the body's relationship with itself and reality, and the *Alphabets* and *Numerals* as focusing on the irreducible elements of referential and abstract language. The flag does nothing to protect us from the deep-seated loneliness that impacts us all. The individual is isolated within society, and, like each star, letter, or numeral, is distinct from others, even as one is joined to the ground.

In paintings such as *Gray Alphabets* and *White Numbers* (figs. I: 6, 7), the letters and numerals simultaneously emerge from and sink back into the ground. As a materialist, Johns acknowledges that the figure is always emerging from and succumbing to the ground, which will eventually overtake him. By refusing to allow his *Alphabets* to spell anything or his *Numerals* to coalesce into a mathematical sequence, Johns declined to use either of these languages in any agreed-upon way and, in doing so, refused society's call to the individual to routinely suppress his or her remoteness from others.

Johns's incorporation of things that pre-exist him, including flags and targets, as well as primary and secondary colors and the tonal range from black to white, signals the artist's recognition that he is an instance in time. In addition, by focusing on the figure/ground relationship, he refuses to align himself with the critical paradigm that believes in progress. For Greenberg, all-over abstract painting represented a historical advance that, among other things, rendered the figure/ground issue obsolete. Johns's explorations of figure and ground suggest that he has never regarded it as a purely formal issue to be solved. Rather, as I see it, the particular figure/ground relationships on which he focuses are keyed to the recognition that the body (figure) inevitably succumbs to dissolution (ground).

Johns repeatedly addresses being alive in time and the changing relationship between the transitory moment and the infinite: givens that we cannot overcome. Because he did not turn his dream of the flag into a narrative, he was able to explore, honestly and radically, a common experience that paradoxically cut him off from others. At the same time, he began to gather a vocabulary that he would continue to recontextualize throughout his career, always intent on gaining further insight into a condition he shares with others, being a thing in time. Like Paul Cézanne, whom he greatly admires, Johns never surrenders his perceptions to the prevailing winds.

CHAPTER 1
NOTES

1. "Clement Greenberg: As the Art World Remembers Him" (interviews with John Russell, Hilton Kramer, William Rubin, Robert Rosenblum, and Linda Nochlin), *The Art Newspaper*, June 1994, p. 4. Linda Nochlin stated, "In a sense it was impossible to think about modern art without him. He thought of modernism as having a telos, some kind of preordained goal." Later, summing up Greenberg's viewpoint, Nochlin said, "The goal of modernist art was to refer with more and more reduction to the means of art itself, to the nature of the art process; that there was going to be more and more reduction, less and less narrative, and that modernist art, by definition, had to move away from reality into the world of abstraction and reveal itself more and more." *www.jasonkauman.com/articles/clement_greenberg_as_the_america.htm.* Other critics and historians influenced by Greenberg, particularly his emphasis on painting's two-dimensionality, and on its having a preordained goal, would include Roberta Bernstein, Michael Fried, Rosalind Krauss, and Barbara Rose.

2. Greenberg's aesthetic ideal was pure form, which he first defined in his essay "Towards a Newer Laocoon" (1940): "The arts, then, have been hunted back to their mediums, and there they have been isolated, concentrated and defined. It is by virtue of its medium that each art is unique and strictly itself. To restore the identity of an art the opacity of its medium must be emphasized." See *The Collected Essays and Criticism, Volume 1: Perceptions and Judgments, 1939–1944*, ed. John O' Brian (Chicago: University of Chicago Press, 1986), p. 32. In 1950 Willem de Kooning began working on *Woman I*, and in 1951 Pollock reintroduced figural elements into a group of black-and-white paintings. By Greenberg's standard, when they began working with figural elements, they retreated from pure form.

3. Jasper Johns, artist's statement, in Dorothy C. Miller, ed., *Sixteen Americans*, exh. cat. (New York: Museum of Modern Art, 1959), p. 22; repr. in *Jasper Johns: Writings, Sketchbooks, Notes, Interviews*, ed. Kirk Varnedoe, comp. Christel Hollevoets (New York: Museum of Modern Art, 1997), p. 20.

4. Quoted in Michael Crichton, *Jasper Johns*, exh. cat. (New York: Harry N. Abrams, in association with the Whitney Museum of American Art, 1977), p. 27.

5. *www.chebucto.ns.cca/Philosophy/Taichi/chuang.html*

6. Neither "Pipe Dream" nor "United States" is visible in any of the reproductions of *Flag*, which suggests one reason they have been overlooked. The fact that *Flag* and much of Johns's painted work loses much of their meaning in reproduction distinguishes his art from that of those he influenced, such as Stella and Warhol.

7. Johns did the pencil drawing *Flag* in 1955, the year he completed the painting of the same title; the drawing has sixty-four stars.

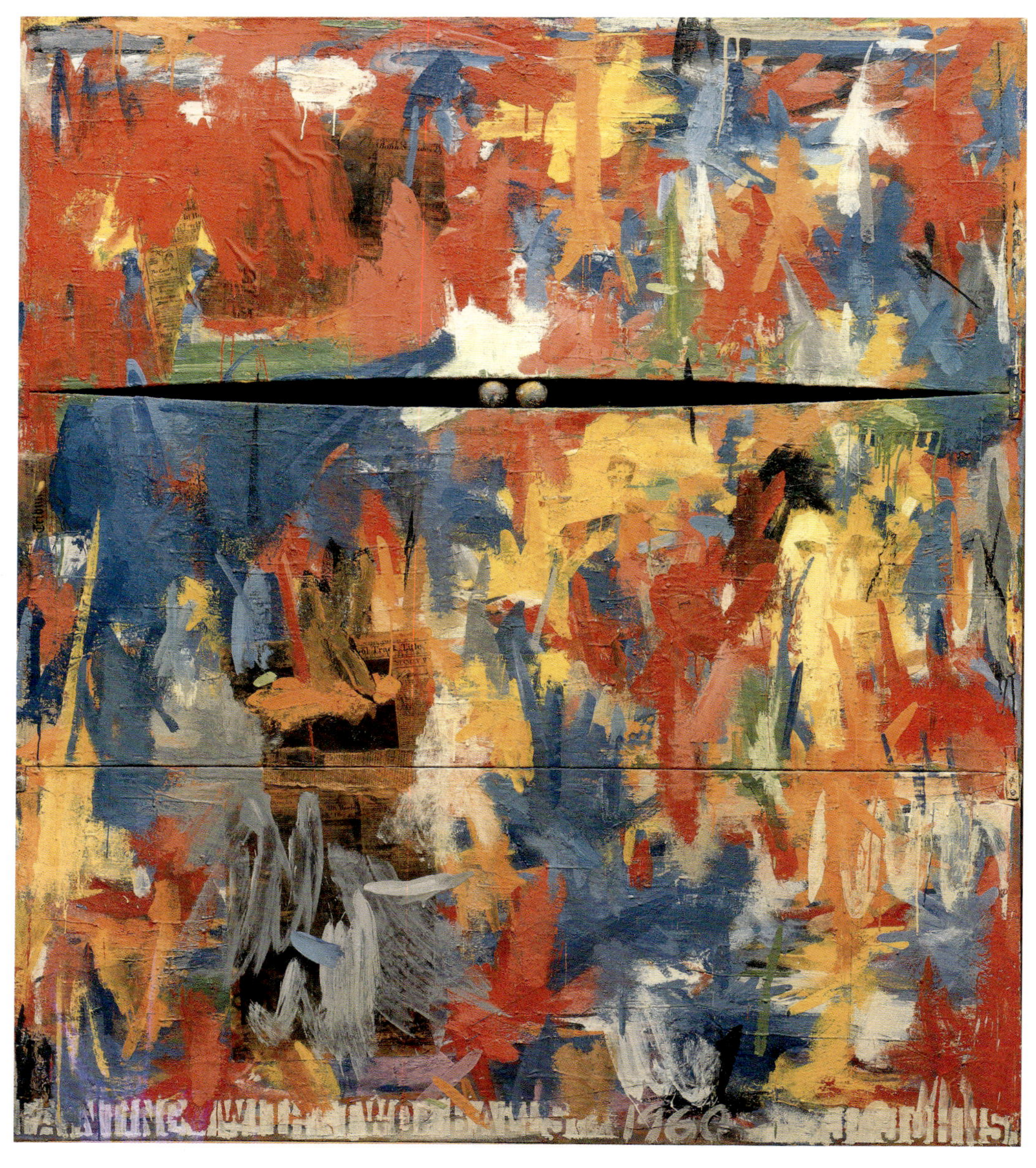

fig. II: 1 **Jasper Johns** *PAINTING WITH TWO BALLS* 1960
Encaustic and collage on carvas with objects 65 x 54 in. (165.1 x 137.2 cm)
Collection the artist

Chapter 2

I.

Throughout his career,
Johns has made a practice of working concurrently
on bodies of work that, on the surface,
might seem to have little to do with one another.

However, once we begin to discern the essential components of his primary preoccupation, as well as his meticulous attentiveness to simultaneity and the bond between figure and ground, we discover that the seemingly disparate directions he took between 1955 and 1961 actually fall into two distinct investigations, the pictorial and the physical. The former includes works discussed in Chapter One, such as *Flag*, *Green Target*, and *Figure 5* (figs. I: 1–3). The latter comprises such unique examples as *Painting with Two Balls*, *No* (figs. II: 1–2), and *Coat Hanger* (1959).

What is remarkable about the physically assertive works is that, with the exception of the spheres appearing in both *Painting with One Ball* (1958) and *Painting with Two Balls,* they are virtually all one-offs in an oeuvre overwhelmingly dominated by motifs Johns subjects to repeated investigations. There is only one coat hanger (that is, there is only one that has not been bent or twisted) hanging from a dowel and only one use of the word "NO" as a dangling sculptural form casting its shadow on the picture's surface. In these Johns likely incorporated ordinary things to expand his vocabulary, to confront a literal figure/ground relationship, and to address the persistent ambiguity of visual concomitance.

If Johns had chosen to use these motifs or objects more than once or, at most, a few times, the initial insight he gleaned from the piece would have been diluted. There was little more he could do with the idea of *No* once he had made it. On the other hand, he could repeatedly investigate a flag because it yielded more perceptions each time he returned to it. This integral linkage of understanding to object reveals much about the artist's character, and why he has proceeded in the way he has. In contrast to that of many of his contemporaries, Johns's project is not geared toward production. Had he hung the coat hanger over a red, yellow, blue, black, or white ground, instead of the gunmetal gray one he used, he would have weakened the meaning as well as thematized the subject. For his single coat-hanger painting, he chose a field of gray encaustic because he wanted to diminish the associative, and therefore manipulative, qualities of more chromatic color.

The understanding of the inseparability of figure and ground revealed by *Coat Hanger* can be found in sculptural works also dating from 1958 dealing with flashlights and lightbulbs (see Chapter Three). To function, a coat hanger, like a flashlight or a lightbulb, requires something beyond itself—be it a peg, a person pressing a button, or someone inserting a bulb into an electric socket. The fact that the hanger is empty evokes a sense of lost time, the interregnum when it is useless. Its emptiness is detached and haunting; a quality of forlornness and vulnerability emanates from the piece. The hanger is helpless to do anything about its material condition. In addition, in *Coat Hanger*, which preceded the two 1960 sculptures titled *Painted Bronze* (figs. III: 4, 5), Johns first introduced his understanding of the individual's existence in time. The coat hanger is suspended between the *after* and the *before*, after it has been used and before it is used again. This understanding of time inverts the more traditional one of *before* and *after*.

For all of his evident delight in making art, Johns never loses sight of his own, inevitable material annihilation. If anything, it is through the medium of art that he is able to examine it with an almost clinical detachment. Johns's determinedly cool point of view paradoxically floods his work with feeling. The passionate acuity of his intellect and touch comes through only when he immerses himself in the task of giving form and substance to reality's dominion over us. By expressing a "helpless statement," he bears witness to his passage through time, scrutinizing it with all the objectivity and dispassion that he can muster in the face of an implicit recognition of mortality. He translates the complexity of reality through content, color, surface sensuality, text, common objects, and uncommon ones.

Jasper Johns *NO* 1961
Encaustic, collage, and Sculp-metal on canvas 68 x 40 in. (172.7 x 101.6 cm)
Collection the artist

fig. II: 2

If, with *Coat Hanger*, Johns underscored the figure's dependency upon the ground by setting a wire hanger on a peg extending in front of the painting's encaustic surface, in *Painting with Two Balls* he arrived at a more complicated understanding of the figure/ground relationship: three stacked panels are joined together by four metal strips, each of which has four openings for screws. The artist used two strips, one at either end, to abut each section to the one adjoining it. Two paint-smeared wooden balls are squeezed into the gap between the top and middle panels, seemingly causing them to open like the slit of an eye. The panels are covered with large sections of newspaper over which the artist brushed mostly vertical passages of encaustic. The palette is predominantly red, yellow, and blue, with some orange, green, lavender, black, white, and gray. Along the bottom, Johns stenciled the title and his name, and wrote "1960," the year he executed the work. Instead of adhering the physical letters to the painting, he collaged the outer or framing parts of the stencil, which made the letters synonymous with the negative shapes. The outer sections are covered in white, with the encaustic going beyond the stencil's edges. In some places, it is clear that the artist applied an additional layer of colored encaustic, which partially covers the white framing shapes and the letters' negative spaces.

Everywhere we look, we see an entangled figure/ground relationship in which something (newspaper, paint) is partially covered by something else (paint, newspaper). The negative spaces of the letters become positive shapes, something legible. If the letters are the negative spaces formed by the physical collage, then what is the relationship between the visual and the physical? Although they are distinct, we see them as indivisible. The title names the painting both linguistically and experientially, bringing language and occurrence into closer proximity. The pair of balls inserted into the painting's cavity further complicates the carefully examined figure/ground relationship. Are the balls an intrusion, one might even say a violation? Or is the painting meant to frame and hold them? Each needs the other to make this unity in which they remain discrete. Something similar happens in the stenciled title, where the sections of collage frame the negative spaces. Within the terms of a figure/ground relationship, the three panels form the ground while the two balls form the figure. And yet, that figure/ground relationship is further complicated by the bond between the colored encaustic and the newspaper collage, and the collaged sections and the negative spaces they form.

While many critics have proposed that *Painting with Two Balls* is a spoof on Abstract Expressionist machismo—"That painting has balls" being both a crude equation and compliment—this view confines Johns's project to commenting on an earlier generation, which makes the work insular. As with *Flag*, it is a view that misses the work's deeper resonance and inclusiveness, as well as failing to address the many kinds of figure/ground relationships that the artist explored in it.

In contrast to *Painting with Two Balls*, the elements of the more serene *Drawer* (1957) imply a harmonious bond between two discrete objects, a drawer and its aperture, each of which depends on the other to achieve a sense of unity while at the same time evoking that which is contained within a body but hidden from view. We cannot ever fully know ourselves, because something will always remain concealed. Johns is not questioning authorship, but he is questioning how much the author can know about a subject when self-knowledge appears impossible to achieve. In the more abstract *Gray Rectangles* (1957; private collection), Johns created another kind of literal figure/ground relationship by inserting three rectangular canvases into the face of a square painting. Each of the small canvases is painted in a primary color (red, yellow, blue) and then overlaid with gray encaustic. In a few spots, pure color peeks through the noticeable physical seam bordering the rectangles and the surrounding gray field. Our attention shifts between the visual surface and the tactile presence of the rectangles, without the two ever completely jibing. In each of the works I have touched upon, the relationship that Johns established between figure and ground is one that explores the bond between the visual and the physical, and certainly is not theoretical.

According to Johns, gray encaustic "seemed to allow the literal qualities to predominate over any others."[2] One of the "literal qualities" is the relationship of the primary-color areas to their gray overlay, which permits what it covers to be both separate and contiguous. The physical seams dividing the smaller rectangles from the larger, containing square are akin to those separating the rings in another virtually monochromatic painting, *Green Target* (fig. I: 2). In *Painting with Two Balls*, Johns highlighted what is latent in *Gray Alphabets* (fig. I: 5), that figure and ground are indivisible yet physically distinct from each other. In front of the encaustic surface of both *Coat Hanger* and *No*, he placed a physical object so that it casts a shadow. The issue for Johns in these works, and it is not solely a formal one, was how to merge figure and ground while retaining the identity of each.

In *No*, by attaching the word "NO" (it is made of Sculp-metal, a leadlike material) from a wire attached to an eyehook inserted near the top of the painting, Johns arrived at an eloquently succinct resolution. The physical letters "N" and "O" create not only multiple shadows on the painting's gray encaustic surface but also multiple linguistic interpretations. In a 1964 sketchbook, Johns noted that the "Japanese phonetic 'no' [means] (possessive 'of')."[3] In addition to signifying "no" and "of," the sound of the word also suggests "know" (to possess information or be aware of something). Given Johns's attention to words, and to all the meanings contained in "no," it is likely that he was also playing with its reverse, "on."

By underscoring the homophonic bond among the words "no," "know," and the Japanese "of," Johns got at the painful consciousness of being human, of realizing that we are encased within a body over whose constantly changing state we can never exercise final control or fully know. However much we may rail against being made of matter, we are still made of it. We may feel separate from the physical world, but we are nevertheless bound to it, and consequently are a discrete part of what Leonardo called the "atmosphere." The unbreakable tension of "no," "know," and "of" is underscored by the shadows of the word "NO" itself, since shadows are cast by solid bodies, not spirits. In addition, both Sculp-metal and encaustic exist in two states, solid (form) and liquid (dissolution). Our bodies are similar.

What are we to make of the outline of Marcel Duchamp's *Female Fig Leaf* (fig. II: 3) to the left of, and slightly below, the eyehook? Duchamp had executed *Female Fig Leaf* by taking a plaster cast of a woman's genitalia. Most likely Johns obtained a bronze version of the sculpture when he went to Paris in 1961 for the opening of his first exhibition in Europe, at the Galerie Rive Droite, which had just issued a bronze edition of Duchamp's object. By heating the bronze and pressing it into the surface of *No*, Johns made a physical impression of the sculpture's base. An "X" is visible inside the outline of the base; the "X" was most likely made after Johns pressed the bronze sculpture into the wax. The outline is part of the ground and distinct from it, which is different from the shadow cast by the metal "NO."

A note Johns wrote to himself some three years after *No* contains the words "encaustic (flesh?)."[4] *Female Fig Leaf* conflates this "flesh" with another material, bronze. Yet like the human body, neither encaustic nor bronze is fixed; each is subject to change, with the two media existing as either solid or liquid, while the body is a constantly altering combination of both. By pressing the heated bronze into the encaustic, Johns registered the latter's susceptibility to shifts in temperature, a fact to which he would return on a number of occasions. The conjunction of the outline, the "X," and the encaustic suggests a sexual encounter, while at the same registering vulnerability. We are made of matter that was produced by matter.

Caught between the *after* and the *before*, we are continually arriving and departing. This is what it means to live in time; we cannot stop it, and much of our experience is transitory. In *Arrive/Depart* (1963–64), Johns linked the erotic moment with art making, matter making matter (see Chapter Nine) with birth and death—all of which are defined by the notions of arrival and departure. Along the right edge of the painting, the artist pressed his palm print into the oil paint, made an outline of *Female Fig Leaf*, and below applied a skull covered with paint to the canvas. Each registered an aspect of the human form: hand, head, procreative organs. Placed at the bottom, the skull suggests an inverted body, with a handprint pressing against the surface and reaching up, near the top of the painting. Our passage through time consists of comings and goings, of the fleeting and changing. The question is, despite all we know, can we remain open to life before chaos swallows us up?

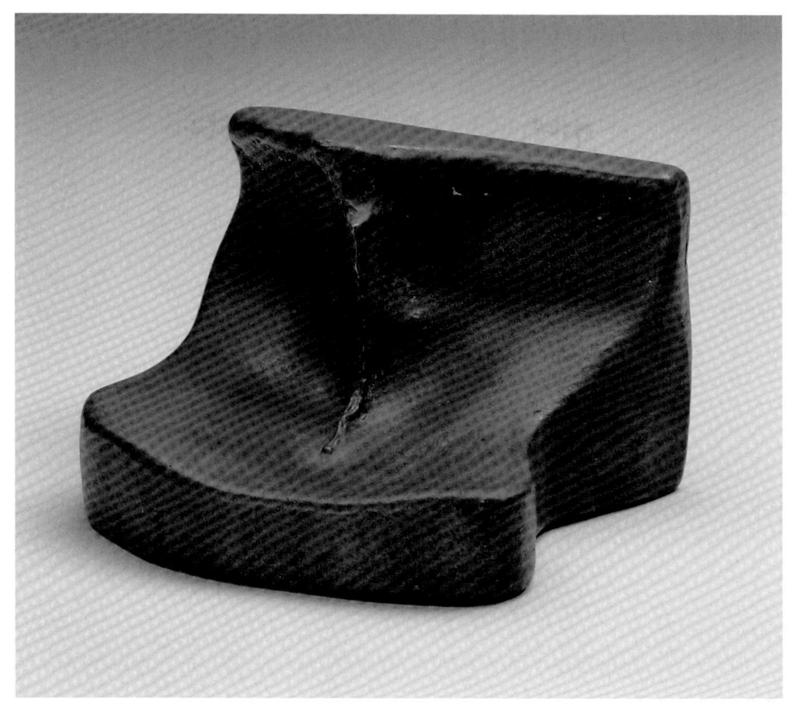

Marcel Duchamp *FEMALE FIG LEAF* 1961 fig. II: 3
Electroplated copper over plaster 3 1/2 x 5 1/4 x 5 in. (8.9 x 13.3 x 12.7 cm)
The Museum of Modern Art, New York. Gift of Jasper Johns

CHAPTER 2
NOTES

1. Other works of this type include *Canvas* (1956), *Gray Rectangles* (1957), *Three Flags* (1958), and *Shade* (1959).

2. Quoted in Richard Francis, *Jasper Johns* (New York: Abbeville Press, 1984), p. 35.

3. Jasper Johns, "Sketchbook Notes," *Art and Literature* (Lausanne) 4 (Spring 1965); repr. in *Jasper Johns: Writings, Sketchbooks, Notes, Interviews*, ed. Kirk Varnedoe, comp. Christel Hollevoets (New York: Museum of Modern Art, 1997), pp. 35, 58.

4. Ibid., pp. 33, 56.

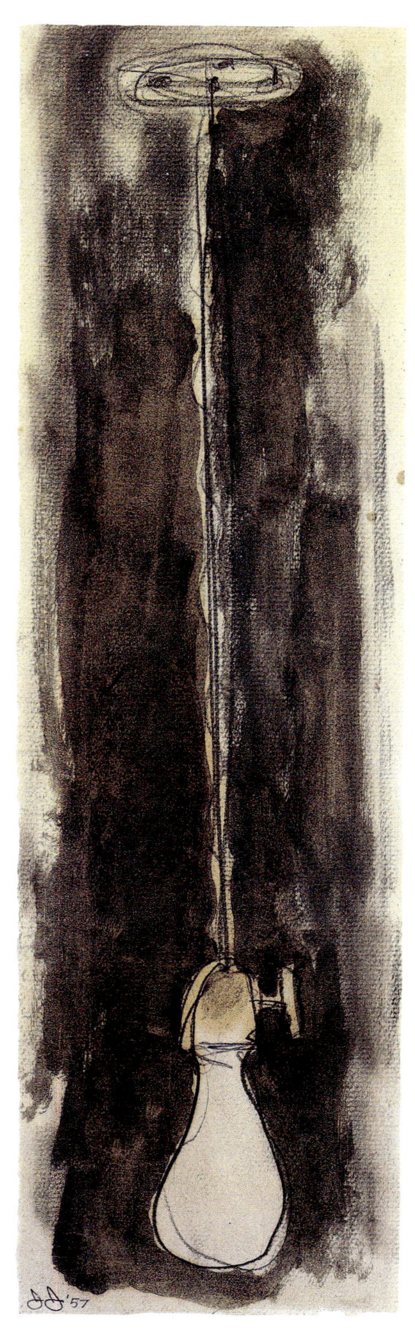

fig. III: 1 **Jasper Johns** *LIGHT BULB* 1957
Graphite, wash, and pencil on paper 15 5/16 x 4 5/8 in. (38.9 x 11.7 cm)
Collection the artist

Chapter 3

I.

In 1957 Johns made a plaster model of a sculpture depicting a lightbulb suspended by an electric cord.

This model proved too fragile and broke. He then made *Light Bulb* (fig. III: 1), a narrow, vertical drawing in graphite, wash, and pencil of the same subject. This is the first work in which the artist focused on a hanging object and on verticality. In the white stars of *Flag*'s (fig. I: 1) blue canton, Johns dealt with things that are suspended or floating, but did not address the effect of gravity. In *Light Bulb*, gravity threatens to separate the bulb from the ceiling; it is the bond between the figure (bulb) and the ground (ceiling). Tethered to the ceiling, the bulb cannot stop itself from falling. Gravity, which is constant, eventually triumphs over us. Verticality enabled Johns to explore the individual's consciousness of falling (feeling helpless) in *Land's End* (fig. V: 1). and the perception of being surrounded by liquid in *Painted Bronze (Ale cans)* (fig. III: 4). In each of these works—one a painting and the other a sculpture—the vulnerable, vertical form is surrounded or bonded to something else; it is not freestanding but contingent. It is suspended in air, turpentine, oil paint, and so forth, and therefore exposed to external conditions. The suspension of a familiar thing registers the degree to which the condition is pervasive and inescapable; we are constantly being pulled down by time, and there is no avoiding it. While art cannot halt time, it can chronicle its passing, as well as clarifying the effect its passage has on us. In Johns's case, the artist never privileges the particulars of his experience over that of others. All of us must endure time's effects.

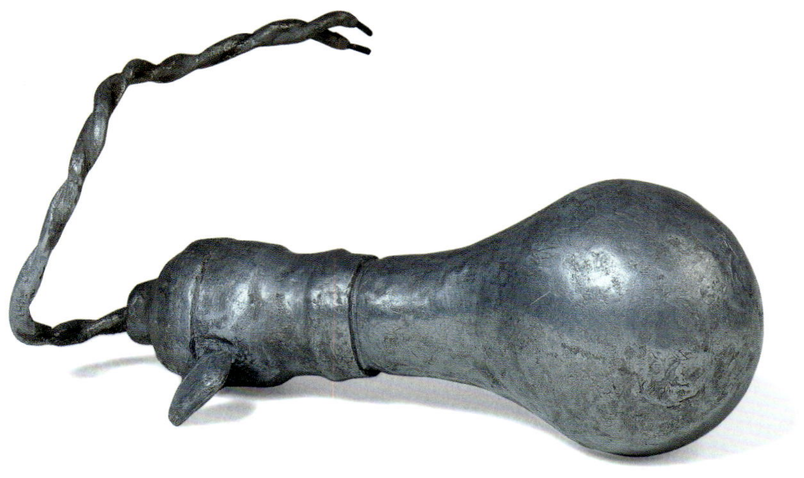

fig. III: 2 **Jasper Johns** *LIGHT BULB II* 1958
Sculp-metal 5 x 8 x 4 in. (12.7 x 20.3 x 10.2 cm)
Collection the artist

Johns would revisit the motif of suspension throughout his career, from works such as *No* (fig. II: 4) and *Watchman* (fig. VI: 1) to *Perilous Night* (fig. IX: 2); and subsequently in the Catenary paintings and related works (see Chapters Eleven and Twelve).[1] In both *Watchman* and *Perilous Night*, the emphasis is on inversion, on something hanging upside down. While this is natural for a lightbulb, so much so that we are apt to accept the position without thinking twice, the inverted chair and legs in *Watchman* and the upended knights in *Perilous Night* feel convulsive and disturbing. For the lightbulb, the condition of inversion is natural, but for the upside-down chair and knights, the situation is frightening because each evokes a human body conscious of itself falling or sinking, a perception the artist directly deals with in *Land's End*.

Between 1958 and 1961, Johns made various sculptures not only of lightbulbs but also of flashlights that explore the figure/ground relationship. In contrast to the seeming self-sufficiency of the Flags, Targets, Alphabets, and Numerals, the lightbulb and flashlight are clearly dependent objects. We sense that, in shifting from the former group to the latter, Johns most likely recognized that he had not yet addressed contingency explicitly enough. The lightbulb must be attached to a power source, and the flashlight needs to be turned on. This bond underscores the mutual dependence of figure and ground, as well as the primal nature of the body's relationship to reality, which we literally depend on to survive. In *Light Bulb II* (fig. III: 2), Johns used Sculp-metal to unify the bulb with the socket, switch, and wire; in *Bronze* (fig. III: 3), a companion to *Light Bulb II*, he cast a section of wire, a socket and switch in the middle, and a bulb, which are attached to a base. Each requires the others to function effectively. In these works, it is obvious that Johns had little use for the widely accepted formalist belief in art's autonomy.

Even so, these pieces do not define Johns's position with quite the clarity of two sculptures from 1960 that carry the same, technically descriptive name: *Painted Bronze (Ale cans)* and *Painted Bronze (Savarin coffee can with brushes)* (figs. III: 4, 5). The first comprises two Ballantine Ale cans mounted on a base. The top of the can on the left bears two triangular piercings from a can opener, while the one on the right is pristine. In an interview, Johns described the genesis of this piece: "I was doing at that time sculptures of small objects—flashlights and lightbulbs. Then I heard a story about Willem de Kooning. He was annoyed with my dealer, Leo Castelli, for some reason and said something like, 'That son of a bitch, you could give him two beer cans and he could sell them.' I heard this and thought, 'What a sculpture—two beer cans.' It seemed to fit in perfectly with what I was doing, so I did them—and Leo sold them."[2]

This story has become the premise for an interpretation of *Painted Bronze (Ale cans)* as a sly spoof on the hard-drinking, anti-commercial Abstract Expressionists, particularly de Kooning. Understood in that way, it fits in with *Painting with Two Balls* (fig. II: 1). Given that de Kooning is the source of the anecdote, we could further deduce that Johns's intention was to critique the work of the Abstract Expressionists, as well as to differentiate his art from theirs. This conclusion seems all the more plausible if we assume that Johns subscribed to the idea that radical art can only be about art, and that

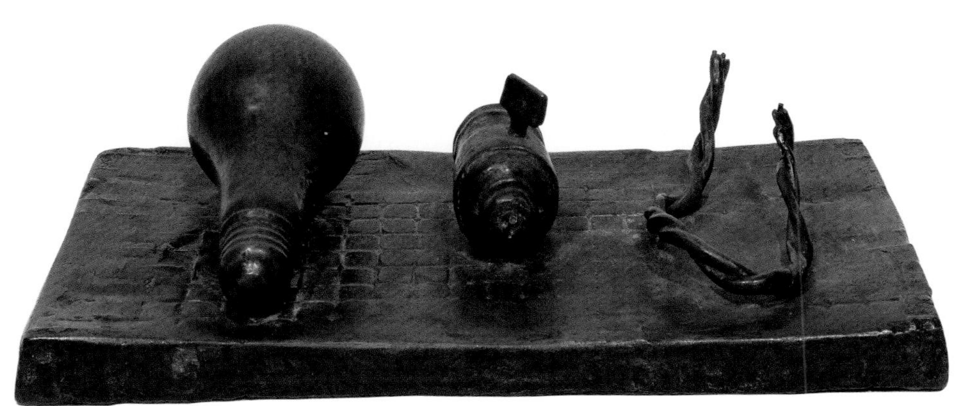

Jasper Johns *BRONZE* 1960–61
Bronze 3 1/2 x 11 1/2 x 6 1/2 in. (8.9 x 29.2 x 16.5 cm)
Collection the artist

fig. III: 3

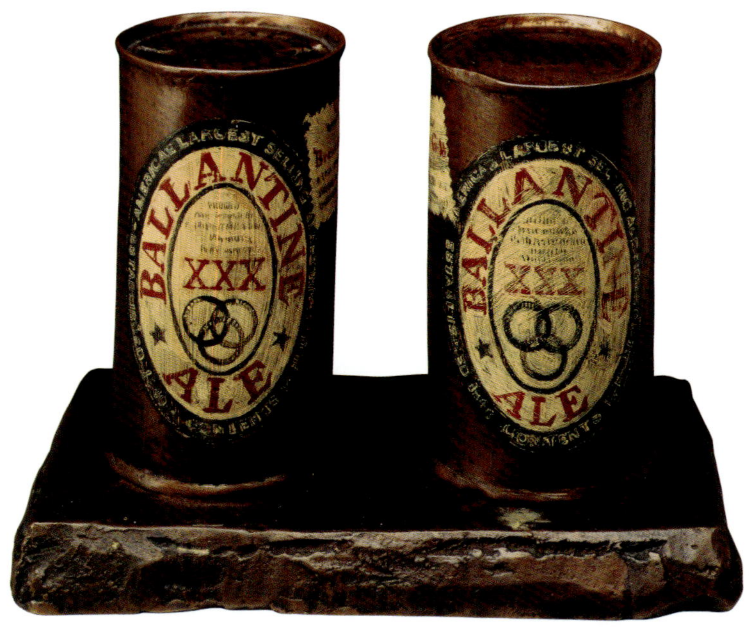

fig. III: 4 **Jasper Johns** *PAINTED BRONZE (Ale cans)* 1960
Oil on bronze Overall: 5 1/2 x 8 x 4 3/4 in. (14 x 20.3 x 12 cm)
Museum Ludwig, Ludwig donation, Cologne

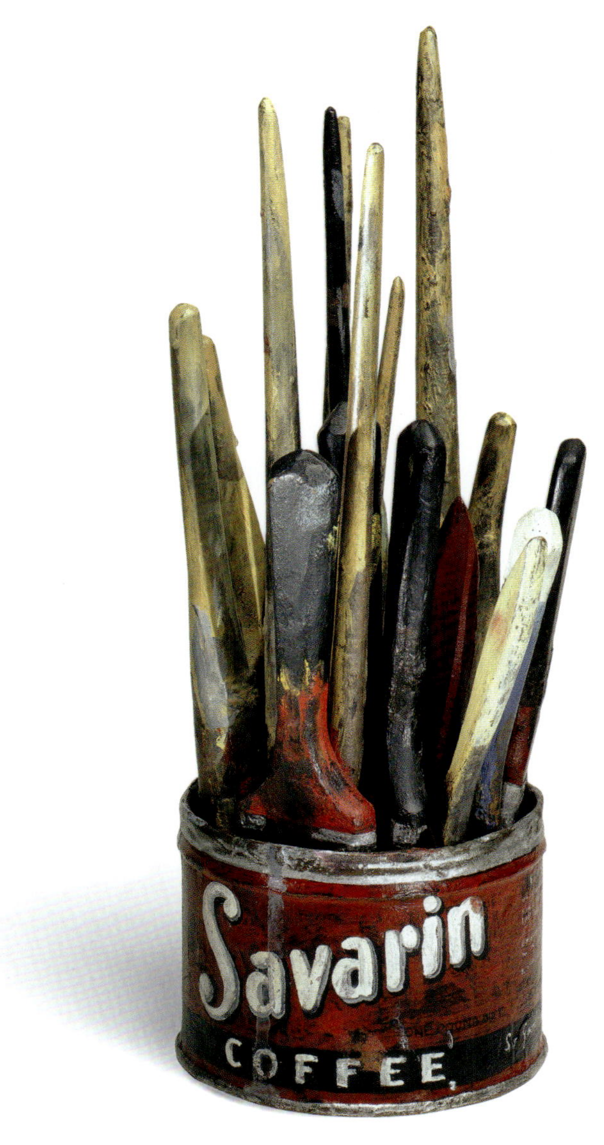

Jasper Johns *PAINTED BRONZE (Savarin coffee can with brushes)* 1960 fig. III: 5
Oil on bronze 13 1/2 x 8 in. (diam. of can) (34.3 x 20.3 cm)
Collection the artist

one way to clear a space for oneself is by parodying, satirizing, or criticizing an earlier generation of artists.

The problem with this reading is twofold: it reduces Johns's sculpture to a reactive stance concerning the art of his predecessors and implies that the piece's strength lies largely in the economy of its witty commentary on that generation's work and drinking habits. In comparison with Andy Warhol's silkscreened plywood Brillo boxes (first shown in 1964), which the critic Arthur Danto believed rendered the difference between art and life meaningless,[3] *Painted Bronze (Ale cans)* seems insular in intent. But this supposes that the goal of art is to dissolve the barrier separating it from life. Danto's reading privileges resemblance while still subscribing to art that does not disturb the timeless zone it inhabits. In *Painted Bronze (Ale cans)*, Johns introduced the element of time passing into the unchanging aesthetic realm that is considered to be synonymous with art. He did not use resemblance to dissolve the barrier between art and life; rather, he underscored his belief that time passing exists everywhere, not just in life.

Both *Painted Bronze* sculptures exist in the *meanwhile*, where a work of art is a moment forever frozen. In their stillness, both sculptures press us to ask what moment Johns froze, and why that particular moment? In *Painted Bronze (Ale cans)*, the container on the left has been emptied, but that on the right has not. This creates a sequence (an indication of time), which in turn suggests that the *now* (the present) can be divided into separate blocks of experience: that which we have done, and that which we have yet to do. But here the usual order of things has been reversed: If we read the sculpture from left to right, as we do a sentence, it reads not *before* and *after* but rather *after* and *before*.

If the customary order of *before* and *after* defines a transformation from one state to another, and thereby hints at the possibility of transcendence, Johns's reversal denies this implication. As his configuration suggests, at some point in time, reality (the present) will consist of only those things that we have not done and will never do, that is, at the moment of our death and thereafter. The unopened can will remain unopened, and the material world will outlive us. This recognition also helps explain why Johns might have been inclined to pick familiar and known things and use a palette consisting of primary and secondary colors, plus the tones from white to black. All of these things precede our arrival and will continue to exist in more or less the same form after our departure. The idea of individuality is an illusion if we believe that it will help us to escape time.

While Johns's engagement with these issues as an artist has afforded him a singular opportunity to plumb their meanings, he knows that he is fundamentally the same as everyone else. He acknowledges that he occupies a helpless body, which requires that he eat, drink, and excrete waste, and that making art does not save him from the passage of time. Johns followed the logic implied in *Painted Bronze (Ale cans)*, and preserved the act of eating in visual form by biting into the encaustic *Painting Bitten by a Man* (1961). His action anticipated the dark equation between looking and eating that he expressed in his "Sketchbook Notes": "'Looking' is & is not 'eating' & also 'being eaten.'"[4] We absorb aspects of reality even as it absorbs us.

At the same time, in direct and conscious opposition to the view of art as an elevated or academic discourse operating on a Platonic or spiritual plane, both *Painted Bronze (Ale cans)* and *Painting Bitten by a Man* acknowledge our biological need to consume. If art does not embrace the baser aspects of existence, Johns seems to have been saying, it is not true to reality. By placing two cans of beer in the realm of art, he suggested that the cycle of consumption and waste is intrinsic to art and life. At the same time, he denied that making art is a more elevated activity than drinking a beer.

Johns's unflinching focus on drawing connections between art and life has led many to believe that he is a literalist concerned only with the surface of things. In his "Sketchbook Notes," the artist proposed an equivalence between seeing and ingesting (which seems to proceed from his alignment of sight with the other senses, as described in Chapter One). He inferred that we eat (and do not eat) when looking, and, at the same time, we are being eaten (and not being eaten). We consume reality and turn it into excrement, just as it consumes us and turns us (and does not turn us) into waste. By qualifying this equation, Johns suggests that the process of consumption and waste is not total, but that it is part of our bond with reality. Thus, transformation is not transcendent, but it is unavoidable and necessary, and hardly likely to be inspiring, at least conventionally speaking. If something other than consumption is to happen, that results from the act of seeing, or what Johns, in "Sketchbook Notes," called "spying."[5] It is the act of seeing that preserves the vital information about our bond with reality that one has gleaned.

Painted Bronze (Savarin can with brushes) also defines a gap in time between the *after* and the *before*: the brushes have been used and are waiting to be picked up again. But, as I see it, this sculpture defines the *after* and *before* very differently from the way *Painted Bronze (Ale cans)* does. Whereas the unopened can evokes a potentiality that will never be realized, the paintbrushes signify that moment of stillness when they will no longer be used again. Just as we are caught in reality, they will be stuck forever in what they are stuck in currently. At some point—and I am convinced that Johns realized this by the time he finished the work, if not before—the sculpture will more closely resemble its real-life counterpart, an artifact in a deceased artist's studio. In real time, *Painted Bronze (Savarin can with brushes)* will one day shift from the category of analogy to that of unembellished fact. Instead of continuing to make work, the artist—his body, we could say—will have become the work. Both time and his art will have swallowed him up. With this understanding of time in mind, *Painted Bronze (Savarin can with brushes)* also offers another reading: one day the artist will no longer be able to clean up after himself and the brushes will remain dirty, rather than being cleansed by solvents.[6] In the ale cans and the Savarin can with brushes, Johns first dealt with evidence of a present that does not include him.

Neither of the *Painted Bronze* sculptures makes the *meanwhile* into an *elsewhere*, a refuge from life and time passing, which Johns defines as an asyndetic joining of formation and dissolution, of consumption and waste. There is no separation between these apparent opposites because, even as we travel through time, time contains us. Underlying Johns's choices of subject is his belief that both material form and dematerialization must be present in his work, disclosing the relationship between the helpless body and reality's constant flux. We find this expressed in as early a work as *Figure 5* (fig. I: 3), as well as, over three decades later, in *The Bath* (1988). In *Figure 5*, the numeral is cut out of printed matter and set into a plane of printed matter, an act that both offsets and merges figure and ground. White encaustic covers but does not hide the printed material. Despite the physical seam between them, numeral and ground exist on the same physical plane. Our ocular processes continue to distinguish the numeral from the ground even as the substances and techniques that the artist used bring them into an ever-closer, Zeno-like proximity. The numeral is poised between visibility and invisibility without ever becoming fully one or the other. Living in time, we are always being swallowed up and emerging.

In both *Painted Bronze* sculptures, Johns went a step further than he did in *Figure 5* by focusing on things that by their very existence flawlessly link formation and dissolution. He chose a sculptural material—bronze—to both mirror and preserve entities that are at once solid and liquid (a can of beer, a can of turpentine). Bronze exists in either a solid or a liquid state, with neither state being permanent. Like encaustic, it first must be melted before it can be employed to create a work of art, after which it cools and solidifies, and quite possibly, as with Michelangelo's ill-fated bronze statue of Julius II, is melted down once more and reused. The open and closed ale cans echo these two states, the liquid that has been poured (dissolution) and the solid cylinder (form) that has yet to be used. Both the drinking of the beer and the pouring of the bronze are acts of consumption. Johns's conflation and mirroring are seamless.

With *Painted Bronze (Savarin can with brushes)*, Johns first realized a configuration to which he has returned repeatedly over the past forty-five years, which is that of a solid body partially submerged in liquid. It is a stratified perception that includes a visible top and a lower, hidden or invisible level. Crucial to Johns's project is our recognition of the latter, which is beneath or beyond what we see, yet we know it is there. It is obvious that this visualization is rooted in experience, and that the artist refuses to turn that experience into either a theme or an iconographic idea. For him there is more to reality and art than their respective surfaces. Johns's preoccupation does not end with the perception of a visible form surrounded by liquid, but rather begins there.

CHAPTER 3
NOTES

1. Two other important works in a similar vein are *In Memory of My Feelings–Frank O'Hara* (1961) and *Fool's House* (1962).

2. Jasper Johns, interview with G. R. Swenson, "What Is Pop Art, Part 2," *ARTnews* 62, 10 (Feb. 1964); repr. in *Jasper Johns: Writings, Sketchbooks, Notes, Interviews*, ed. Kirk Varnedoe, comp. Christel Hollevoets (New York: Museum of Modern Art, 1997), p. 94.

3. Arthur Danto, *Encounters and Reflections: Art in the Historial Present* (New York: The Noonday Press, 1991), pp. 288-289.

4. Jasper Johns, "Sketchbook Notes," *Art and Literature* (Lausanne) 4 (Spring 1965); repr. in *Jasper Johns: Writings* (note 2), pp. 37, 59.

5. Ibid.

6. The cycle of dirt and cleaning is also central to *Fool's House* (fig. VII: 4), *Racing Thoughts* (figs. IX: 2, 3), and *The Bath* (1988), where a bathtub is a motif.

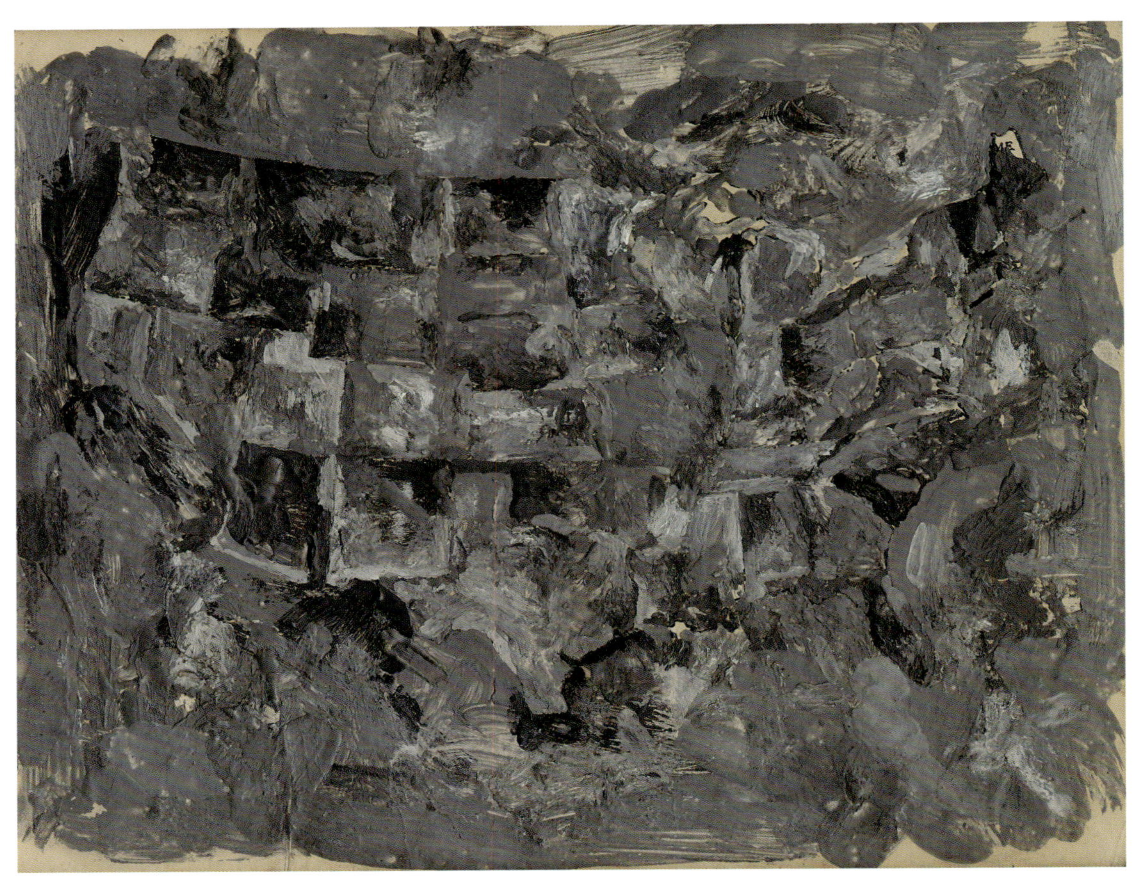

fig. IV: 1 **Jasper Johns** *MAP* 1960
Encaustic on printed paper, mounted on board 8 x 11 in. (20.3 x 27.9 cm)
Robert Rauschenberg Foundation collection

Chapter 4

I.

In a 1960 *Map* (fig. IV: 1), Johns used gray encaustic to paint over a small outline map that depicts the United States as an emblem, without indicating adjacent bodies of water or neighboring countries.

This led to three large compositions, all bearing the title *Map*, representing the continental United States, as well as the Atlantic and Pacific oceans: the first dates to 1961, the second to 1962, and the third to 1963 (fig. IV: 2). Formally, the large Maps are related to *Flag on Orange Field* (1957), and *Alley Opp* (1958) in that in each the motif and the monochromatic field are distinct and indivisible. There are two things about *Flag on Orange Field* that are particularly relevant to the Maps. First, the artist used "on" in the title, suggesting that the flag is a thing rather than an image. Second, he chose an orange field, and did not go on to make one on a green, yellow, black, or white field; he did not turn the subject into a theme.

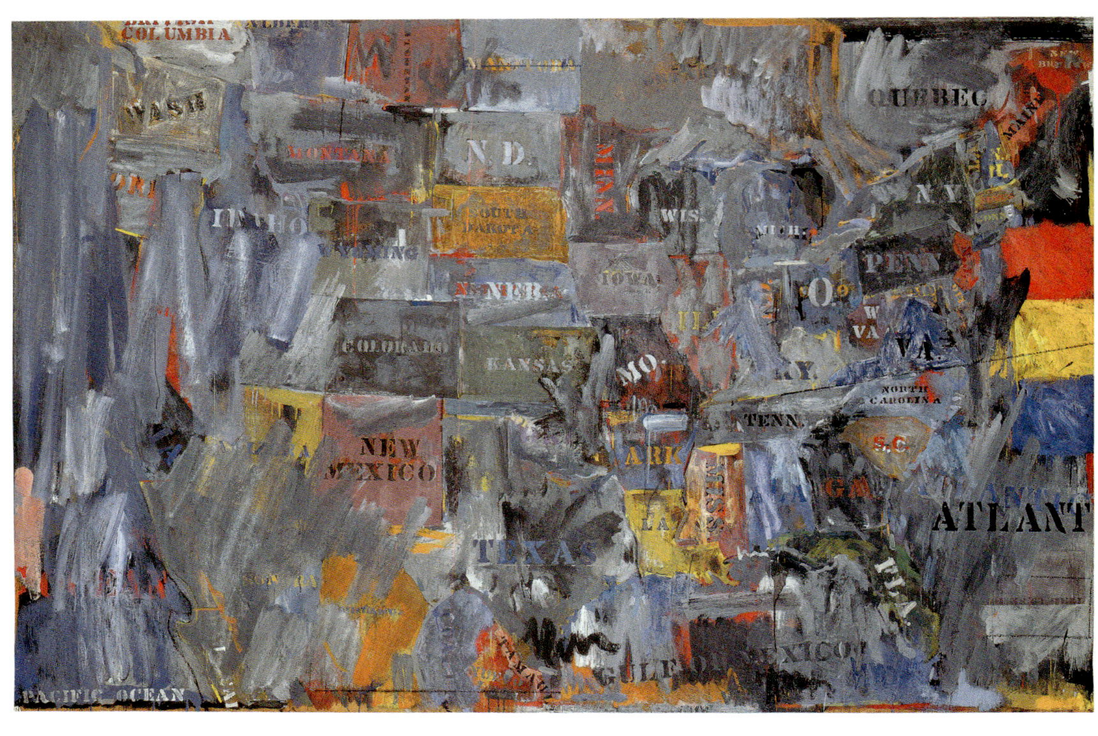

fig. IV: 2 **Jasper Johns** *MAP* 1963
Encaustic and collage on canvas 60 x 93 in. (152.4 x 236.2 cm)
Private collection

Like a flag and a target, a map is a two-dimensional icon, but one that possesses its own set of graphic signifiers. Coinciding with the geographic divisions that the boundaries of the puzzlelike shapes on the map represent, it seamlessly joins form (landmass) and formlessness (ocean), the slowly changing and the constantly shifting. The map thus offered Johns another found object with which he could further explore his preoccupation with a solid body partially immersed in liquid. In addition to defining this motif using the inherent nature of his medium (oil in the first large *Map*, and encaustic in the other two), Johns must have challenged himself to discover how much he could inflect a found object—a map—with meaning while remaining objective and detached.

The last large *Map*, in encaustic and collage, is the most elaborate of the three. Its color and brushwork also make it the most turbulent. Over a grayish-violet Atlantic Ocean, the artist stenciled "ATLANT" in black letters abutting the painting's lower-right edge, cutting off the last two letters of the word (fig. IV: 3b). Above the cropped word, Johns stacked three irregularly edged rectangles in primary colors (from the top: red, yellow, blue), their right sides flush with the painting's right edge.[1] And above these, situated sideways and also flush with the same edge, is the collaged fragment "*New York Post*, Friday, October." These three details, along with the elements described below, present what might be considered the key to the painting.

Directly below the rectangles and "ATLANT," Johns stenciled "JOHNS '63" and "HELL" in a continuous horizontal row (fig. IV: 3c). Around the text, he drew a three-sided rectangle (the left side is open, literally, to the agitated encaustic brushstrokes signifying the ocean) that echoes the three colored rectangles above. Some of the steeply slanting strokes sweep over the top line of the rectangle, while others cover the "J" of "JOHNS," forcing us to read the letters as "OHNS '63 HELL." We can hear in "OHNS" two other words, "one's" and "owns," which leads to the possibility of "one's hell" and/or "owns" or "owns hell," and from there to "one's own hell." By connecting the Atlantic Ocean and "HELL," Johns described dissolution (the effects of time on the body) as hell. It is uncharacteristic of the artist to be so unambiguous, and he has not repeated the idea elsewhere in his oeuvre. This may be because he realized that to do so would be to dilute its impact—another instance of the restraint he showed earlier in the more physically emphatic works like *Canvas* (1956) and *Drawer* (1957). The alignment of "JOHNS" and "HELL" is, I suspect, the other reason the artist has not returned to this equation: it is too extreme, at once emotional and personal, and in that regard does not quite fulfill the conditions of his project. At the same time, for all of his reticence, here is an early instance of the artist transgressing his own boundaries. His choice not to do it again suggests that he was aware that repeating this equation would turn it into a theme, as well as imply a conclusion. It would give him a reason to become closed and stop looking.

In counterpoint to the "Atlantic" side of the painting, Johns layered grayish-blue encaustic strokes over California and Arizona. It is as if a tsunami has washed over the Pacific coastline and submerged these states.[2] The Map paintings make it plain that nature and/or reality is unmanageable and cannot be contained by the names or boundaries we apply to it. The three-sided rectangle around "JOHNS '63 HELL," which protects

[a]

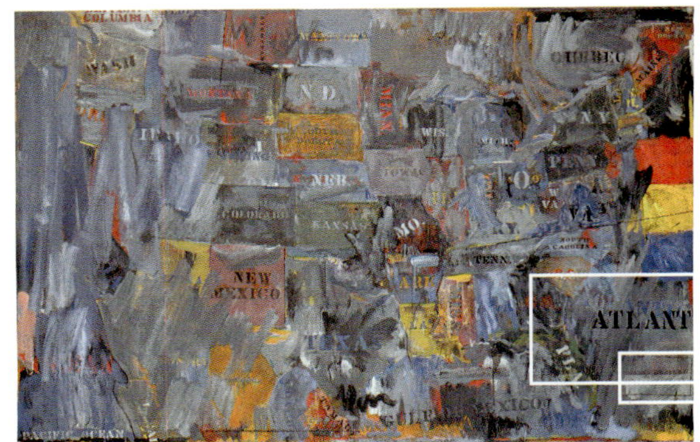

detail [b]

detail [c]

[b]

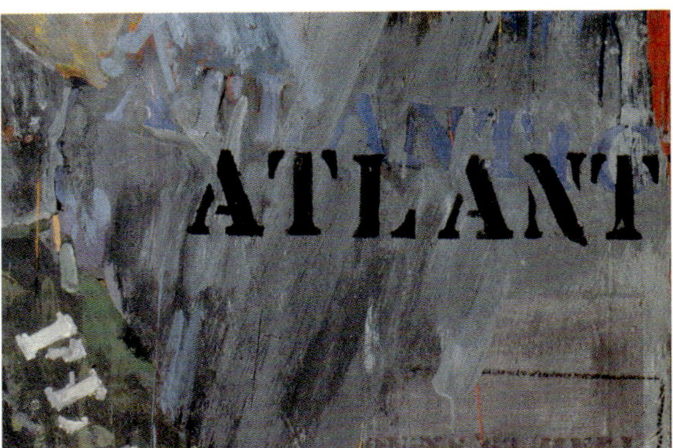

[c]

figs. IV: 3a–c **Jasper Johns** *MAP* [a] and two details [b, c] 1963

See fig. IV: 2.

neither the artist's name (identity) nor the date (a discrete moment—i.e., memory—singled out from an infinity of memories) from dissolution by the ocean, echoes this understanding of reality, or what the artist has called "a sense of life."[3] Water engulfs Johns's name and the western coastline. We live in the infinite and what we experience is only a tiny part of reality. Unable to stop time, we must be open to its passage and its ravages.

Taken as a progression, the three large Map paintings register an increasing sense of agitation and openness. Had Johns inflected each subsequent Map—*Double White Map* (1965) and *Green Map above White* (1966–67)—with stronger evidence of the ocean's inescapable havoc, he would have risked stepping beyond the impartial perception that the device offered him, shifting him away from objective consideration toward subjective expression. For the artist, the goal is to remain utterly objective no matter what he is contemplating, including his own mortality, which he views not as a theme but as a fact that necessitates visual facts.

Contrary to Stephen Koch's assertion that Johns produced a "sumptuous surface on which meaning was significantly refused,"[4] I would argue that the artist's integration of subject (map), materials (encaustic, oil, newspaper, etc.), and technique (stenciling, discrete layering of encaustic, collage) is predicated on the exact opposite: that meaning is embedded in things and eventually becomes evident. One reason that Koch and other critics have looked at Johns's work denotatively is that they have not completely separated themselves from some of the formalist positions of the 1950s. For them a map's identity rests in its two-dimensionality, rather than in being both a map of a landmass bordered on two sides by water and a flat thing. And, they would say, the map motif provided Johns not only with an image that could be incorporated into a two-dimensional surface but also with an array of separate states that enabled him to create a kind of alloverness, because each has its own graphic weight.

The critical refusal to look beyond formal innovation in Johns's art explains why many have not recognized that, in making the large, six-panel *According to What* (fig. VI: 2), he was not asking a question, but chronicling the material terms by which the world (including the artist) becomes known. By incorporating into this composition what Johns called the "watchman," or unthinking figure (an inverted body cast attached to a chair) (see Chapter Six)[5]—as well as elements that are textual (sculptural letters and stenciled words) and ocular (primary and secondary colors), things that have been simultaneously changed and preserved (silkscreened newspaper), indications of time passing (metal pulled away from the surface), and a visually established system (in a panel registering the tonal shifts from dark to light gray)—Johns detailed the simultaneity of material conditions that must be in play for a work to be true to reality. In the far-left panel, the watchman appears directly above a small stretched canvas that has been turned upside down and attached to the painting's surface with eyehooks (both the watchman and the canvas are inverted). The canvas can be detached to reveal the surface it hides. On the back, the artist stenciled the painting's title, "ACCORDING TO WHAT," which we must read (our intelligence). Traces of the title, written in pencil, are also upside down. Thus, if we look at *According to What* from left to right, we begin with the body (the falling watchman) and the mind (the spy who reads and is conscious that something remains unseen). As with poetry, the meaning of an artist's work is found in that individual's language, syntax, and vocabulary—in other words, the givens with which a piece is constructed.

Not only does a pre-existing critical discourse circumscribe how something is read or seen, but it also limits the ability to read or see what is actually there. Today, the act of reading a work of art and explicating it is thus restricted, for the most part, to only a few, proscribed lines of thought, a number of which have to do with the aesthetics of emptiness that Johns helped establish. And yet, in ironic contrast to the stable stripe abstractions of Frank Stella, who, as noted above, said, "What you see is what you see," and to the silkscreens of Coca-Cola bottles, with their supposedly witty social commentary, of Andy Warhol, who claimed all one needed to know is on "the surface of [his] paintings,"[6] Johns's Maps convey a state of flux, of formation and disintegration. If they are his "landscapes," as one art historian has stated, then their vistas are buffeted by change.[7] As with *Flag,* the map afforded Johns the possibility of discovering, through the inherent behavior of his materials—oil and encaustic—where appearance and reality overlap.

For Johns, seeing is a complex act that is not confined to the ocular. The two *Painted Bronze* sculptures (figs. III: 4, 5) and the Map paintings invite us to move past surface and image into an awareness of the object's tactility and physical presence as a thing. *Map* (1963) is not a purely visual experience: the layers of collage and the stenciled words require that we literally read some details of the painting, which extends the experience of it into the realm of textual apprehension. The tactile surface tempts us to touch it—the only avenue of art appreciation available to the blind, as opposed to the ocular and the textual. By conjoining these discrete and seemingly incompatible modes of comprehension, Johns acknowledges the limitations of the visual. Sight alone is an inadequate conveyor of knowledge. Our bond with reality involves all our senses, as well as our intelligence and our capacity to dream.

Johns may have paved the way for the aesthetics of emptiness, but he has never adhered to what many have defined as its underlying principles and assumptions. The real irony is that he appears to have lost critical currency for stepping into history—in his case, by making it—and just as quickly stepping out of it by remaining true to a vision of living within the immediacy of his own experience, which cannot be distilled into formalism or any other critical or theoretical discourse. Those critics who believe in historical progress and maintain a tacit allegiance to Marxist theory are unable to access Johns's work. Consequently, his iconoclasm has been downgraded to hermeticism, and the subject he has explored with an unparalleled ferocity has largely been ignored. It seems that reality, not to mention our unbreakable bond with it, is the last thing we want to have on our minds.

In Johns's art, a thing and a vision are interchangeable—the work is the palpable materialization of a vision; in Johns's vision of reality, each of us is a thing among things. Central to this vision is the moment when a solid form and dissolving reality inhabit each other, as in the letter "J" obliterated by encaustic in *Map* (1963). In the same painting, Johns went so far as to frame his perception of time's isolating effects upon us all when he named the liquid state (Atlantic Ocean) "HELL." Johns might be, as Michael

Kimmelman stated, a "virtuoso control freak,"[8] but one of his recurring subjects is the inevitable loss of control. Both *Map* (1963) and *Painted Bronze (Savarin can with brushes)* share a subject (brushes stuck in turpentine and a map of North America bordered by the Atlantic and Pacific oceans) that mirrors the liquid and solid states of the materials (encaustic and bronze) from which they are made. Echoing the artist's own words, we have the sense that he chose these materials out of "necessity," rather than desire. His mastery is not ego-driven, but subject-driven. This is why there are awkward passages in his work, and why he has refused to develop a style, which all too often becomes a machine that reduces everything to the same bland consistency.

CHAPTER 4
NOTES

1. *Map*'s stacked rectangles are restated in paintings such as *Land's End* and *Periscope (Hart Crane)* (figs. V: 1, 5) with the words "RED," "YELLOW," and "BLUE" superimposed on them but not necessarily on the color they designate. This suggests that our actual experiences are at once connected and disconnected, and that we cannot order reality into neat categories.

2. In *Map* (1962), Johns partially covered the stenciled word "CALIFORNIA" with a layer of encaustic. He had done the same in *Map* (1961), using blue oil paint.

3. *www.yale.edu.opa28.n17/story4.html*

4. Stephen Koch, *Stargazer: The Life, World, and Films of Andy Warhol* (New York/London: Marion Boyars, 1973; repr. 1985, 1991), p. v.

5. Jasper Johns, "Sketchbook Notes," *Art and Literature* (Lausanne) 4 (Spring 1965); repr. in *Jasper Johns: Writings, Sketchbooks, Notes, Interviews*, ed. Kirk Varnedoe, comp. Christel Hollevoets (New York: Museum of Modern Art, 1997), pp. 37, 59–60.

6. Stella: Interview by Bruce Glaser with Frank Stella and Donald Judd, broadcast by WBAI-FM, New York, Feb. 1964; published as "Questions to Stella and Judd," ed. Lucy R. Lippard, *ARTnews* 65, 5 (Sept. 1966), pp. 55-61. Warhol: Interview in *East Village Other* (1966), repr. in *I'll Be Your Mirror: The Selected Andy Warhol Interviews: 1962–1987*, ed. Kenneth Goldsmith (New York: Da Capo Press, 2004), p. 89: "If you want to know about Andy Warhol, just look at the surface of my paintings and films and me, and there I am. There's nothing behind it."

7. Roberta Bernstein, untitled essay, Jasper Johns: *The Maps*, exh. cat. (New York: Gagosian Gallery, 1989), p. 8.

8. Michael Kimmelman, "Catenary," *New York Times*, May 27, 2005, p. B32.

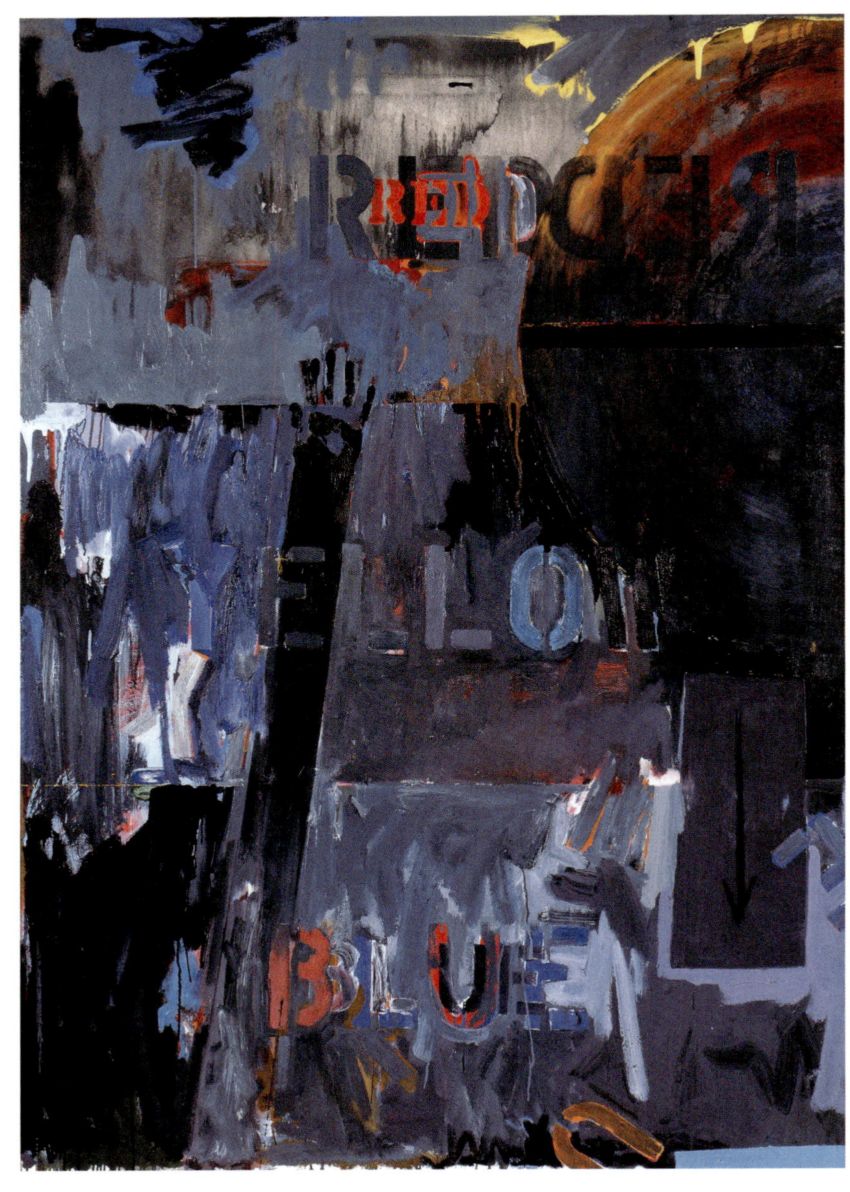

fig. V: 1 **Jasper Johns** *LAND'S END* 1963
Oil on canvas with wood 67 x 48 1/4 in. (170.2 cm x 122.6 cm)
San Francisco Museum of Modern Art. Gift of Mr. and Mrs. Harry W. Anderson

Chapter 5

I.

For the purposes of this book,
I have divided the paintings that Johns completed
between 1955 and 1966
into three loosely defined groups.

The pictorial work is examined in Chapter One, and the physical in Chapter Two. The third group explores groundlessness. I want to emphasize that these groupings are not hard and fast, and that there are many obvious exceptions to them.[1] Nonetheless, in addition to his three large Maps (see Chapter Four), between 1961 and 1963 Johns completed a number of rich, complex paintings in which ready-mades do not figure prominently. Often executed in oil rather than encaustic, these works mark a radical departure from his pictorial Flags, Targets, and Maps, as well as from his more physical gray encaustics.[2] They convey the feeling that a partially visible figure is hovering above or descending into a bottomless quagmire in a conflation of the temporal and the infinite. Included in this group are *Land's End* and *Periscope (Hart Crane)* (figs. V: 1, 5). The arm reaching up in *Land's End* has nothing to grab on to; it cannot stop itself from falling further. Time's passing pulls each of us closer to chaos, which in *Land's End* and *Periscope (Hart Crane)* is equated with reality, with what lies beyond the painting's edges. We become absorbed into something far larger than ourselves, and we lose our identities.

Until 1960, however, when he completed the two *Painted Bronze* pieces (figs. III: 4, 5), Johns had not directly addressed the impact time's passing may have on our consciousness. It should also be mentioned that the oceans in his Map paintings and the turpentine in *Painted Bronze (Savarin can with brushes)* evoke, through surrogates, dissolution, i.e., the ravages of time. However, neither the paintings nor the sculptures utilize a figure or part of a figure to indicate the individual's "helpless" relationship to reality. In these works, the artist seems to have been exploring whether he could find objective counterparts to dissolution and the effects of passing time without recourse to a ready-made or surrogate. Perhaps a deeper concern was whether, without something preformed, he could use the medium of painting itself to visualize his concept of helplessness.

Much of Johns's earlier work is based on his critical investigation of an existing thing, placing him in an observational position, a situation he might have concluded was too dependent on external circumstances. Having employed bronze and encaustic to encapsulate his view of the inseparable union of form (a coffee can crammed with brushes, the continental United States) and chaos (turpentine, the ocean), he might have wanted to move beyond this bond to a set of correlatives that define the body's entrapment in time. Another equally pressing reason why he might have changed his approach was his awareness that, if he continued using ready-mades,[3] he would risk repeating himself and diminishing the scope of his work from the specific to the generic. He might have concluded that casting about for another example of a solid body partially immersed in liquid would mean looking for a subject to a predetermined idea. Throughout his career, Johns has not only resisted this temptation but has gone to great lengths to circumvent what could be termed "directed looking" in order to remain detached, objective, and open.

Johns seems to have recognized that he had not yet placed a human figure in his work, with the exception of the fragments in *Target with Four Faces* (1955) and *Target with Plaster Casts* (fig. I: 4). Given that he is not, nor has he ever been, a purely abstract artist, in considering how to incorporate the figure into his work he must have sought to avoid repeating either his earlier innovation or the historical conventions governing the depiction of figures in painting. Moreover, he had to have wondered what solutions would be consistent with his dedication to the immediacy of palpable things and lived experience, which implicitly disallows illusion, description, anecdote, or any form of stepping back. It is a challenge to which he responded with unexpected means and conclusions.

In 1962 Johns made a suite of four drawings, all which he titled *Study for Skin* and sequenced using Roman numerals. For each drawing, he applied oil to his head and hands and pressed them against a sheet of drafting paper. He then rubbed charcoal over the paper; the charcoal adhered to the oil-soaked areas so that it appears as if someone with unrecognizable features were trapped within the sheet, becoming a ghostly physical presence. In *Study for Skin I* (fig. V: 2), Johns turned his head, resulting in a faint impression of his face, without eyes, while his left and right cheek and ears splay outward, like flayed skin. In this drawing, as well as in *Study for Skin II* (1962), Johns's handprints also appear, pressing against the paper as if it were an invisible barrier. Employing a process that is both direct and objective, he achieved something eerie and disturbing. As with *Flag,* the

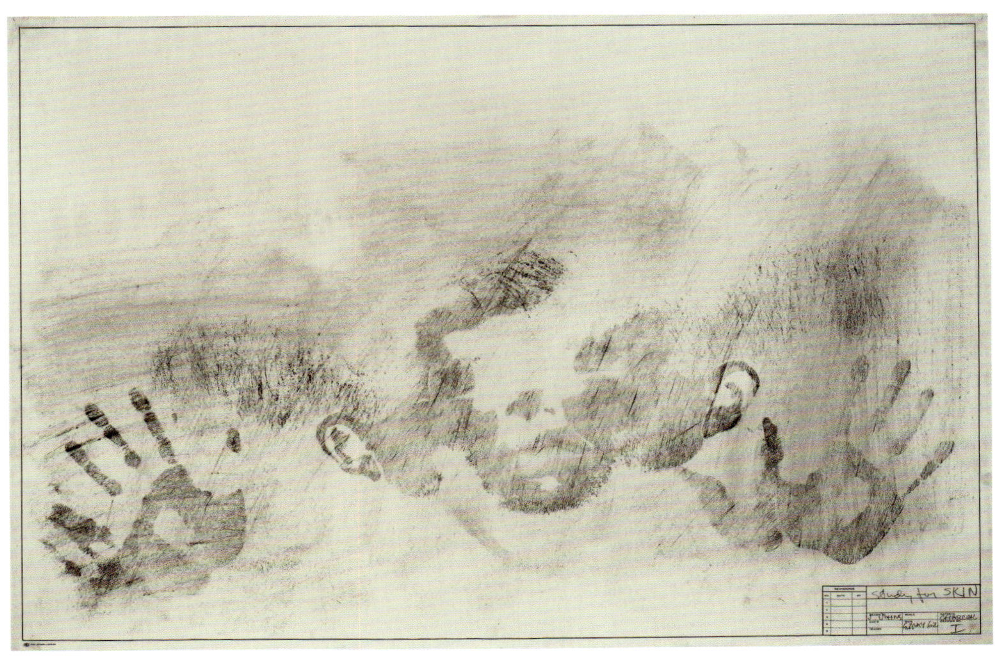

Jasper Johns *STUDY FOR SKIN I* 1962 fig. V: 2
Charcoal and oil on drafting paper 22 x 34 in. (55.9 x 86.4 cm)
Collection the artist

viewer sees a layered thing, at once image and physical evidence, a parallel world rather than an illusionistic representation.[4]

It is instructive to turn to a relatively minor and isolated work within Johns's oeuvre that nonetheless reveals the thoroughness with which the artist objectively explores his perception of the individual's relationship to reality and time. Done the same year as the enigmatically physical *No* (fig. II: 2), *Good Time Charley* (fig. V: 3) includes an inverted can, on which the painting's title has been stamped, and a downward-angled ruler. The title evokes an affable fellow who lives without regard to the future or to the consequences of his actions and who does not recognize that he is a vulnerable thing among things. The ruler has scraped away a wide arc of encaustic on the painting's surface, evidence of time's irreversibility, and has come to rest on top of the inverted container, suggesting that its rotation has tipped the can over. What's done is done, and nothing can alter it. Here, as in *Painted Bronze (Ale cans)*, Johns linked one activity with another: a ruler used for measuring and a can for carrying liquid. Is the artist's life really so different from that of a "good-time Charley"? After all, what they both do is irreversible. In *Good Time Charley* and *Weeping Woman* (1975) (see Chapter Eight), Johns drew parallels between his actions as an artist and those of others.

In making the transition from ready-mades and encaustic to devices and oil, Johns can be said to have enlarged his approach, moving from the pictorial and the physical to the realm of action, which introduces an intrinsically time-based element into his work. Viscous, slow-drying oil paint enabled him to both chronicle and preserve the effects of a physical act; he made the semicircle, for example, by attaching one end of a ruler or stretcher strip to the painting's surface and then dragging it through wet paint, uniformly smearing the gummy surface much as a wiper can produce patterns on a car windshield in a storm. The device that created the smear is also contained within the circumference of the semicircle it has made. Our influence on and engagement with the vastness of reality are minimal, at best.

Along the upper-right and upper-left edges of *Device* (fig. V: 4), Johns attached two wooden strips and dragged them through the field of oil paint, creating two inward-directed semicircles of uniformly smeared pigment. The strip on the left hangs at a slight angle, while the one on the right is rotated about a quarter of the way in, pointing downward at an angle. Except for a narrow ribbon of space along the bottom-right edge, the painting is covered with bursts of red, yellow, and blue.

On the lower-left side of the painting, a large area of mostly vertical blue strokes extends down from the lower perimeter of the semicircle, with at least one stroke extending into and over it, to nearly the bottom of the composition. Across the painting's lowest section, Johns stenciled "DEVICE," using brushwork and color to distinguish each letter. For example, the "D" is blue over orange, the "I" is mostly red and nearly merges with the red and orange ground, and the second "E" is green, with blue filling the spaces between the letter's three prongs. In order to read the title, we must keep adjusting our focus, at least in our mind's eye, to separate the letters (figure) from the brushwork (ground). In places they seem to be virtually merged together so that the acts of reading and looking are conflated, one constantly being inflected by the other.

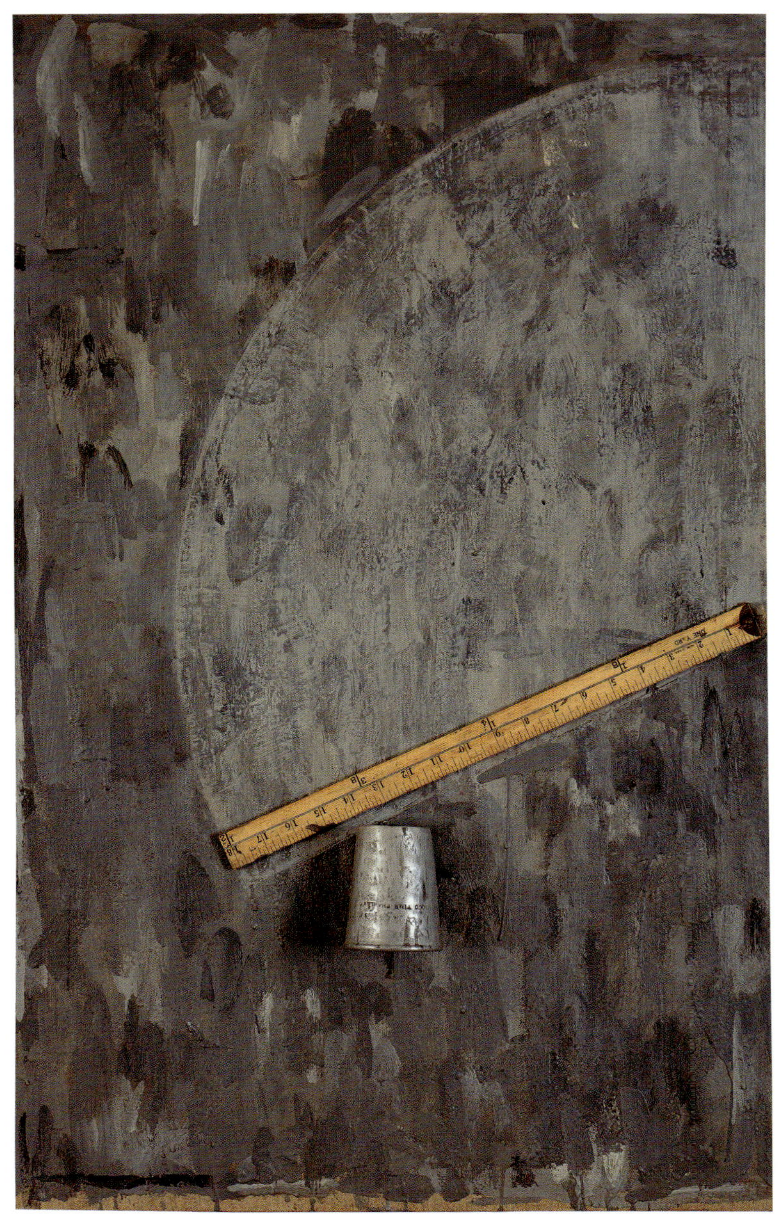

Jasper Johns *GOOD TIME CHARLEY* 1961 fig. V: 3
Encaustic on canvas with objects 38 x 24 x 4 1/2 in. (96.5 x 61 x 11.4 cm)
Philadelphia Museum of Art

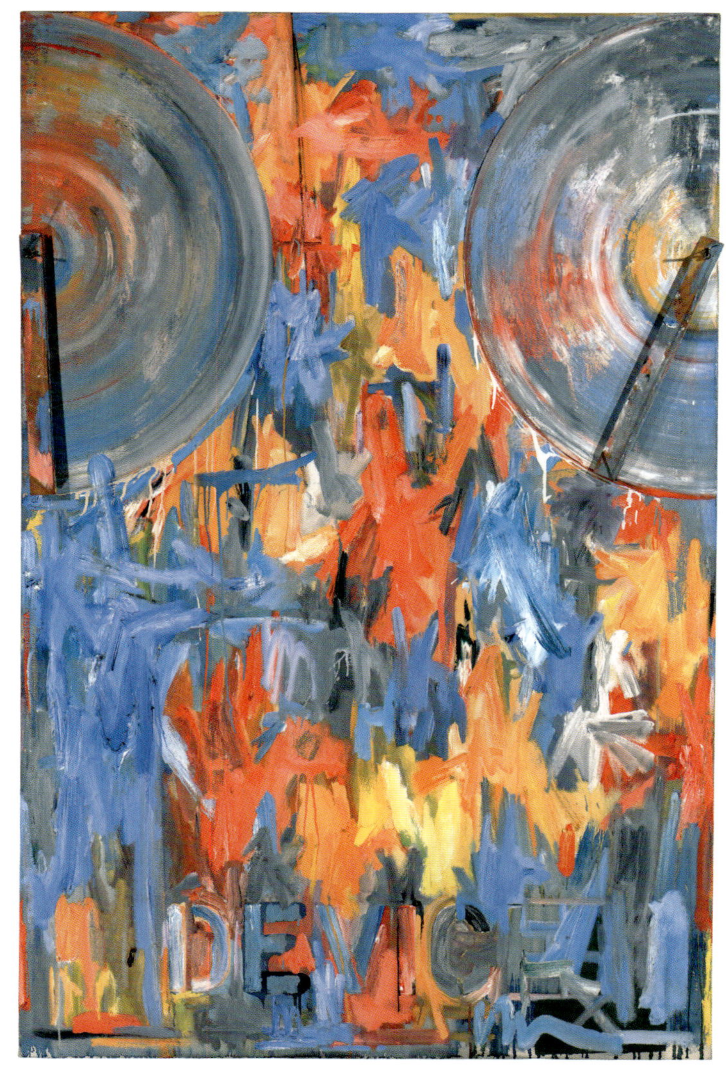

fig. V: 4 **Jasper Johns** *DEVICE* 1961–62
Oil on canvas with wood 72 1/16 x 48 3/4 x 4 1/2 in. (183 x 123.8 x 11.4 cm)
Dallas Museum of Art. Gift of the Art Museum League, Margaret J. and George V. Charlton, Mr. and Mrs. James B. Francis, Dr. and Mrs. Ralph Greenlee Jr., Mr. and Mrs. James H. W. Jacks, Mr. and Mrs. Irvin L. Levy, Mrs. John W. O'Boyle, and Dr. Joanne Stroud in honor of Mrs. Eugene McDermott

space in which he could also establish a wide range of appositions (the time of the newspaper and that of the flag as a symbol). Crane did this in "Cape Hatteras," where asyndetic expressions such as "star-glistered" and "larval-silver" abound. In the poet's joinings without conjunctions and the artist's compressions of encaustic and newspaper collage, brush and turpentine, we sense a shared understanding of their respective media, something Johns likely comprehended when he read Crane's poetry. In *Land's End* and *Periscope (Hart Crane)*, the asyndetic joinings consist of actions performed by the artist (handprint, stenciling, uniform smearing) that are registered in the pigment, as well as the combining of palm print and semicircle, name and color, and the correct and reversed spelling of names.

Johns purposefully does not attempt to resolve the dualism of time and space because it implies a stable world that keeps chaos and memory at bay. Nothing, not even art, can stop or even slow life's passing, much less relieve us of our memories. In fact, what interests Johns is conveying an awareness of both time and reality that includes the momentary and the infinite. The stenciling of the words "RED," "YELLOW," and "BLUE" in areas of color that may not be what the word indicates defines our predicament: the act of naming may have once connected Adam to nature, and even suggested his dominion over its inhabitants, but it no longer does so for us. The arm and palm print in *Land's End* simultaneously rise and fall along the painting's surface, as if protesting the nature of existence. They could be the arm and hand of Job held up stiffly in vain complaint, and they could be sliding inexorably down. This sense of helplessness and resistance, acceptance and rejection, is what makes *Land's End* so poignant. Rather than one action or the other—submission or defiance—it is both at once. Johns's ambiguity is disquieting because it does not tell us how to read the hand and arm. It is we who decide whether it is falling, or rising, or both.

In *Land's End*, *Periscope (Hart Crane)*, and a number of other works done between 1961 and 1963, Johns found a way to chronicle the conjunction of the body and two kinds of time without resorting to a ready-made. Through the device of reversed and "falling" words, he also evoked memory and gravity. We are always being pulled down, even as our minds wander forward and backward. While words are abstractions that signify reality, Johns's stenciled words are physical, signlike things pressed against a physical surface. Given this joining, we are led to ask, what is real and what is abstract? Do name and thing always exist in separate but connected realms? And if so, do we exist only in the world of language? Johns understands that reality seems to be made of language, that it is a constantly morphing description of itself. The stacking of red, yellow, and blue suggests that we are beyond land's end, and that the ocean (or dissolution) is not only before us, but around us. The color areas also suggest the spectrum, but, in contrast to Goethe, who believed that prismatic light was evidence of spiritual presence, Johns's stenciling and reversals remind us that it is we who name, however inadequately. In *By the Sea* (1961), Johns joined four narrow, horizontal canvases vertically. He stenciled the top three with "RED," "YELLOW," and "BLUE," and the bottom with the three words superimposed one above the next, making them nearly impossible to decipher. Considered from top to bottom, the work implies that order cannot overcome gravity, which inevitably leads to disintegration. The overlaid letters, and the difficulty we have distinguishing one from the others and from the ground, underscore the artist's vision of our indivisibility from our circumstances.

In *Land's End* and *Periscope (Hart Crane)*, Johns layered and interpenetrated different visual states, none of which dominates. The stenciling and superimposing of words evoke a shifting focus in terms of spatiality and distance. It is as if we are trying to locate something, perhaps ourselves, in relationship to our milieu, which includes memory. In the bottom rectangle of *Periscope (Hart Crane)*, for example, the letters of "BLUE" are inverted and slide down the canvas, figuratively detaching from it while naming the section in which they exist. Instead of emphasizing the two-dimensionality of the picture plane, Johns interrogated it. As he wrote in a sketchbook, "Take an object. Do something to it. Do something else to it."[13] In this case, the object is a painting.

The vertical arrangement of the color names, each located within its own demarcated section, also suggests a landscape, with "BLUE" at the bottom implying the ocean, the place from which, in *Land's End*, the arm and hand rise up and sink down. Presumably, the arm and hand are connected to a body that exists outside the area charted by the painting. For Johns the relationship between the viewers and the artwork is as between here and there; we are not separate entities but are joined. The implied figure literally has no place or plane on which to stand, suggesting that the ground under our feet is hardly secure. The only outcome of time of which we can be sure is that we will all succumb to the formless (or liquid) world.

By the early 1960s, Frank Stella had defined a painting as an insistently flat, self-contained, and autonomous object, while Andy Warhol, particularly in his grids of Coca-Cola bottles and green stamps, implied that what is within a painting endlessly replicates itself beyond its edges. For Stella art is about art, and for Warhol it was about availability, display, and social critique. Both artists believed that everything one needs to see is on the surface, and thus they rooted their art in the ocular. For Johns art is concerned with matter. He makes specific, tactile things that must be experienced on their own terms. They must be scrutinized. What happens to the things that extend beyond the canvas, such as the arm in *Land's End*, is never revealed.

In their heartrending crystallization of acceptance and resistance, suspension and immersion, future and past, *Land's End* and *Periscope (Hart Crane)* exhibit a visual perception that runs through Johns's oeuvre. In them something has been either partially submerged in or suspended above something else. Time has passed, and continues to pass. We live in both time and our memories, and neither consoles us.

CHAPTER 5
NOTES

1. For example, *Painting with Two Balls* (fig. II: 1) may be an assertively physical figure/ground painting, but its surface comprises pictorial bursts of mostly primary colors and large sections of collaged newsprint peeking through. And in their examination of the figure/ground relationship, simultaneity, and the different senses by which we apprehend reality, *False Start* (1959) and *Jubilee* (1959), in which colors and words are inseparable, form their own category.

2. Also to be mentioned in relationship to this type are *Canvas* (1956), *Drawer* (1957), *Coat Hanger* (1958), and *Gray Rectangles* (1959).

3. By 1961 these included the American flag, targets, numbers, the alphabet, a coat hanger, flashlights, lightbulbs, a coffee can and paintbrushes, ale cans, wooden balls, the map of the United States, body parts, a music box, stretcher bars, a book, a drawer, a thermometer, and a ruler, as well as the words "The," "No" (in three dimensions and in shadow), "Tennyson," "black," "gray," and "white," and the names of all of the primary and secondary colors.

4. Johns left his handprints as well on *By the Sea* (1961), which preceded the *Study for Skin* suite, as well as on *Land's End* (fig. V: 1), *Periscope (Hart Crane)* (fig. V: 5), the painting *Diver* (1962), and the drawing *Diver* (1963). All of these works share a concern for verticality, suspension, gravity, and falling.

5. Hart Crane, *The Poems of Hart Crane*, ed. Mark Simon, intro. John Unterecker (New York: Liveright, 1986), pp. 77–78.

6. Quoted in Michael Crichton, *Jasper Johns*, exh. cat. (New York: Harry N. Abrams, in association with the Whitney Museum of American Art, 1977), p. 50.

7. Crane (note 5), p. 78.

8. The most recent example of linking Johns's art to an aspect of his life about which he has said little can be found in James Rondeau, "Jasper Johns: Gray," in James Rondeau, Douglas Druick, et al., *Jasper Johns: Gray* (Chicago: Art Institute of Chicago, 2007), pp. 45–47. See also Kenneth Silver, "Modes of Disclosure: The Construction of Gay Identity and the Rise of Pop Art," in Paul Schimmel and Donna De Salvo, eds., *Hand-Painted Pop: American Art in Transition, 1955–1962*, exh. cat. (Los Angeles: Museum of Contemporary Art, 1992), pp. 179–203, esp. pp. 186–188. The most extensive attempt to link Johns's biography to his art can be found in Jill Johnston, *Jasper Johns: Privileged Information* (New York and London: Thames and Hudson, 1996).

9. Quoted in Crichton (note 6), p. 27.

10. Crane (note 5), p. 78.

11. These are the last words of Beckett's novel *The Unnamable*, trans. the author (New York: Grove Press, 1958).

12. Erwin Panofsky, "Über das Verhåltnis der Kungstgestiche zur Kunsttheorie," in ibid., *Aufsätze zu Grundfragen der Kunstwissenschaft*, ed. Hariolf Oberer and Egon Verheyen (Berlin): B. Hessling, 1974). For an insightful discussion of this essay, see Anita Albus, "From the Rainbow to the Earth," in idem, *The Art of Arts: Rediscovering Painting*, trans. by Michael Albus (Berkeley: University of California Press, 2001), pp. 114–15. I would like to thank Squeak Carnwath for alerting me to this book.

13. Jasper Johns, "Sketchbook Notes," *Art and Literature* (Lausanne) 4 (Spring 1965); repr. in *Jasper Johns: Writings, Sketchbooks, Notes, Interviews*, ed. Kirk Varnedoe, comp. Christel Hollevoets (New York: Museum of Modern Art, 1997), pp. 31, 54.

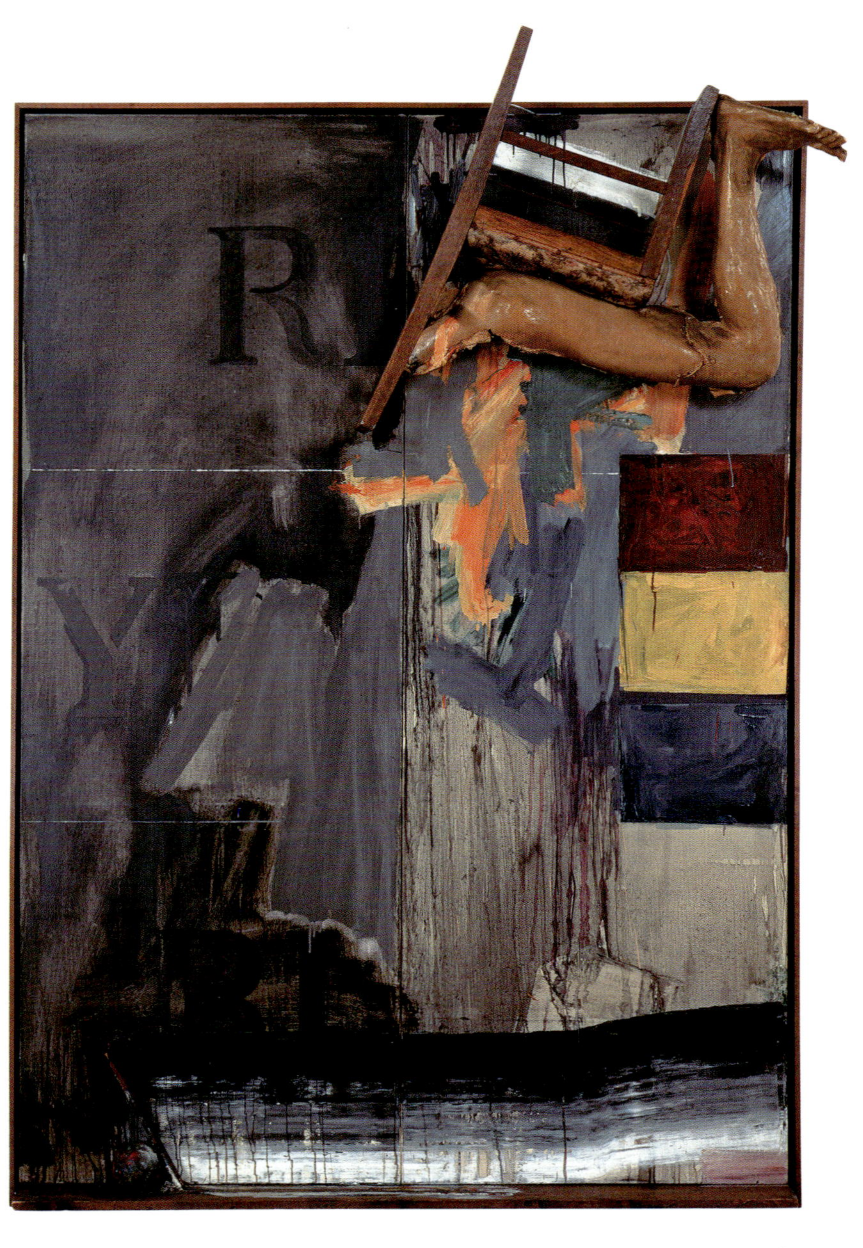

fig. VI: 1 **Jasper Johns** *WATCHMAN* 1964
Oil on canvas with objects (two panels) 85 x 60 1/4 in. (215.9 x 153 cm)
The Sogetsu Art Museum, Tokyo

Chapter 6

I.

In the spring of 1965,
Johns published "Sketchbook Notes"
in a quarterly magazine,
Art and Literature.[1]

Rather than seek asylum in a previously established discourse and align himself, however obliquely, with tradition, Johns took it upon himself to develop terms—at once limited and open-ended—that would allude to the states that he felt constitute the individual's existence in time, the randomness of sensations, and the uncontrollable nature of one's thinking. "Sketchbook Notes" is not a manifesto; rather, it is a notebook entry made public. In it the artist wrote about two figures: the "watchman" and the "spy." Never once using the word "I," Johns made it clear that these figures were not his alter egos, but a phenomenon common to many, including himself.

Johns seems to have asked himself whether could he visualize what it means to be a thing borne along by time. This would require that he develop through language a window that offered the reader a view of the ways he comprehended reality. Yet, by grounding his art in an understanding carefully defined in language, Johns most likely realized that he risked being branded solipsistic. After all, he was not setting out to explain his art or to disclose what it was about. He was working out stipulations that suggested something about the permanent links between the individual and reality, a subject that has engrossed philosophers for centuries.

Johns must have recognized that, if time isolates individuals from others, and to some degree from themselves, he had to construct a language that could suitably account for that separation. In addition, he had to acknowledge that any language he constructed would be something that others could read, that its very existence implies a reader, and thus that understanding by others is possible. It also had to be as calm and obdurately matter-of-fact as his Flags and Lightbulbs. It had to be a language of impartially stated details, rather than a treatise of opinions. After all, he was attempting to describe a condition that all of us inhabit: time's passing. Otherwise, he would be claiming to be the sole inhabitant of this isolation, as well as that the real force motivating his actions was a need for approval. The language had to be efficient and specific yet accessible, and the proposals had to be consistent with the originating terms he developed. They had to reflect his vision of reality.

Johns's terms posit something about the individual's relationship to what the philosopher Ludwig Wittgenstein called a "state of affairs."**2** Although "Sketchbook Notes" consists of three dense paragraphs followed by a list, I want to focus on the first paragraph, which is simultaneously poetic and theoretical, associative and logical:

> The watchman falls "into" the "trap" of looking. The "spy" is a different person. "Looking" is & is not "eating" and "being eaten." (Cézanne?—Each object reflecting the other.) That is, there is a continuity of some sort among the watchman, the space, the objects. The spy must be ready to "move," must be aware of his entrances & exits. The watchman leaves his job & takes away no information. The spy must remember & must remember himself & his remembering. The spy designs himself to be overlooked. The watchman "serves" as a warning. Will the spy & watchman ever meet? In a painting named Spy, will he be present? The spy stations himself to observe the watchman. If the spy is a foreign object, why is the eye not irritated? Is he invisible? When the spy irritates, we try to remove him. "Not spying, just looking"—Watchman**3**

Elsewhere in his 1965 sketchbook, Johns made two other observations worth noting: "encaustic (flesh?)" and "Beware of the body and the mind. Avoid a polar situation."**4** As I suggested earlier, one connection between encaustic and flesh is that both are vulnerable to changes in their environment. This susceptibility is highlighted by encaustic's reaction to heat. The "polar situation" Johns sought to avoid is the work of art that does not acknowledge the body's existence in time. The mind (or our capacity for idealization) should not be separated from the body (our unthinking material self), for this would lead to a purely intellectual art, that is to say a kind of looking that does not take into account the body's vulnerability to change and runs the risk of becoming cut off and solely aesthetic, not to mention false to reality.

On a simple level, "watchman" is Johns's term for the body, while "spy" is his term for the mind. Each engages reality differently; the watchman passively "falls 'into' the 'trap' of looking," while the spy is an invisible presence who is actively "spying." Looking is a "trap" because it is done without consciousness. The watchman, or body, tends to take in appearances without regard to their meaning. He appreciates the beauty of the sunset but does not probe its embodiment of time's relentlessness and indifference. "The spy stations himself to observe the watchman" in order to achieve a state of painful attentiveness similar to what Rainer Maria Rilke described near the beginning of the "The First Elegy" of the *Duino Elegies*:

> For beauty is nothing but the beginning of terror, which we are still
> just able to endure,
> and we are so awed because it serenely disdains to annihilate us.[5]

As demonstrated in *Flag* (fig. I: 1) and the Maps (see fig. IV: 2), one of Johns's central preoccupations is recognizing that instant of perception when the appearance of beauty, which in the artist's case comes in the form of ordinary and pre-existing things, and reality's serene disdain are identical. The spy, obsessed with discovering the reality of all situations, must see through what the watchman is content to look at. The body does not remember ("The watchman leaves his job & takes away no information"), while one's consciousness (or spy) "must remember & must remember himself & his remembering" and "station[s] himself to observe the watchman." The spy must discover the information that the watchman misses, even though it is right before his very eyes. Johns's project demands that he be attentive, even as it subtly accuses him of not being attentive enough.

Two of the verbs Johns used to describe the watchman are "falls" and "serves." Both imply a condition that is unavoidable ("helpless"); they are not actions we necessarily choose to do, but typically ones we cannot help but do. The state of falling is critical to *Land's End* and *Periscope (Hart Crane)* (figs. V: 1, 5), as we have seen, and to the artist's largest drawing, *Diver* (1963), the paintings *Watchman* and *According to What* (figs. VI: 1, 2), and many works from the early 1980s to the present. No matter what we are doing, we are always falling, always approaching that moment when we will disappear forever into the earth.

Caught in time, the body's susceptibility to change "'serves' as a warning." "The spy stations himself to observe the watchman" and to confirm these shifts on the defenseless body. Although the tone of the text is cool, it seems evident that Johns's awareness of time is excruciatingly intense. In the sentence "The watchman leaves his job & takes away no information," Johns disclosed the motivating factor of his art. Unlike a watchman, a spy's

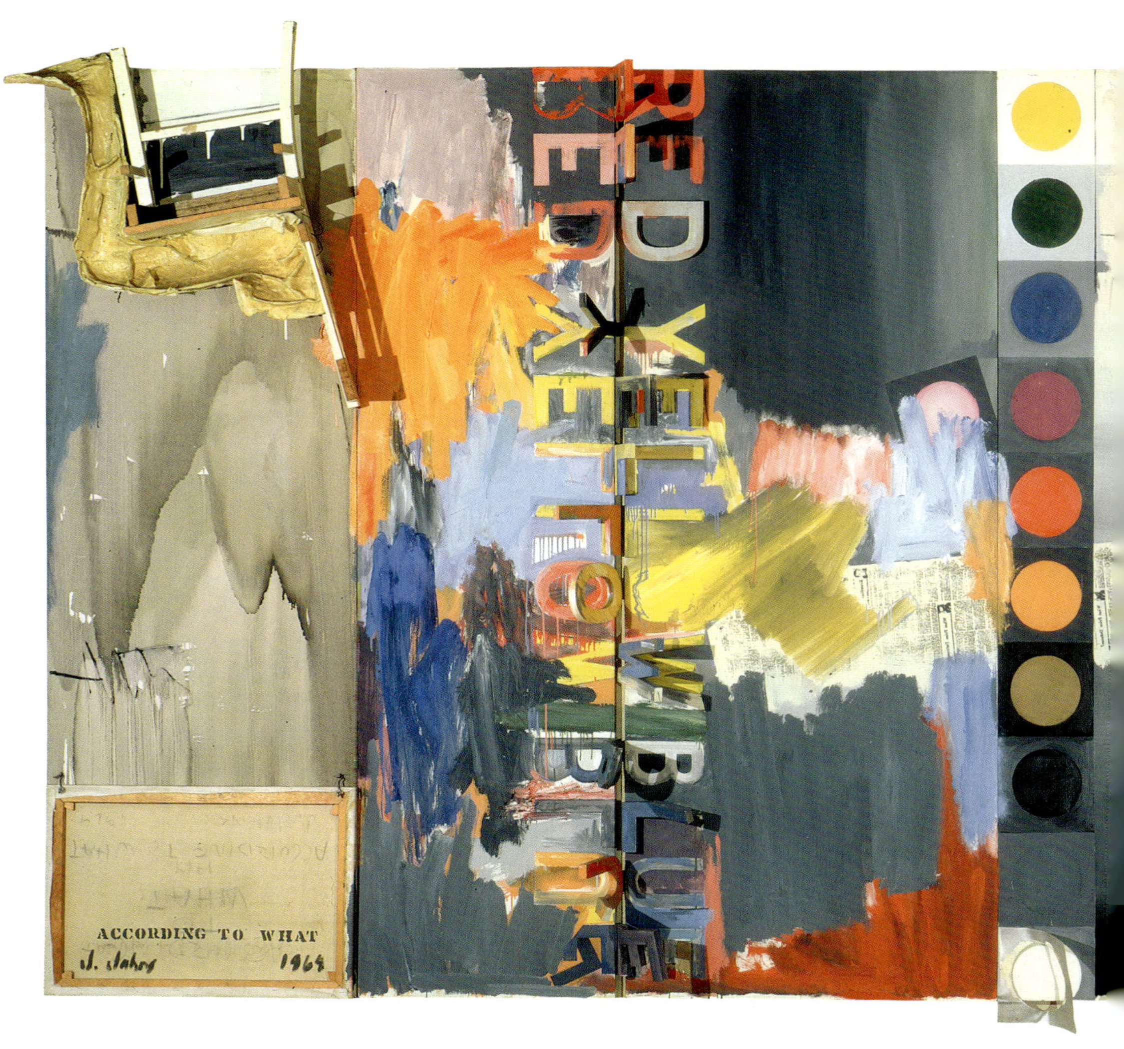

ACCORDING TO WHAT
J. Johns 1964

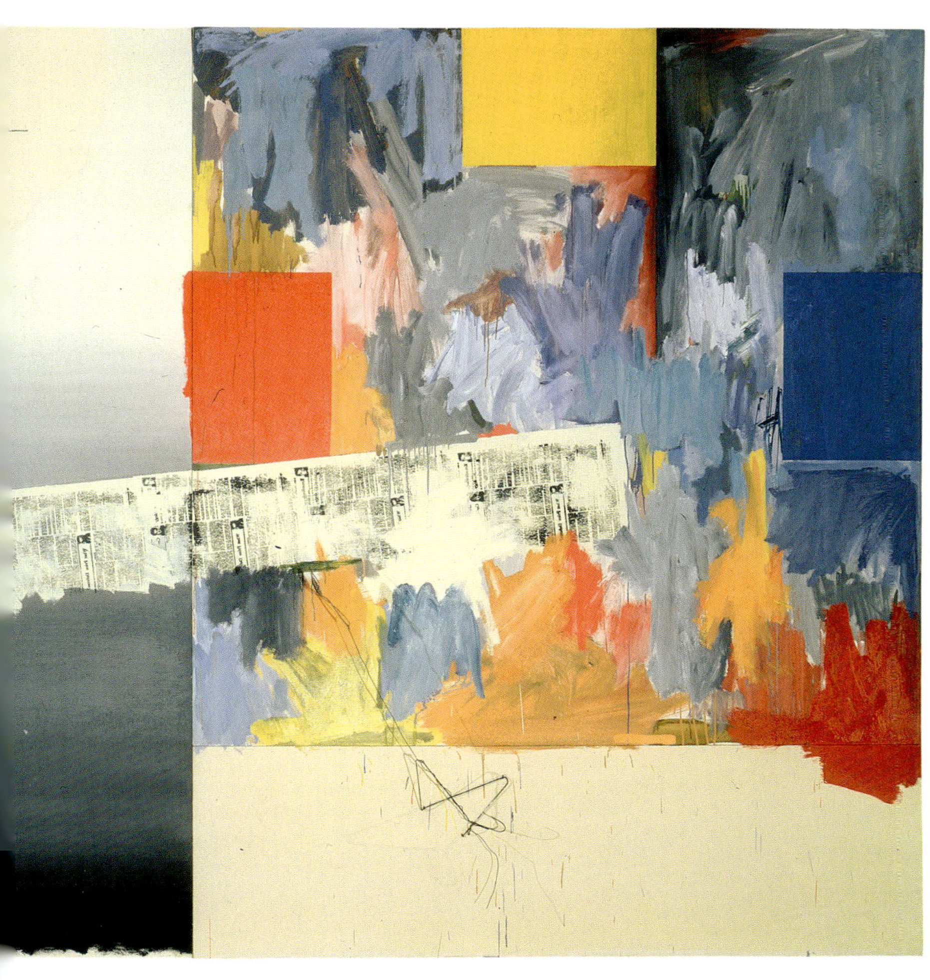

Jasper Johns *ACCORDING TO WHAT* 1964 fig. VI: 2
Oil on canvas with objects (six panels) 7 1/3 x 16 ft. (2.24 x 4.88 m)
Private collection

primary task is to ferret out the whole story, however disturbing it might be. By naming our consciousness the "spy," Johns underscored that he is not content with looking, but, like a spy, is compelled to sort fact from fiction.

To quote Johns's terms, which seem to derive from spy and mystery novels, it was the watchman who dreamed he was painting the American flag and who had fallen "'into' the 'trap' of looking"; but it was the spy who observed the watchman and disentangled the reality that lay beneath the appearance of what he was looking at. The watchman and the spy are alike in that they are both engaged with and by the material world. In the spy's case, however, the application of certain interrogative techniques to what has been looked at, as well as a sensitivity to a material's inherent behavior, frames the nature of the examination: how he will be able to clarify what the watchman has experienced, but not comprehended. The watchman had the dream, but the spy had to discern its meaning. The inseparable proximity of the watchman and the spy is imperative to Johns's aims; by bringing together "looking" and "spying" ("seeing through"), Johns found verbal equivalents for the indispensable bond between appearance and reality. His preoccupation with the nature of this union began with *Flag* and has continued through "Sketchbook Notes" to the present.

II.

Johns's abiding concern with the relationship between appearance and reality is one reason he was drawn in the early 1960s, before writing "Sketchbook Notes," to the works of Wittgenstein.

In *Philosophical Investigations*, posthumously published in 1953, Wittgenstein examined, among a range of topics, the issue of subjective and objective experience. He was concerned with discovering the basis of knowledge: how one knows what one knows. While Johns did not make the six-panel painting *According to What* in direct response to his reading of Wittgenstein, the work clarifies some of the objective measures basic to his investigations of the relationship between facade and veracity: primary colors are the basis of all other colors, grisaille is the standard way of measuring light and dark, the body is vulnerable to circumstance (the inverted chair and figural cast in the upper-left-hand corner), figure and ground are inseparable, and certain techniques have the ability to both preserve and transform something (the silkscreened newspaper that stretches across three panels). All of these measures are both conventional and accessible, which is one reason why Johns repeatedly uses them in his art. He deliberately eschews the subjective and the expressionist, as well as anything that might be seen as an attempt to develop a private language, as this would result in both a hermetic and a highly subjective view of reality.

In an earlier four-panel painting, *4 the News* (fig. VI: 3), Johns seems to have responded directly to something he read in *Philosophical Investigations*. In one passage in this collection of numbered, rather gnomic statements, Wittgenstein, exploring the unreliability of memory and its relationship to reality, described a man trying to corroborate his recollection of the time a train departs by calling to mind the image of the timetable. Among other things, Wittgenstein used this example to point out the fallacies to which such solipsistic thinking might lead—and certainly this is a pitfall into which art can also stray. If we cannot count on memory, how do we determine what is true, particularly if what lies outside our memory may also not be helpful in discerning the truth? Wittgenstein reinforced his understanding of this dilemma with the following: "As if someone were to buy several copies of the morning paper to assure himself what it said was true."[6] Repetition does not constitute truth, only repetition.

In contrast to Wittgenstein's example of "several copies of the morning paper," Johns wedged a single, rolled newspaper between the top two panels of *4 the News*. Nonetheless, like Wittgenstein, the artist focused here on what is simulacrum and what is truth, using the newspaper as an illusion of reality. Along the bottom panel, Johns stenciled the painting's title and "PETO JOHNS." Near the bottom-right side of the same panel, he pressed his left hand into the paint. Its placement suggests that someone is reaching across his body, as well as underscores that the painting is both visual and tactile. We reach for the news, but what does it tell us? In the middle of the bottom panel, he stenciled the word "THE" twice, superimposing the smaller version over the larger one.[7] The last line of Wallace Stevens's poem "The Man on the Dump" may have inspired the artist's doubling of the word "THE": "Where was it one first heard of the truth. The the."[8]

As in Stevens's poem, Johns's doubling of "THE" proposes that there is no such thing as an overarching truth, just "The the." Grammatically, we often use "the" before something or someone that has already been mentioned, as well as to distinguish that example from all others. The apposition of the two denies the possibility of ultimate truth without settling for complete relativism. Is there a way of thinking and being that does not align itself with a "The the," as Stevens succinctly stated? Given the close attention Johns pays to the relationship between appearance and authenticity, this question seems pertinent.[9]

"PETO" refers to the nineteenth-century American trompe l'oeil artist John F. Peto; this is the first time that Johns openly acknowledged the influence of another artist on his work. The title *4 the News* derives from Peto's painting *The Cup We All Race 4* (fig. VI: 4),[10] in which the artist depicted, in a hyper-realist style, a dented tin cup hanging from a hook affixed to a wooden panel. On the work's painted wooden frame, Peto inserted the title, executed in such a way as to resemble letters gouged out of the wood by a knife. Above the cup, on the top slat of the frame, Peto depicted a brass plate stamped with his name. To the right, four nails hold four torn paper corners—evidence that something, possibly a postcard, has been ripped from its place. As the painting's title and style suggest, paint became the most precise way for Peto to explore the discrepancy between

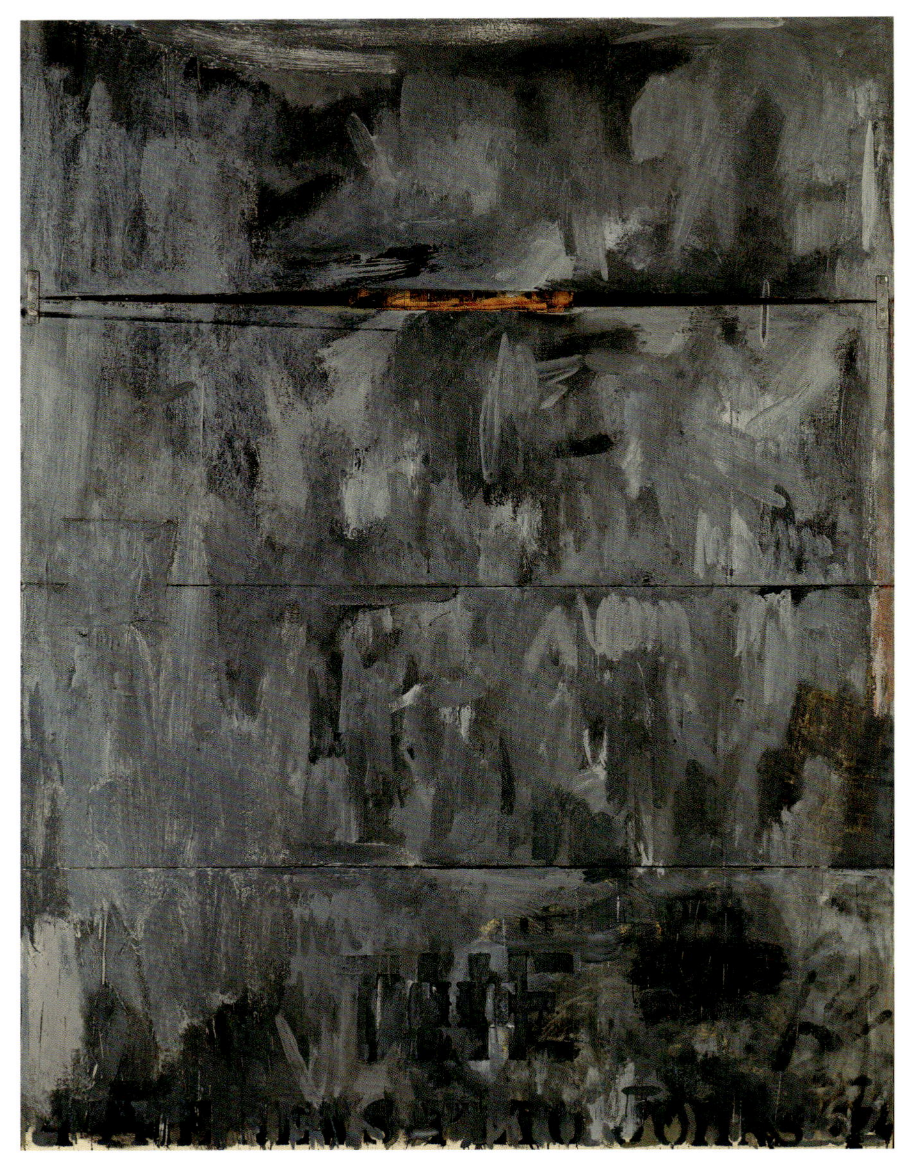

fig. VI: 3 **Jasper Johns** *4 THE NEWS* 1962
Encaustic and collage on canvas with objects 65 x 50 in. (165.7 x 127 cm)
Kunstsammlung Nordrhein-Westfalen, Düsseldorf

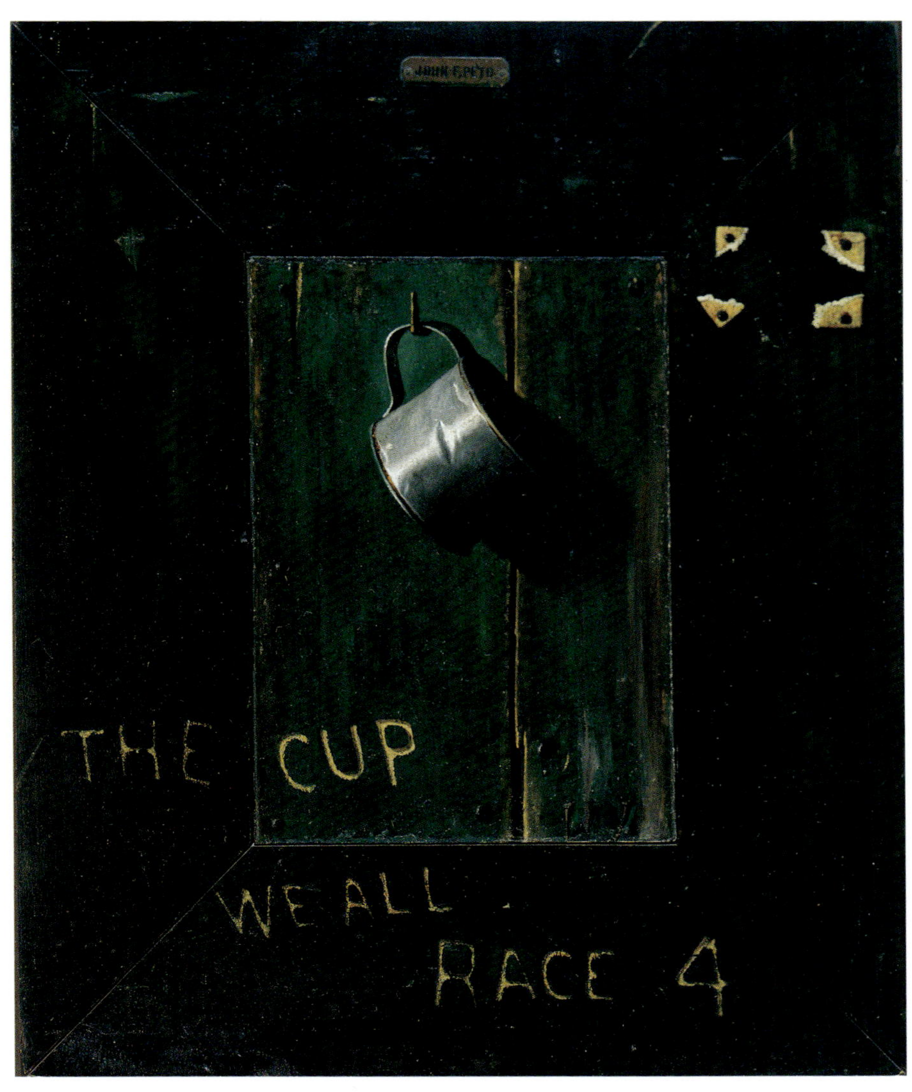

John F. Peto *THE CUP WE ALL RACE 4* c. 1900 fig. VI: 4
Oil on canvas and wooden panel 25 1/2 x 21 1/2 in. (64.8 x 54.6 cm)
Fine Arts Museums of San Francisco. Gift of Mr. and Mrs. John D. Rockefeller 3rd

appearance and reality. Everywhere in the composition, he chronicled the effects of time. The prize we all race for is a dented tin cup. In Johns's painting, what we race for is the newspaper, which does not lead to veracity, but away from it.

In less than a decade, Johns had gone from what seem to be single sources of inspiration to composites of multiple ones, in this case Peto and possibly Wittgenstein and Stevens. Despite working in very different traditions and media, each man focused on the relationship between the subjective and the objective, paying particular attention to how one can uncover the objective. Like Johns's spy, both the philosopher and the poet sought the information that reality can be made to disclose. In order to extract it from the sensory world, in their work they carefully reconstructed the perception, rather than the object, of their attention. Not concerned with mimesis, they were able to reveal the assumptions and false conclusions inherent in acts of apprehension that many of us do automatically.

In reaching for a newspaper—that particular manifestation of the "news"—do we overlook or ignore our relationship to reality? A newspaper gets older by the minute. The paper in Johns's painting was already old news when he incorporated it into the work; it chronicles the past, rather than responds to or engages with the changing present. The news items are closed to reality, while the painting with its breach actually is open to time (the newspaper ages). The present tense is Johns's primary concern: How do we remain alert, even as we fall toward dissolution? The spy observing the watchman is his answer.

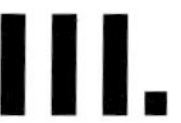

In the catalogue for the 1959 exhibition "Sixteen Americans"
at the Museum of Modern Art, New York,
Johns cited his interest in "three academic ideas"
that could be traced back to these sources:
Paul Cézanne and Cubism, Marcel Duchamp, and Leonardo.

He was taken with "Leonardo's idea (Therefore, O painter, do not surround your bodies with lines...) that the boundary of the body is neither part of the enclosed body nor part of the surrounding atmosphere."[11] Nearly six years later, in "Sketchbook Notes," Johns developed what he called an academic idea into a decidedly non-academic possibility: "That is, there is a continuity of some sort among the watchman, the space, the objects." By stressing "a continuity of some sort," the artist continued the thinking implicit in his understanding of Leonardo's concept of the "boundary." And, in his emphasis on continuity, Johns contradicted those commentators who regarded his works from 1964 to 1971 as being "unsettled and eclectic."[12] For the artist, the "continuity" is the bond between form and formlessness, a material thing and change.

In *Watchman* the artist attached and inverted a partial body cast (thigh and calf) seated on a chair in the upper-right-hand corner of the painting, the unseen head presumably pointing down. Along the bottom is a wooden board that extends into the viewer's space, like a shelf. In a "Sketchbook Note" from 1964, Johns had written: "Put a lot of paint & wooden ball or other object on a board. Push to the other end of the board. Use this in a painting."[13] If we ask ourselves why the artist followed the note's instructions in *Watchman*, the answer might be found in the two sculptures titled *Painted Bronze* (figs. III: 4, 5); and the condition of the *after* and *before* they bracket (see Chapter Three). The wooden strip Johns used to push the paint-covered ball left a grisaille trail across the bottom of *Watchman.* Inverted above the smear is the watchman; the implication is that he is suspended and, it would seem, waiting to fall. The ball, strip, and smear define the *after*: they were utilized to do something that cannot be reversed. The inverted body inhabits the *before*; it is still suspended, and the action its position implies has not been completed. Johns's interpretation of time's continuum is embodied in the connection between the *after* and the *before*. In contrast to conventional narratives of before and after, with their emphasis on happy endings or transcendence, Johns's view shifts the focus to the present, with the understanding that we live between these two states, where the moment after the before is chaos and death, the "HELL" of dissolution that we read in *Map* (1963).

CHAPTER 6 NOTES

1. Jasper Johns, "Sketchbook Notes," *Art and Literature* (Lausanne) 4 (Spring 1965), pp. 185–92; repr. in *Jasper Johns: Writings, Sketchbooks, Notes, Interviews*, ed. Kirk Varnedoe, comp. Christel Hollevoets (New York: Museum of Modern Art, 1997), pp. 25–37, 49–60. The first English translation of Maurice Merleau-Ponty's essay "Cézanne's Doubt" appeared in the same issue of *Art and Literature*, as did poems by Ted Berrigan and Frank O'Hara. Johns alluded to work of both poets long before they became well known. Johns's painting *In Memory of My Feelings–Frank O'Hara* (1961) takes its title from a poem by Frank O'Hara; one year after Grove Press published *The Sonnets* by Ted Berrigan, the artist silkscreened the book's title page and blank facing page in his painting *Screen Piece 3* (1968).

2. Ludwig Wittgenstein, *Tractatus Logico-Philosphicus*, trans. David Francis Pears and Brian McGuiness (New York: Routledge Classics, 2001), pp. 6–7. The following sentence from Wittgenstein's book is highly relevant: "A state of affairs (a state of things) is a combination of objects (things)."

3. *Jasper Johns: Writings* (note 1), pp. 37, 59–60.

4. Ibid., pp. 33–34, 56.

5. Rainer Maria Rilke, *The Selected Poetry of Rainer Maria Rilke*, trans. Stephen Mitchell (New York: Vintage Books, 1989), p. 151.

6. Ludwig Wittgenstein, *Philosophical Investigations*, 2nd edition, trans. by G. E. M. Anscombe (New York: MacMillan Company, 1958), p. 265.

7. Johns embedded the word "The" once before, in the encaustic painting *The* (1957; private collection).

8. *The Collected Poems of Wallace Stevens* (New York: Alfred A. Knopf, 1957), p. 203.

9. Johns told the author that he first read Stevens's poem when he was a teenager. More than three decades later, he made an etching that was used as a frontispiece to a limited edition of Stevens's poems, published by Arion Press in 1985, with an introduction by Helen Vendler, who also selected the poems. The etching led to the painting *Winter*, which eventually became part of a cycle, *The Seasons* (figs. X: 8–11).

10. Also related to Peto are two paintings Johns completed between 1983 and 1984, both of which he titled *Racing Thoughts* (figs. IX: 3, 4). Johns told the author that he first learned of Peto's work from a reproduction that the dealer Ileana Sonnabend sent him, most likely in 1961.

11. Jasper Johns, artist's statement, in Dorothy C. Miller, ed., *Sixteen Americans*, exh. cat. (New York: Museum of Modern Art, 1959), p. 22; repr. in *Jasper Johns: Writings* (note 1), p. 20.

12. See for example Kirk Varnedoe, *Jasper Johns: A Retrospective*, exh. cat., with an essay by Roberta Bernstein (New York: Museum of Modern Art, 1996), p. 223.

13. *Jasper Johns: Writings* (note 1), p. 58.

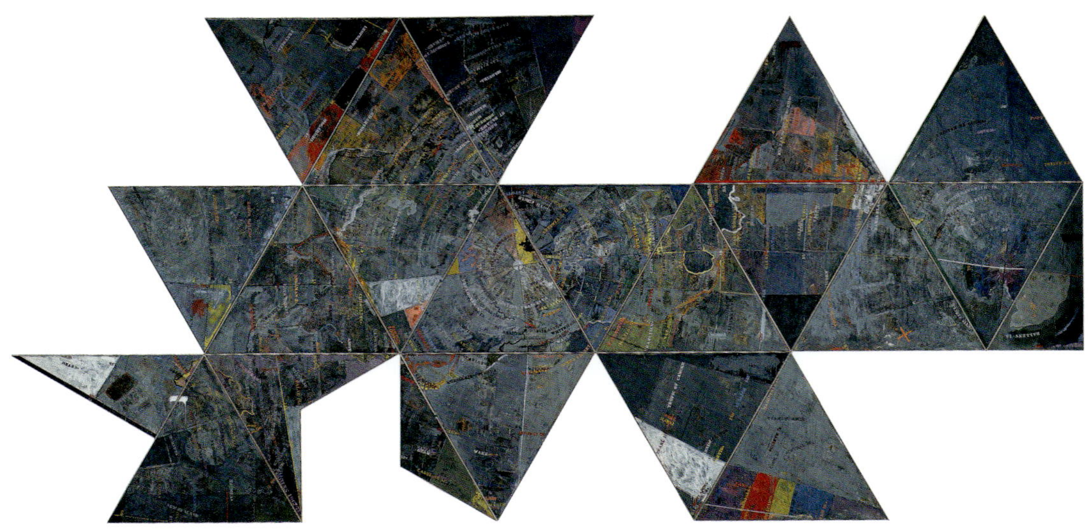

fig. VII: 1 **Jasper Johns** *MAP (Based on Buckminster Fuller's Dymaxion Air Ocean World)* 1967–71
Encaustic and collage on canvas (twenty-two parts) 16 ft. 4 7/8 in. x 32 ft. 9 11/16 in. (5 x 10 m)
Museum Ludwig, Cologne

Chapter 7

I.

Before discussing Johns's use of the crosshatch, I want to return to the Map paintings, specifically one on which he worked from 1967 to 1971: *Map (Based on Buckminster Fuller's Dymaxion Air Ocean World)* (fig. VII: 1).[1]

By far the largest painting to date in his oeuvre, it consists of twenty-two triangular sections, which can be realigned to make different two-dimensional configurations of the globe. Fuller's *Dymaxion Air Ocean World* is a projection of the world onto the surface of a polyhedron, which is then opened up and flattened out. He believed that this map resulted in less distortion than the Mercator projection, where the globe is laid out on a cylindrical form. Fuller's is a two-dimensional map that, in its adjoining triangular shapes, retains a trace of being a three-dimensional object. In Johns's version of the Dymaxion, the earth's continents are shown as a nearly always connected landmass entirely surrounded by the oceans. Fuller's polyhedron can be unfolded in different ways; one configuration, for example, shows the oceans surrounded by the continents, with the exception of Antarctica, which is enveloped by water.

In its ability to shift from two dimensions to three, Johns's *Map (Based on Buckminster Fuller's Dymaxion Air Ocean World)* led to his *Usuyuki* paintings and works on paper (1977–81) (see fig. VII: 5). In addition, the fact is that a flat thing made up of equal-size sections that can be rearranged must have been on Johns's mind when he developed his crosshatch paintings and the systems underlying their organization. It may also be that Johns, during the five years he worked on *Map*, had time to consider how a planar object might be broken up and reconfigured, and how he might make this evident in the painting itself. *Map* not only prepared Johns for the crosshatch but also may have helped him recognize how a cluster of similarly colored parallel lines could be useful.

II.

In *Untitled* (fig. VII: 2), a four-panel painting from 1972, Johns introduced a new motif, colored clusters of parallel lines or hatch marks resembling an abstract handprint.

According to the artist, he had seen something similar on a passing car, and knew at once that he would use the pattern. Later, in an interview, he said, "It had all the qualities that interested me—literalness, repetitiveness, an obsessive quality, order with dumbness, and the possibility of complete lack of meaning."[2] This last observation signals that Johns is interested in meaninglessness as something into which meaning can be introduced.

Untitled includes cast body parts attached to paint-spattered strips of wood on the right panel and a flagstone pattern on the middle two. Crosshatching fills the entire panel on the left. The flagstone pattern is repeated, with the left half of the middle-left panel reappearing in the right half of the middle-right panel. This shift in placement suggests a sequential reading from left to right, implying that both panels belong to a bigger pattern that cannot be fully grasped. In this reading, the "conclusion" is the panel with the cast body parts and wooden strips. The body fragments evoke chaos and destruction as the unavoidable, final destination. The literalness of this statement is unique in Johns's work, and he refrained from doing it again. Like the word "HELL," which we find in *Map* (1963) (fig. IV: 2), the fragmented body casts appear only once in his work. To do so more than once would have thematized them, as well as suggested that they were conclusive. The sense of movement in the flagstone panels can also imply that we cannot see the actual right portion of the middle-right section, which has slid beneath the panel of body parts. From this slippage, we can infer that what remains visible in both flagstone panels is a glimpse of something larger.

The process of shifting is embodied in the actual materials used in the flagstone panels: Johns executed the one on the left in oil and the one on the right in encaustic. The shift that he registered in these two sections, as well as the recurrence and disruption of the flagstone pattern, is not confined to an ageless visual realm; it takes place in time, just

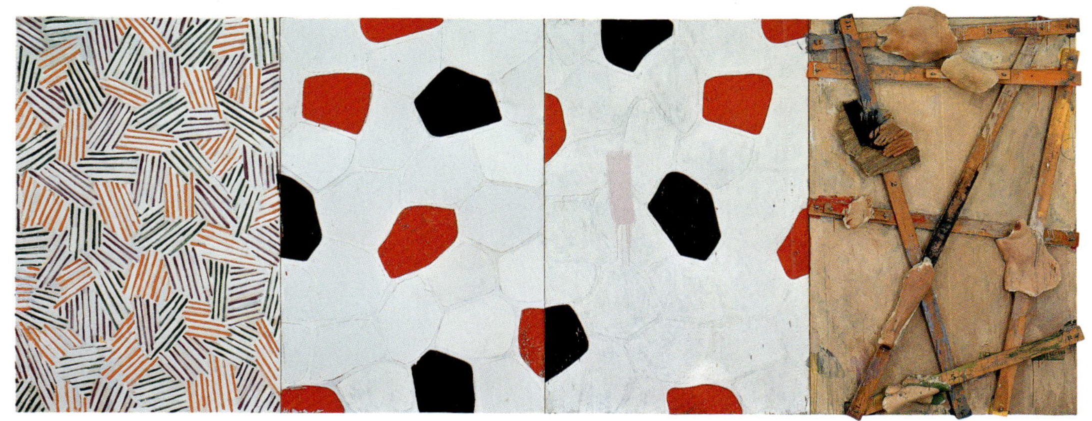

Jasper Johns *UNTITLED* 1972 fig. VII: 2
Oil, encaustic, and collage on canvas with objects (four panels)
6 ft. 1/16 in. x 16 ft. 1 in. (1.83 x 4.9 m)
Museum Ludwig, Ludwig Donation, Cologne

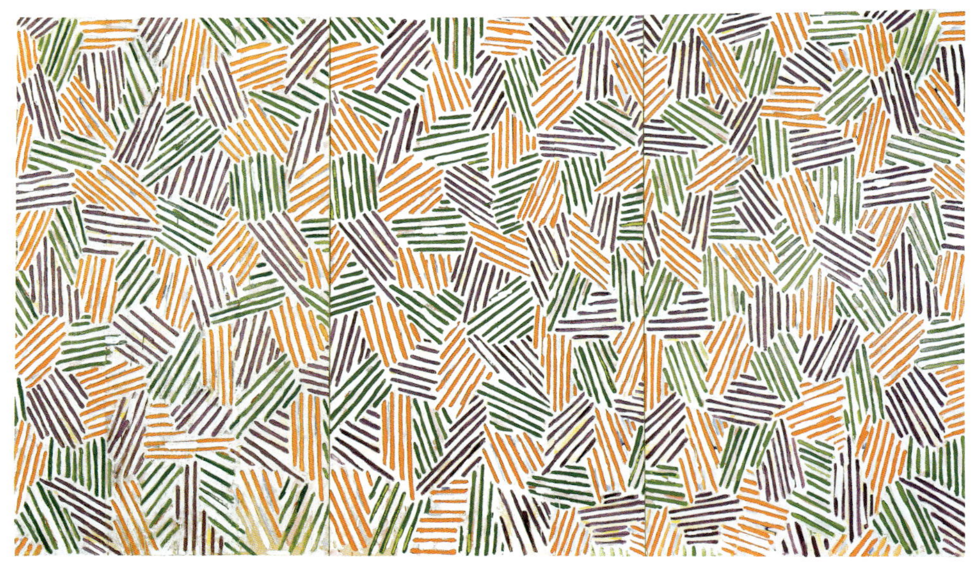

fig. VII: 3 **Jasper Johns** *SCENT* 1973–74
Oil and encaustic on canvas (three panels) 6 ft. x 10 ft. 6 1/4 in. (1.83 x 3.21 m)
Ludwig Forum für Internationale Kunst, Aachen

as a patch of dripping violet—a singular, out-of-place element on the flagstone pattern—evokes both irreversibility and gravity. Johns pressed an iron near the bottom of the seam between the right flagstone pattern and the body-cast section. Its imprint connects the panels like a hinge, while revealing encaustic's vulnerability to heat. All of the elements seen and invoked in *Untitled*—patterning, slippage, materiality, time, irreversibility, gravity, helplessness—reappear as major factors in Johns's future crosshatch paintings, reminding us that uniqueness and repetition are inseparable aspects of reality.

In *Scent* (fig. VII: 3), which Johns started after he completed *Untitled*, he synthesized the crosshatch pattern and a schematic structure derived from his flagstone panels. The work's palette of purple, orange, and green (secondary colors) suggests that the "scent" was derived from something mixed with something else. Johns's schematic structuring of the hatch marks, as well as their color, enabled him to define every inch of a painting while rejecting the means of those working in the ocular tradition, where sight is privileged above all other senses. We cannot simply lose ourselves in the looking (falling into the trap of looking without taking away any information). By ignoring previously explored paths to all-overness (which included the pouring of paint), Johns enlarged painting's possibilities. For one thing, his deliberate placement of the crosshatch requires us to read the work in two interconnected ways, from examining the surface to apprehending it in tandem with its underlying structure. Following the distinction Johns made in "Sketchbook Notes," we could call these two approaches looking and spying.

For nearly a decade, beginning with *Scent* and ending with the last of his works titled *Between the Clock and the Bed* (1982–83), Johns used the crosshatch as the primary component of his paintings. They can be divided into three groups. In the first (this includes *Scent*, as well as the *Usuyuki* series), he shifted the modular structure filled with crosshatches, as in the two flagstone panels of *Untitled*. The artist used this schema to organize the different crosshatches into what initially appear to be abstract fields. However, it becomes readily apparent, upon close examination, that Johns carefully placed the crosshatches according to predetermined arrangements (worked out in diagrams or in writing), in which symmetry and asymmetry are embedded one within the other. The carefully planned shifts and disruptions become critical features of our experience of the work.

In the second group, which includes thematically related (and similarly titled) paintings such as *Corpse and Mirror* and *Dancers on a Plane*, Johns employed a different method to construct a symmetrical/asymmetrical system. *Corpse and Mirror II* (1974–75) comprises three panels stacked on the left and one on the right.[3] Along the two physical seams separating the stacked panels, the hatch marks change direction but not hue. Although there are no physical seams on the right-hand side, the marks echo their counterparts on the left side in changing direction but remaining the same color along an invisible seam, which they in effect define. In *Dancers on a Plane* (1979), four panels stacked on the left mirror those on the right. However, along the three horizontal seams between the stacked panels, Johns did the following: along the top seam, the hatch marks change color and direction; along the middle seam, they continue in the same direction but change color; and along the bottom seam, they change direction but not color. In this group, Johns broke down the larger pattern into smaller ones, each of which defines a particular relationship to those adjacent to it.

In the third group, comprising such works as *Weeping Women* (fig. VIII: 1) and *The Barber's Tree* (1975), *Between the Clock and the Bed* (see fig. VIII: 6), and *Tantric Detail III* (fig. VIII: 5), a more immediate and noticeable disruption occurs even when there is no apparent underlying structure for the placement of the colored hatch marks. In *The Barber's Tree*, which was inspired by a photograph of a barber's pole that the artist saw in a magazine,[4] the title stenciled along the bottom left and the artist's name and date stenciled along the bottom right add a textual element to what initially seems to be a purely ocular painting. The scattered drips of melted encaustic bring sight and tactility into close proximity; the painting is simultaneously visual and visceral. The drips, which are also apparent in *Corpse and Mirror* (1974), *The Dutch Wives* (1975), and *Weeping Women*, evoke a state of change and eventual dissolution.

In the crosshatch paintings, it seems to me that the artist asked himself how he could make a literal, repetitive mark that is largely without meaning function within a figure/ground relationship that is not purely formal, but one that reflects on the individual's rapport with reality. In his early citation of Leonardo's caution against separating the figure from its surrounds, the artist revealed his preoccupation with determining where a thing ends and another begins. Are there clear demarcations between one phenomenon and another? What are the properties that connect or disconnect a thing or event to or from another? In all of these concerns, one detects a recurring sense of apprehension in confronting our inevitable loss of control.

Instead of suppressing or displacing this common but genuinely personal fear, which is what society teaches us to do both individually and collectively, Johns repeatedly finds ways to simultaneously acknowledge and question it that extend beyond the personal. He is determined to record the vanishing present he inhabits, even as it is pulls him toward his own demise. And yet, while the sources of his deep-rooted anxiety could have led him to develop an art built upon an expressive "I," which would suggest that he alone endures these indignities, he has gone to great lengths to recognize his fears as an ordinary state of helplessness. Many critics have seen Johns's choice of pre-existing motifs as evidence of his work being impersonal, cold, or aloof, but this is not the case. The artist's commitment to commonplace things posits a world of shared experience. His decision to work with a palette of primary and secondary colors, as well as the tonal range from black to white, downplays a personal color range (such as those of a Pierre Bonnard or a Mark Rothko). Johns's boldly distilled, fiercely anti-illusionistic colors are a central thesis in his lifelong argument with the realm of appearances, which tends to offer false impressions that will lure us into the trap of looking rather than encouraging us to see. As is acutely apparent in the objectivity and literalness of his work, Johns adamantly rejects society's innumerable fantasies that we can stop or slow down time.

Johns employed the crosshatch to make paintings whose subjects included changing, invisible phenomena, as well as feelings of premonition (*Scent*): the ethereality of lightly falling snow (the *Usuyuki* series); winged insects that emerge from a seventeen-year underground hibernation only to mate and die (*Cicada* [1979]); art's mirroring of reality (*Corpse and Mirror*); substitutes, surrogates, and stand-ins (*The Dutch Wives*); extreme emotional states (*Weeping Women*); figures in movement (*Dancers on a Plane*); the inevitability of mortality (*Tantric Detail*); and being caught in time (*Between the Clock and the Bed*). Whereas ephemeral experiences were not the primary focus of earlier paintings such as *Green Target* (fig. I: 2) and *Map* (1963), they are central to a number of the crosshatch paintings. Unlike *Flag* (fig. I: 1), which suggests that dreaming is a personal experience that underscores the isolation of the individual and society's denial of that fact, the crosshatch paintings address external states familiar to everyone—shared experiences, rather than isolating ones. Often these experiences are transitory; they register something passing and changing into something else.

In the crosshatch, Johns found a form that is specific, allows a high degree of flexibility and openness, and is as meaningless as one can get; it is also both visual and tactile. By arranging these marks according to a system, juxtaposing that system with words, layering it with other, differently sized crosshatches, or combining it with figural elements, Johns was able to conjoin spying and looking. As he wrote in his "Sketchbook Notes," "There is a continuity of some sort among the watchman, the space, the objects." In that same paragraph, he also said, "The spy stations himself to observe the watchman." And finally, he connected two kinds of seeing associated with the mind (spy) and unthinking body (watchman), "'Not spying, just looking.'"[5] Consequently, rather than being the subject of attention (such as a flag, map, or coffee can crammed with brushes), the crosshatch became Johns's means to explore his perceptual preoccupations with reality; it also generated a new paradigm through which to approach content. The pattern enabled him to explore the figure/ground relationship in new ways, using repetitions and shifts that make it nearly impossible to discern where the figure ends and the ground begins. As we know from his earlier work, the artist's interest in figure/ground is not purely formal, and his perceptions are anchored in things and experiences.

The crosshatch pattern has long been featured in Western art as a way to create the illusion of three-dimensional forms by suggesting light and shadow on the topography of a surface. Johns, however, dislodged the motif from its historical context by making it describe nothing. Like flags or maps, his crosshatch patterns are literal and clearly human-made, and they hypothesize an ordinary world (or reality) that we all inhabit. Johns has never shown any interest in depicting a figure within a hollowed-out spatial setting. Rather, consistent with his earlier work, the space in the crosshatch images is condensed and layered. He enhances his surfaces by seeming to atomize them into distinct but related parts using patterning, as well as collage, to convey a compressed and tactile spatiality, often in a state of implied movement. The crosshatches (brushstrokes) amplify what is true of encaustic, which bonds rather than blends together. The inherent behavior of encaustic is consistent with Johns's view of reality and his citation of Leonardo.

III.

In his essay in *Jasper Johns: Works since 1974,* the catalogue that accompanied the artist's exhibition in the American Pavilion of the 1988 Venice Biennale, Mark Rosenthal judiciously detailed three types of responses to Johns's crosshatch paintings.

The first response defined the crosshatch as pure abstraction. As Rosenthal put it: "Some are content to explore these lush abstractions for their subtlety of composition and structure, claiming that the artist has momentarily become a nonobjective painter."[6] Nearly a decade later, Kirk Varnedoe, then chief curator of painting and sculpture at the Museum of Modern Art, New York, aligned himself with the view that the crosshatch works are non-objective abstractions:

> Johns is rarely discussed as an abstract artist, but cross-hatch paintings such as this one [*Corpse and Mirror*], *Scent*, *Weeping Women*, and several others are among his central works, and constitute a singular chapter in the history of modern abstract art; outside the standard categories of geometric order or gestural expressionism, but partaking of aspects of both. They hold a special interest within the framework of the relationship—usually described as antithetical—between Johns's aesthetic and that of New York School painting of the early 1950s; the allover compositions of Johns's abstract painting of the 1970s would seem to represent in part a measured (in the literal sense of "quantified" or "geometricized") response to Jackson Pollock's poured paintings.[7]

According to Rosenthal, the second response considered the crosshatch paintings as parodies of abstractions. Here, he cited Barbara Rose, who called them "pseudo-abstractions—impersonations of an abstract style," and went on to claim "that each is a picture 'of an idea, a purely intellectual construct.'"[8] For the third viewpoint, which focused on the artist's biography, Rosenthal cited Charles Harrison and Fred Orton, who believed that "something is camouflaged or hidden" in the crosshatches. Orton, for example, read Johns as a gay artist who was dissembling that fact while making anti-masculine art.[9]

Thus, for these writers, the crosshatch paintings are either art about art—whether straightforward abstraction or the "idea" of abstraction—or they are Johns's attempts to cover up or encode aspects of his personal life. The former paradigm assumes that pure abstraction is a worthwhile goal that to some degree has been defined by others, while the latter presupposes that there is a stable, private "I" that finds it necessary to remain hidden from the public. Both models limit what art can address. However, like Johns's earlier paintings and sculptures, the crosshatch paintings not only resist historical categories but also underscore their limitations. In response to the first and second responses that Rosenthal detailed, I would argue that the crosshatch works are neither pure, non-objective paintings nor riffs on abstractions. They definitely are not based on "a purely intellectual construct," because this suggests that the generating idea is divorced from experience and reality. As Johns wrote in his "Sketchbook Notes," "Beware of the body and the mind. Avoid a polar situation."[10]

In terms of the third response to the crosshatch, which argues that something is being obfuscated, particularly in terms of the artist's biography, I would argue that once again we must consider this assertion in light of what is concealed in Johns's earlier work. In both *Map* (1963) and *Painted Bronze (Savarin can with brushes)* (fig. III: 5), he disclosed one aspect of his preoccupation, which is the indivisible bond between figure and ground, form and chaos. I would further argue that the idea of "camouflage" is wrong because it suggests that he is hiding something about himself; as I have argued, Johns is not interested in the bounded, social self, but in the individual's connection to reality. Ever since *Flag*, Johns has been anti-"I," anti-autobiographical, in his art. His use of primary colors, grisaille, pre-existing objects, and things that are repetitive and without meaning is intended to evoke a reality inhabited by all of us. This has to do with the artist's vision of material reality, rather than a concern with social reality. The surrogate figures in Johns's art—the upraised arm and hand in *Land's End* (fig. V: 1) and the charcoal-covered face and hands pressed against the paper in *Study for Skin I* (fig. V: 2)—are everyman representations of the human race, not the statements of a gay or straight man. This is not to suggest that there is nothing erotic in Johns's art: his dripping encaustic and his incorporation of works by other artists such as Duchamp's *Female Fig Leaf* (fig. II: 3) are two among several tactics with sexual overtones that come to mind.

In *Scent*, which is definitely not what Rose designated a "pseudo-abstraction," Johns seems to have asked himself whether appearance (looking) and reality (seeing) can be brought into proximity when the subject is not a recognizable thing of or from the world (such as a flag or map). At the outset of his career, he rejected the idea that painting was something meant only to be looked at, or what Greenberg and his legatees called pure, non-relational abstraction. It seems to me that, by the time he painted *Scent*, Johns would not have found it necessary to make abstractions, whether pure or fake, because, as others had defined these possibilities, such works would not take into consideration our relationship to reality. Rather, the crosshatch pattern, with its "lack of meaning," afforded Johns the freedom to explore the rapport between figure and ground without exploiting a pre-existing subject. He could interrogate the nature of a common event or a familiar occurrence. In contrast to *Map* (1963), which Johns inflected through the application of paint, in *Scent* he utilized structure, repetition, and disruption to amplify, as well as give meaning to, the pattern's neutrality. On a number of occasions, the artist has said that he uses gray because it is neutral and does not direct our eyes. To avoid the latter, Johns chooses known things and dispassionate means, encouraging us to disentangle ourselves from what he has called the "'trap' of looking." This holds true for the crosshatch paintings.

In *Scent*, Johns's first work entirely covered in crosshatches, material difference and visual similarity are made to coincide. The work consists of three joined panels, each of which is distinguished by its medium. The artist executed the middle panel and that on the far right in oil, one on unsized canvas with a matte surface, and the other on sized canvas with a noticeable amount of gloss. He painted the panel on the far left in encaustic. Each crosshatch, or unit of parallel lines, is rendered in a single secondary color: orange, purple, or green. Some of the units appear similar in their configuration, while others seem unique. This is most immediately evident in the areas adjacent to the seams between the middle and outer panels. What at first glance looks like random patterning becomes, on closer inspection, a deliberately plotted schematic, in which a vertical band of the crosshatches along the right and left side of the middle panel, about one-third of the middle panel's width, are moved to the adjacent area of the outer panels. This alteration is repeated in each of the outer panels, where a vertical band of crosshatches, again about one-third of the panel's width, is shifted from the outer third of the panel on the far left to the outer third of that on the far right. In each panel, the middle third is not repeated.

The overlapping of similarities and dissimilarities occurs in *Scent* on both a material and a visual level, making it difficult to ascertain these distinctions in ways that are neat and comforting. There is a certain escapist pleasure in looking at the painting when we forget what we have learned or do not bother to scrutinize it closely, forgoing a deeper apprehension of what connects with what and exactly where disruptions occur. While this kind of looking might seem like a complicated game, it is not, because the painting's subject, as its title makes clear, has to do with an actual experience rather than with abstraction or an elevated sense of visual perception. Continuous seeing, which Greenberg and others advocated in championing all-over, non-relational composition, is an aesthetic pleasure that Johns undermined in *Scent*. However, the artist's purpose was neither to criticize formalist aesthetics nor to refer to Pollock's abstract painting *Scent* (c. 1955). In fact, when Johns learned that his title was the same as Pollock's, he briefly considered changing it. The reason he did not is because his title specifies the phenomenon he was exploring.[11]

The alignment of similarity and difference in *Scent* focuses on a figure/ground relationship where the middle third of each panel is unique, while the flanking areas are repeated. We can get lost in the looking or we can move between looking and spying out the schematic structuring that is embedded within the painting. For all its repetitions, the work's visual field never settles into stasis; there is dynamism in the painting, a continuum of change that has been slowed down and particularized into distinct elements, as well as speeded up. Looking at *Scent* involves noting which areas are repeated, while trying to distinguish where replication ends and divergence begins. The shifts are never demarcated; Johns may have repeated part of a mark, but once the mark extends beyond an invisible border, it becomes unique. The great lengths to which Johns went to conceal the repetition forces us into a highly conscious state of looking (spying). We must harness distinct modes of comprehension in order to engage fully with the painting. Thus, ideally, our experience of *Scent* is not confined solely to looking. Johns's overlapping systems of unities, repetitions, and disparities do not culminate in a visual puzzle, but embody an attempt to register a phenomenon as elusive and potent as scent. As the title suggests, we have to scent out what will happen (figure and ground merge), as well as distinguish a scent (presence) from something larger (ground).

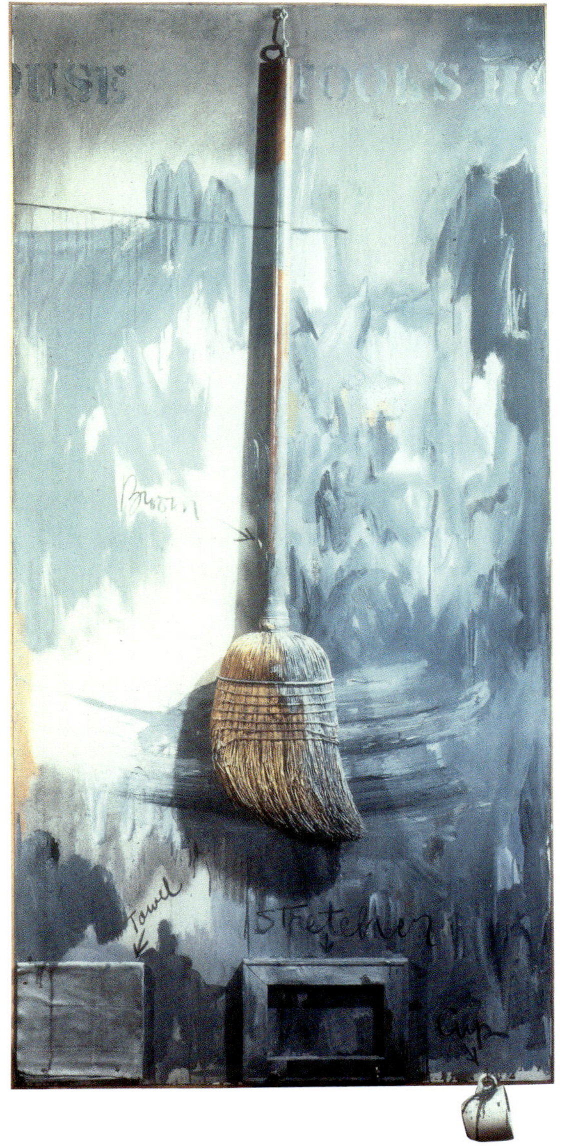

Jasper Johns *FOOL'S HOUSE* 1962 fig. VII: 4
Oil on canvas with objects 72 x 36 in. (182.9 x 91.4 cm)
Collection Jean Christophe Castelli

At the same time, we can imagine curling the flat, three-paneled painting end to end into a cylinder in which the crosshatches on the overlapping outer edges would align. The suggestion that a flat painting can be cylindrical occurred in Johns's art as early as 1962, in *Fool's House* (fig. VII: 4), where the stenciled title "FOOL'S HOUSE" is broken up, so that "FOOL'S H" appears along the painting's upper-right edge with the "O" cropped at that edge. Along the left's side upper edge, the "O," truncated by the left edge, is followed by "USE." By making the title circle back on itself, as well as dividing the words so that we read "FOOL'S" and "USE," Johns conveyed something about the repetition of cleaning (a paint-smeared broom hangs from middle of the top edge), and the affinity between painting and cleaning up. We paint today and then clean up so we can paint tomorrow, and so on. These activities occur and reoccur in and over time and cannot be reversed.

Until the rise of non-objective art, the picture plane was considered to be the prepared surface on which the artist typically rendered volumetric forms in two dimensions, with crosshatching as one of the means through which this transformation took place. *Scent* carries on this tradition in suggesting that it can be turned into a cylinder. The work possesses a vertical, volumetric dimension that has the potential to become a figural presence. In addition, the bond that Johns establishes between two- and three-dimensionality further underscores his exploration of figure/ground and the lack of clear demarcation between form and its surrounds. Johns's use of the crosshatch in effect flew in the face of current belief in flatness as painting's essential condition.

Among the meanings of the word "scent," which is both a noun and a verb, is the indication that something is about happen. One can detect in this painting's repetitions, shifts, and discontinuities a rigorously conceived attempt to address mortality and change—the moment when the figure becomes fully absorbed by the ground. But the issue of our inevitable end would not become Johns's primary focus until his later years. If in *Scent* figure and ground are one, can we think of the figure as a scent surrounded by, as well as inextricable from, the atmosphere? There is something both pleasing and discomfiting about *Scent*; its meticulous planning visualizes a diagram of a constantly changing faculty that is invisible yet universal.

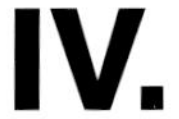

In *Water Freezes* (1961), Johns placed a thermometer in a groove between two largely bluish-gray encaustic panels on which he stenciled the painting's title, one word onto each surface.

The juxtaposition of the thermometer and encaustic underscores the latter's susceptibility to exterior conditions. Like encaustic, water hardens or melts at a certain temperature. Over fifteen years later, the artist extended the possibility of diagramming an incessantly altering natural phenomenon into a more complicated and rigorous paradigm in a series of paintings titled *Usuyuki* (1977–81), which is the Japanese word for "light snow." Snow

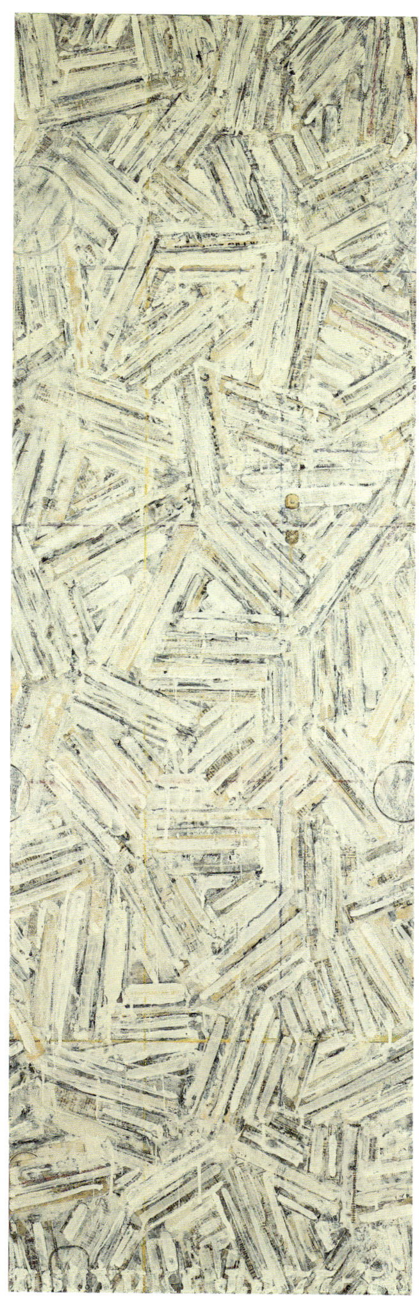

Jasper Johns *USUYUKI* 1977–78

Encaustic and collage on canvas 56 3/4 x 18 in. (144.1 x 45.7 cm)

Collection Kenneth and Judy Dayton

fig. VII: 5

is water vapor frozen into ice crystals, falling to earth in the form of unique flakes. It is either solid (ice crystal) or, having melted, liquid (water), and in that regard echoes encaustic's two distinct states.

In all of the *Usuyuki* paintings, Johns established a complex set of topographic rules connecting the arrangement of crosshatch units to an additional layer of predetermined marks. These consist of circles and round-edged rectangles made by a tin can and a can of turpentine, respectively, pressed into the waxy surface. Placed at specific intervals, often truncated at the edges of separate panels but also within the surface of the painting itself, the circles and rounded rectangles are cropped by the clearly defined rectangles of the painting's edges and "continued" on the other side of the division or the opposite edge. The divisions of the circles and rectangles are not even, however. *Usuyuki* (fig. VII: 5) is a schematic model of falling, swirling snow. In addition to divided circles, linear and horizontal divisions mark its surface, which consists of three compressed layers (collaged newspaper strips; encaustic crosshatching; and the stenciled title, artist's name, and date). Located at the bottom, the stenciling endows the painting with gravity, as well as adds another textual factor to that of the newspaper strips. The layers provoke shifts in attention and make us ask whether the snow is the figure and/or the air through which it falls to the ground, whether the circles impressed into the surface are the figure and the crosshatch patterns the ground, or whether the ground is the layer of newspaper, which forms a diagram that acts as a kind of preliminary drawing for the encaustic pattern.

In the *Usuyuki* paintings and related works, pure looking is not simply denied; it was never possible. Throughout his career, as we have seen, Johns has defined the acts of looking and seeing as two distinct but connected conditions; he expects the viewer to move from the brief, initial moment of innocent looking to a prolonged state of mindful inspection and reflection. However, unlike a painting, which, in a sense, renews itself each time a new viewer encounters it, that viewer cannot return to a state of innocent looking. The painting embodies time's irrevocability and the transitory nature of experience on a material and a pictorial level. In *Scent* and the various works titled *Usuyuki*, Johns broadened his preoccupation with mortality to engage experiences that are elusive and fleeting. And although the moments of beauty that we experience are transitory, Johns does not mourn their passing.

CHAPTER 7
NOTES

1. I would like to thank Tom Micchelli for bringing Fuller's *Dymaxion Air Ocean World*, and its possible connection to Johns's *Usuyuki* series, to my attention.

2. Quoted in Sarah Kent, "Jasper Johns: Strokes of Genius," *Time Out* (London), Dec. 5–12, 1990, p. 15; repr. in *Jasper Johns: Writings, Sketchbooks, Notes, Interviews*, ed. Kirk Varnedoe, comp. Christel Hollevoets (New York: Museum of Modern Art, 1997), p. 259.

3. The second *Corpse and Mirror* painting dates from 1974; the two *Dancers on a Plane* paintings date from 1979 and 1980.

4. Michael Crichton, *Jasper Johns*, exh. cat. (New York: Harry N. Abrams, in association with the Whitney Museum of American Art, 1977). According to Crichton, Johns was inspired by a 1973 *National Geographic* photo of a Mexican man painting a "barber's tree."

5. Jasper Johns, "Sketchbook Notes," *Art and Literature* (Lausanne) 4 (Spring 1965); repr. in *Jasper Johns: Writings* (note 2), pp. 59–60, pl. 11, p. 37.

6. Mark Rosenthal, "Crosshatch Paintings, 1974–82," in *Jasper Johns: Works since 1974*, exh. cat. (New York/London: Thames and Hudson in association with the Philadelphia Museum of Art, 1988), p. 14.

7. Kirk Varnedoe, *Jasper Johns: A Retrospective*, exh. cat., with an essay by Roberta Bernstein (New York: Museum of Modern Art, 1996), p. 269.

8. Barbara Rose, "Jasper Johns: Pictures and Concepts," *Arts Magazine* 52, 3 (Nov. 1977), p. 149.

9. Charles Harrison and Fred Orton, "Jasper Johns: Meaning What You See," *Art History* 7, 1 (Mar. 1984), p. 88. For Orton on Johns's homosexuality, see Fred Orton, "Jasper Johns: The Sculptures," in *Jasper Johns: The Sculptures*, exh. cat. (Leeds: Centre for the Study of Sculpture at the Henry Moore Institute, 1996), pp. 9–70.

10. Johns, "Sketchbook Notes," (note 5); repr. in *Jasper Johns: Writings* (note 2), pp. 34, 56.

11. David Bourdon, "Jasper Johns: 'I Never Sensed Myself as Being Static,'" *Village Voice*, Oct. 31, 1977, p. 75.

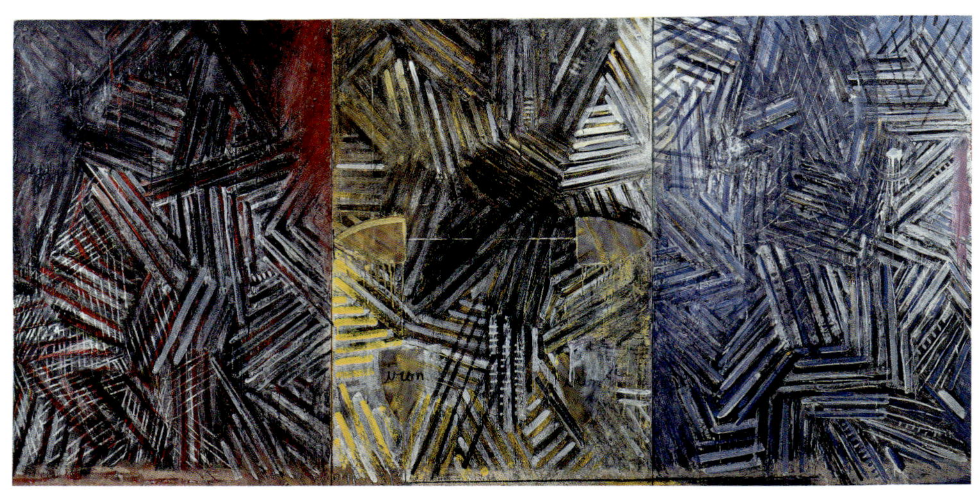

fig. VIII: 1 **Jasper Johns** *WEEPING WOMEN* 1975
Encaustic and collage on canvas 50 x 102 1/4 in. (127 x 259.7 cm)
Collection David Geffen, Los Angeles

Chapter 8

I.

In *Weeping Women* (fig. VIII: 1), Johns shifted his focus from transitory phenomena to figural presences, which was to be the primary theme of the crosshatches until he finished the three *Between the Clock and the Bed* paintings (fig. VIII: 8) and began moving in another direction.

Weeping Women is a triptych in which each panel is dominated by a primary color; from left to right, we see red, yellow, and blue. Along with these principal colors, Johns applied bands of black, gray, and white. Also, in a number of places, the encaustic dripped down the painting's tactile surface. Stretching across the bottom of all three sections is a loosely painted, creamy-pink band, which, in the center and the right panels, is overlaid with a thin black line. Evoking gravity and a base or pedestal, the band and line shift the painting from two dimensions to a more indefinite zone that is neither flat nor volumetric. Each panel presents a different configuration of marks—some semi-transparent, others scratched into the wax surface. The center section contains collage elements and four imprints made by an iron, two of which are labeled "iron." The panel on the right is marked by circles, which were created by pressing a tin can into the wax. That on the left displays no such markings. Thus, in each panel the artist conveyed three distinct presences.

According to Johns, in *Weeping Women*, unlike *Scent* or *Usuyuki*, he used no system to arrange the crosshatch pattern.[1] The only repetition is a triangular arrangement of hatched lines in the upper third of the painting, which is more clearly visible in the red and yellow panels, and a little less so in the blue. The triangular form is never centered, denying any overt association to a human head. In contrast to Pablo Picasso, who first used broad hatch lines in *Les Demoiselles d'Avignon* (1907) to simplify into flat planes the breast and doglike face of the woman standing at the far right and those of the woman seated directly below, Johns layered and overlapped the crosshatches to create a space in which the marks can sit. The viewer both sees and sees into the painting. Instead of turning volume into planes, as Picasso did, Johns used a linear pattern of encaustic crosshatches and incised lines to merge form and space to the point that it is difficult to discern where one ends and the other begins.

There are a number of sources for Johns's painting. In 1975, when he was in Paris—where he had gone to work on the prints for *Foirades/Fizzles*, his collaboration with Samuel Beckett—he saw an etching of Picasso's *Weeping Woman*.[2] The motif of the crying woman is a theme that had absorbed Picasso for more than six months in 1937. In almost all of his works with this subject, Picasso focused primarily on the model's head. Often her eyes resemble saucers tipped at sharp angles, with tears streaming down her cheeks like trails of honey.

Done shortly after Picasso had completed *Guernica* (1937), *Weeping Woman* is related to the distraught woman in that painting. For the print, Picasso produced more than sixty proofs of various states, many of them consisting largely of densely textured lines, on different plates. He began working on a large plate on July 1, 1937, and made more than forty proofs of the seven separate states. Of these, only in states III and VI did he number the impressions, fifteen of each. In the later states, he often made deep incisions to describe the creases of the woman's skin, the curve of her cheek, the weave of her handkerchief, and each strand of her hair.

Later on, Picasso added drypoint to the etching. The addition of drypoint, combined with the aquatint, transformed the surface into a shrouded, linear darkness. Three days later, on July 4, he redrew the motif on a smaller plate. Here Picasso made the boldest move of the series, redrawing his subject so that she simultaneously wipes away her tears and bites her handkerchief. The image contains fewer lines and is flatter than in the prints made from the larger plate. Picasso then redrew the woman, reversing the head (July 4, 1937, state IV) (fig. VIII: 2). Her hair is matted, her visage more contorted and incised with lines. Instead of placing her against a black ground, as he did in the previous etching, Picasso echoed the exaggerated lines of her face, hair, and handkerchief by turning the walls and ceiling into a kind of striped frame. The use of straight lines to describe the room and curving ones to shape the face brings figure and ground into closer proximity. My sense is that it is this state Johns saw in Paris.[3]

One of my reasons for thinking so is that the woman is biting (eating) the handkerchief (or cloth), while the handkerchief is absorbing (or eating) her tears. Johns described the symbiotic relationship of consumption and absorption in his "Sketchbook Notes":

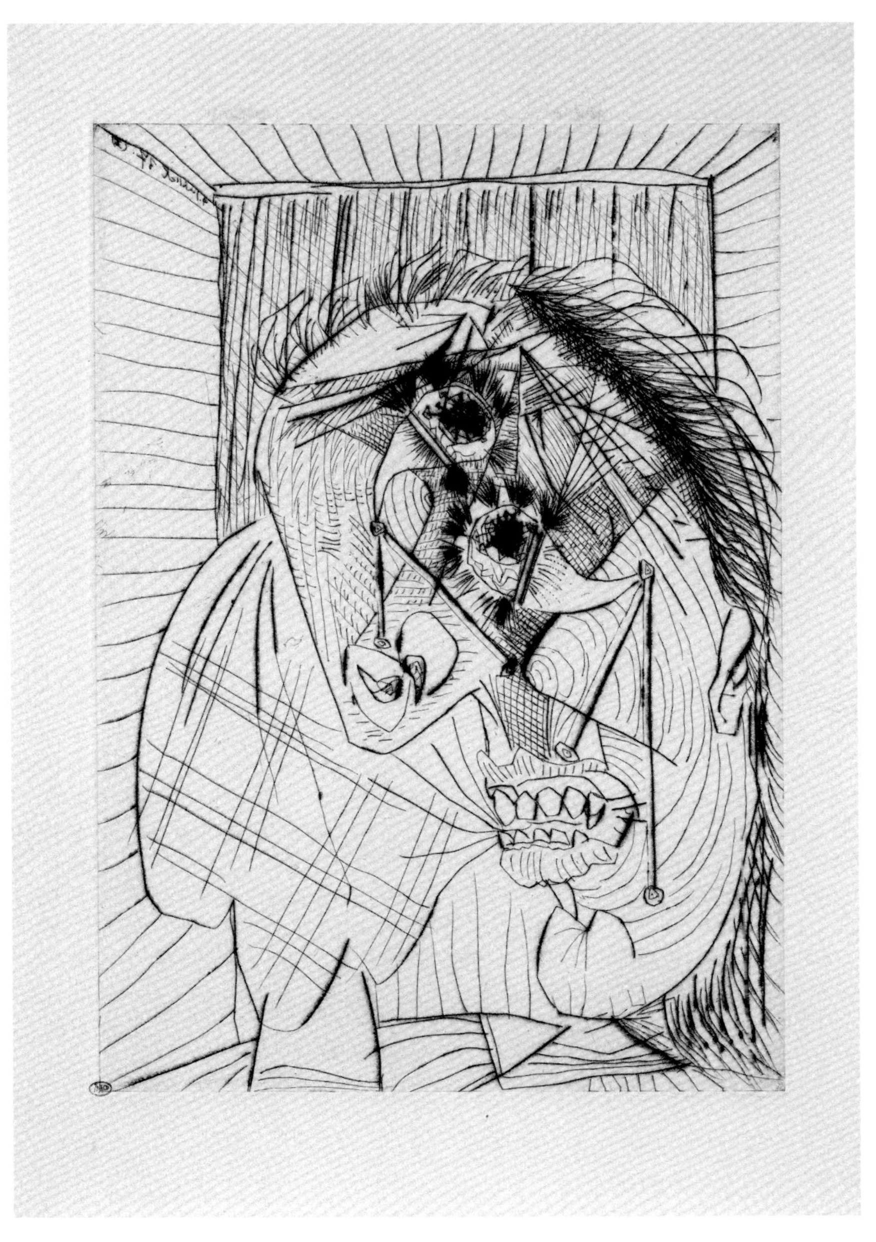

Pablo Picasso *THE WEEPING WOMAN (4 July 1937, State IV)* 1937 fig. VIII: 2
Drypoint on paper 13 5/8 x 9 7/8 in. (33 x 48 cm)

"'Looking' is & is not 'eating' & also 'being eaten,'" a motif found as well as in his *Painting Bitten by a Man* (1961).[4] The weeping woman's biting a piece of fabric also recalls Johns's use of the bedsheet in *Flag* (fig. I: 1) to merge figure, ground, and time. The literal and actual spark Johns's metaphors, which in his painting *Weeping Women* underscore the enduring union of solid and dripping wax, of flesh and tears.

In contrast to Picasso's many works on the weeping woman, Johns shifted the emphasis away from distortions of form to the interaction of line, pattern, and the inherent behavior of encaustic, thus rooting his vision in materiality. Since he had equated flesh and encaustic in his "Sketchbook Notes," it is possible that he made a further association between tears and melted wax. In *Weeping Women*'s middle panel, Johns pressed an iron into the encaustic surface four times, leaving four distinct impressions, two of which point downward. These forms, which also resemble breasts, suggest another work by Picasso, *Woman in an Armchair* (1913) where we see similar triangular breasts. When this painting was owned by the New York collectors Victor and Sally Ganz, Johns would have seen it any number of times, prominently displayed in a room of the couple's apartment, where his largest drawing, *Diver* (1962), also hung.

In writing the word "iron" over the two breastlike shapes, Johns not only identified the implement that made the mark, introducing an element of self-consciousness, but also connected the painter's actions to domesticity (as well as to the labor of a laundress, a subject Picasso also treated in *Woman Ironing* [1904]), which includes cleaning and ordering. Like a woman ironing, an artist using encaustic tries to eliminate wrinkles. Characteristic of Johns, there is a wicked humor in this conjunction: if encaustic is a correlative of flesh, removing wrinkles is a vain (in both senses of the word) attempt to slow the passage of time. Need we recall that Johns created three weeping women by employing only crosshatch patterns, lines that we might also regard as wrinkles?

Johns's definition of the artist as a laborer emphasizes a commonality of experience, which is consistent with his use of pre-existing signifiers and primary and secondary colors, as well as black and white. Johns would have us believe that an artist, as much as a laborer, produces something useful—as useful, in fact, as clean, ironed shirts. The "iron" also reminds us of Duchamp's statement "Use a Rembrandt as an ironing board."[5] Here, I would suggest that, for Johns, Duchamp was not denying the past, but rather challenging himself to make a Rembrandt relevant to the present. It is also worth noting that more than a decade before he executed *Weeping Women*, during the early 1960s, when he was incorporating strips of wood, spoons, a broom, rulers, and other devices and domestic tools into his work, Johns painted *Iron* (1962), where he pressed a heated iron against a small wooden board on which he had applied gray encaustic, melting the encaustic away. In the imprint left by the iron, Johns wrote "iron." In *Weeping Women*, he was able to enlarge the way we would read the act of pressing a heated iron against the painting.

In the largely blue panel on the far right of *Weeping Women*, Johns applied a heated tin can to the encaustic in three places, leaving grooved imprints. In the middle of the circle on the right, a gob of white encaustic has dissolved into three streams running down the surface. The streams' color prompts association with breasts dripping milk, a conjunction linking helplessness with sustenance. Although we associate the materials and marks in *Weeping Women* with Johns's oeuvre, they are not in and of themselves special. One could go so far as to say that there is something almost anonymous and neutral about them. Linking flesh and encaustic, weeping and melting, the liquefaction signals an inherent and unavoidable end. Because heat is necessary to seal and protect the painting, while retaining the capacity to disfigure it, *Weeping Women* suggests that inevitability and defenselessness are synonymous. This imbues the work with an acute feeling of discomfort and pain. At the same time, in contrast to Picasso's almost exclusive focus on the woman's head, its orifices evoking her sexuality, Johns's painting encompasses the women's bodies, which are largely indistinguishable from the ground, defining mortality as inescapable as well as the primary source of our pain.

Johns's use of crosshatch to evoke a figural presence that is both layered and pervious easily lends itself to a reading of each panel as a splayed figure whose skin has been tightly stretched and scarred by the iron and tin-can markings. Picasso, as Roland Penrose pointed out, never revealed the source of his subject's grieving.[6] Johns, however, did, suggesting that misery is inherent to our existence. This is why he did not depict a head or face; grief is synonymous with the body.

II.

Johns's three paintings titled *Tantric Detail*, done between 1980 and 1981 (see figs. VIII: 4, 5), were inspired by a seventeenth-century Nepalese painting, *The Mystical Form of Samvara with Seventy-four Arms Embracing His Form of Samvara with Seventy-four Arms Embracing His Sakti with Twelve Arms* (fig. VIII: 3), which had been in the collection of Ajit Mookerjee, the author of a number of books on Tantra art.

Johns first saw a reproduction of *The Mystical Form of Samvara* in Mookerjee's *Tantra Art: Its Philosophy and Physics,* which first appeared in 1966 and has been reprinted several times since.[7] The painting depicts the dark-skinned Samvara (Lord of Death) and the red-skinned Sakti (the active female principle or life force), facing each other and making love. Standing on two prone figures, Samvara holds Sakti, who has wrapped her legs around his hips. According to Mookerjee, such coupling figures represent a state of unity called *yuganaddha*: "Here there is neither affirmation nor denial, neither purity nor impurity, neither form nor formlessness; it is a synthesis of all these dualities."[8]

The literalness of Johns's title suggests that it would be wrong to assume that the artist, by choosing this subject, had become a devotee of Tantric principles. For one thing, rather than depicting the entire scene, Johns focused his attention on a detail, located in

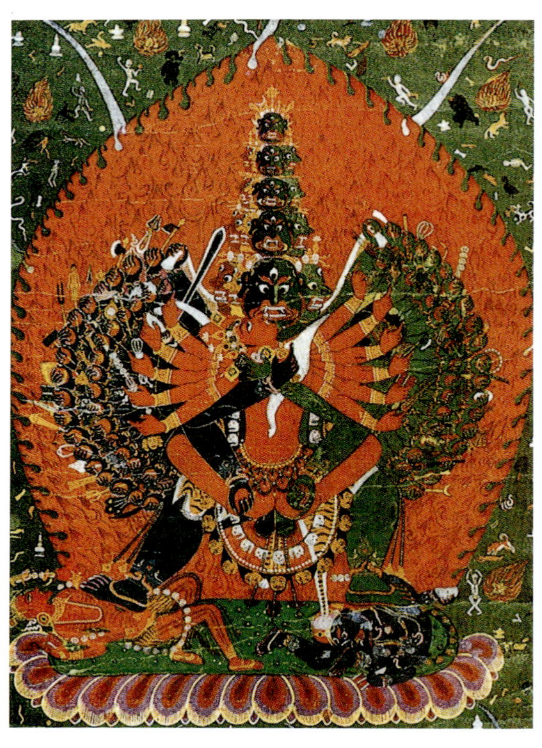

fig. VIII: 3 *MYSTICAL FORM OF SAMARA WITH SEVENTY-FOUR ARMS EMBRACING HIS SAKTI WITH TWELVE ARMS* c. seventeenth century
Gouache on cloth 28 x 19 in. (71.1 x 48.3 cm)
Formerly collection Ajit Mookerjee. Present location unknown

the lower part of the painting. It comprises the area from Samvara's scrotum and part of his penis (visible just below Sakti's buttocks) to the garland of skulls and severed heads suspended near the ground. Strings of white beads (which can also be read as sperm) also hang down, with one strand seeming to come from behind the scrotum and passing through a skull and a severed head below.

Johns's *Tantric Detail* paintings retain the alignment of these elements in the Nepalese work, integrating the scrotum, part of the penis, skull, and a vertical row of the white beads into a compositional structure consisting of three stacked rectangles, each of which is articulated by a series of crosshatches. This, rather than a schematic diagram, suggests the works' underlying structure. Johns had used stacked rectangles as early as 1961; *By the Sea* (1961) features four vertically stacked panels. In the three *Tantric Detail* paintings, however, the division is implied rather than literal. While the scrotum is visible near the top of the middle rectangle, most of the penis has been "cut off" by the rectangle above. The image of a flattened skull hovers at the top edge of the bottom rectangle, directly below the scrotum, with the dome of its cranium "cut off" by the bottom of the middle rectangle. A vertical line of short, white strokes (beads) falls from the skull's lower jaw to the painting's bottom edge. The crosshatch patterning changes direction at the lines separating the rectangles, but always continues in the same colors. While Johns did not rely on a system to determine the distribution of the crosshatches, it is worth noting that, in *Tantric Detail II* (1981) and *Tantric Detail III* (fig. VIII: 5), the placements are very similar.

Throughout the paintings and works on paper in the series, Johns kept the same arrangement, with the genitalia at the top of the middle panel and the skull at the top of the bottom rectangle. Three movements are implied: up, down, and into. In the case of the skull, the subtle articulation of its gray shapes within gray crosshatches suggests that appearance and disappearance are indissoluble. The beads, which form a spine, anchor the skull to the painting's bottom edge. If the top rectangle were curled over until it met its bottom counterpart, the paintings would constitute a form with skull, spine, and genitalia. If there is a body, however, it has either disappeared beneath one of the panels or been flayed and stretched into a vertical plane comprising the three horizontal rectangles. The details Johns chose distance his painting from the subject matter of its source. Rather, depicting the scrotum as hairy and cartoonish while rendering the skull in a flat, emblematic manner, Johns underscored the disjunctive quality of this dismembered body. The stylistic differences between penis and skull emphasize the distinct, sometimes opposed, but ultimately connected states we inhabit.

While the testicles and skull are familiar symbols of life and death, by now we have learned that the simplest or quickest reading of a work by Johns is likely to be the least rewarding and may, in fact, obscure the artist's vision. As symbols of the life force and mortality, testicles and skull signify beginnings and endings, which the painting echoes through its structure. As with *Scent* (fig. VII: 3) and the other crosshatch paintings, the artist was examining the nature of the bond between figure and ground. However, in contrast to *Scent* and even earlier paintings like *Flag* (fig. I: 1), where figure and ground conjoin, it seems

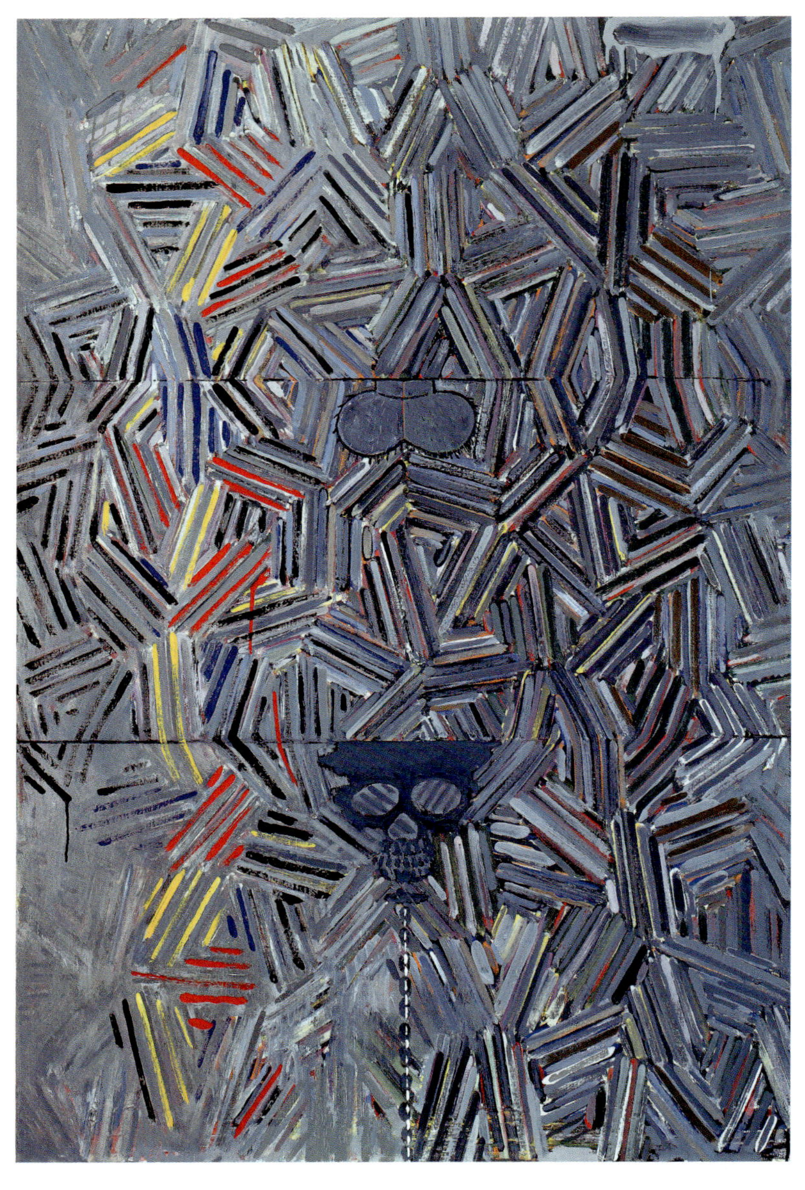

fig. VIII: 4 **Jasper Johns** *TANTRIC DETAIL I* 1980
Oil on canvas 50 1/8 x 34 1/8 in. (127.3 x 86.7 cm)
Collection the artist

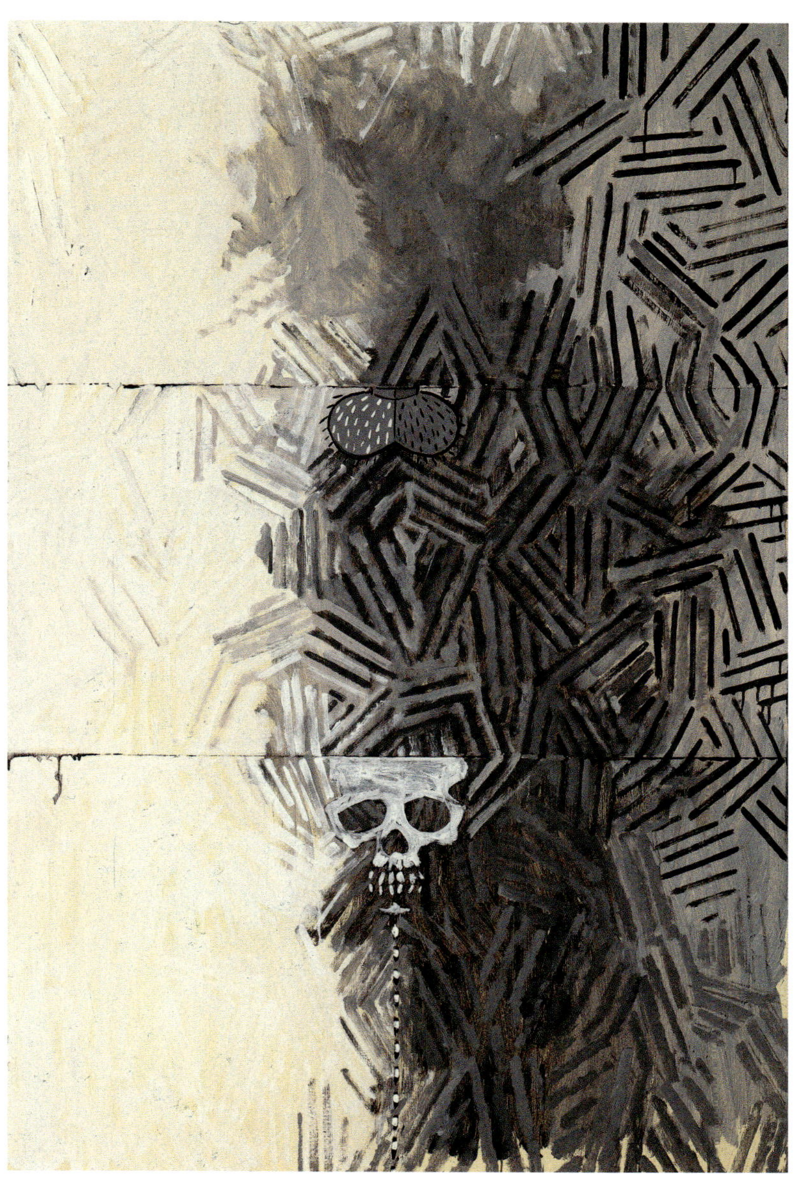

Jasper Johns *TANTRIC DETAIL III* 1981
Oil on canvas 50 x 34 in. (127 x 86.4 cm)
Collection the artist

fig. VIII: 5

obvious in *Tantric Detail I* that the testicles and skull can be considered figures and the crosshatch, the ground. In fact, the placement of the testicles and skull within the crosshatch patterns implies that, despite the fluctuations of the forces of life and death, the body is already merged with the ground. By dividing the painting into three stacked rectangles and aligning the skull and scrotum so that each appears to have partially slipped beneath the rectangle above, Johns gave each rectangle a tangible presence; it is a thing of some depth rather than a flat and, in that regard, idealized surface.

In this series, Johns also connected the two experiential states he defines as looking and spying. Once we move from looking at the oil-on-canvas *Tantric Detail I* to scrutinizing it, we see a horizontal, drippy brushstroke along the top-right edge. Falling and irreversibility are inherent to the material world, including the one inhabited by this painting. On the left-hand side of the lowest rectangle are ghostly traces of crosshatches, as if they have been shrouded. This layering underscores the thinglike nature of each of the rectangles. Also, reds and yellows, brighter than the colors on the right side, which is dominated by blues and grayish blues, mark the left side of the canvas. On the left side of the lowest section, adjacent to the red, yellow, and red strokes, are ghostly gray brushmarks. It is as if a process of submerging is taking place, and this echoes the skull and penis slipping beneath the ground. In *Tantric Detail III*, the white crosshatches on the right side are difficult to distinguish one from the other, conveying a state of merging.

The *Tantric Detail* series invites us to move beyond scrutinizing and into a state of contemplation. The contemplation of one's death is a central tenet of Tibetan Buddhism, something Johns likely knew. While he may have picked up on the subject matter of his source in this regard, the artist did not locate his motifs within a cosmology, but rather within an experiential realm. Body parts are swallowed up, evoking a state of change, erasure, and dissolution. The present we and the work share is shaped by the past and the future, by acknowledging that there was a beginning and there will be an ending, and that, as the painting implies, this conjunction is true of all moments in time. The penis slipping beneath the rectangle above is both; it is simultaneously making love and being subsumed. The white, spermlike beads suggest that life goes on without us, that our beginning and ending is part of a larger beginning and ending. Birth and death, form and decomposition coexist.

III.

Johns began his *Between the Clock and the Bed* paintings (1981–83) (see fig. VIII: 6) shortly after he became aware that his own crosshatch pattern very closely resembled the red and blue hatching of the Lapland coverlet that Edvard Munch had depicted in his *Self-Portrait between the Clock and the Bed* (fig. VIII: 7).[9]

Executed shortly before his death, the painting shows the elderly artist standing erect, but with a somewhat resigned expression on his face, between a grandfather clock and a small, single bed. The insistent verticality of the clock and the artist contrasts with the bed's horizontality, as if to oppose the forces of action and life with those of inaction and death. Behind Munch a doorway opens onto an adjacent room, probably his studio, with a number of paintings, presumably his, on the wall. But the bedroom Munch occupies is dark—his work is behind him, both literally and figuratively. Art, Munch's painting makes evident, becomes a part of its time, as well as a part of one's past, but time is always present and continuous. We live between the past and the future, between the after (time started, as represented by the clock) and the before (time stopped, as represented by the bed).

In all three of his triptychs on the subject, Johns layered at least two different-size crosshatch patterns, with long, wide units extending across the entire composition and smaller, narrower ones confined to a minor portion of the surface. In each the smaller crosshatch pattern, often in primary colors, appears in the lower right, the spot where Munch located his bed. In two of the paintings, Johns also included a smaller crosshatch pattern where Munch depicted the grandfather clock. And in the only oil (the other two are in encaustic), he silkscreened onto the canvas the image of his 1979 *Usuyuki* print. The location of the silkscreen corresponds to the door in Munch's painting, while its slightly diagonal tilt echoes the placement of two rectangles in previous works, one with a red and green circle (*Eddingsville* [1965]) and the other made up largely of white lines (*Harlem Light* [1967]). The diagonal tilt conveys movement, even falling, as well as hints at spatiality, which is also suggested by the layering of crosshatches of varying size.

The large crosshatch patterns in the left and right panels are arranged as mirror images of each other, while those in the middle section are distinct. As seen in previous crosshatch works, this mirroring suggests that the painting can be folded over, causing the section in the middle to become covered by the two joined sections. This conveys the possibility of two things melding together to become one. The placement of the smaller crosshatch patterns is connected to specific elements in Munch's composition. In contrast to *Weeping Women*, which, as noted above, was inspired by Picasso's etching of a woman's head framed by indeterminate space, Johns's *Between the Clock and the Bed* paintings allude to a composition in which perspectival space, something that previously had never played a part in this artist's work, became an essential structuring device.

Johns's primary preoccupation, in doing the three *Between the Clock and Bed* paintings, was with the figure/ground issue. In the middle panel of both the first and second works, the artist filled the interstices between the bluish parallel lines of the crosshatch with

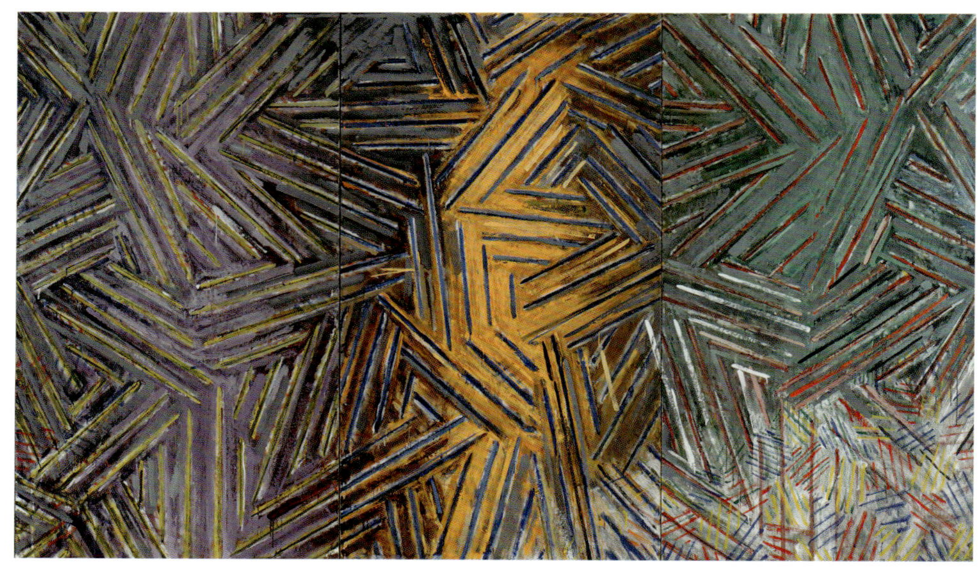

fig. VIII: 6 **Jasper Johns** *BETWEEN THE CLOCK AND THE BED* 1981
Oil on canvas 6 ft. x 10 ft. 6 1/4 in. (1.83 x 3.2 m)
The Museum of Modern Art, New York

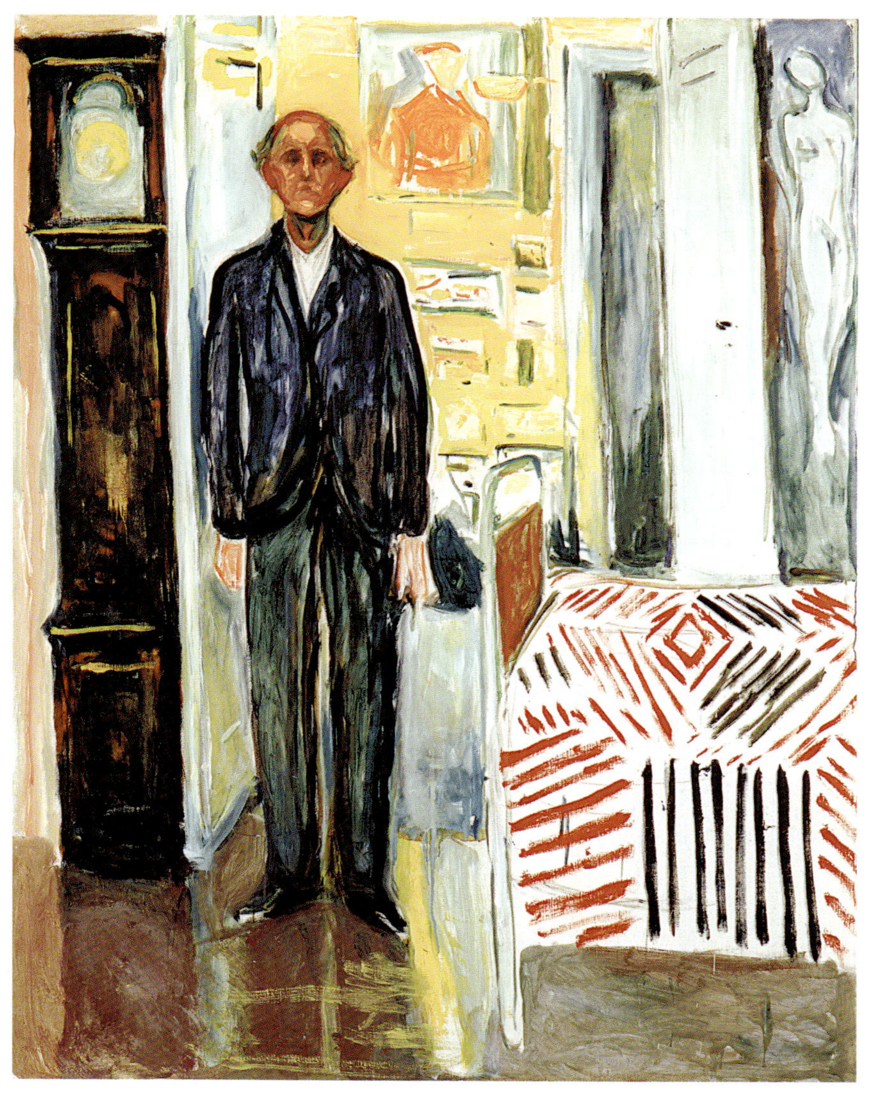

Edvard Munch *SELF-PORTRAIT BETWEEN THE CLOCK AND THE BED* 1940–42 fig. VIII: 7
Oil on canvas 58 3/4 x 47 1/2 in. (149.2 x 120.6 cm)
Munch Museum, Oslo

orange to evoke a figural presence. The orange appears trapped behind the slanting blue lines, lending the work a ghostly, disembodied feeling that recalls his suite of four drawings *Study for Skin* (1962). In both paintings, a field of smaller crosshatches in blue, red, and yellow extends from the bottom right of the figural presence to the painting's rightmost edge. The proximity of the smaller crosshatches to the orange figural presence suggests that the figure is intersecting or will fall into the horizontal pattern of primary colors (the bed). In the second *Between the Clock and Bed*, the diagonal tilt of the largely white silkscreen of the *Usuyuki* print brings into play the perception of falling and descending that has preoccupied Johns since at least 1963, with *Land's End* and *Periscope (Hart Crane)* (figs. V: 4, 5).

Through his layering of two different crosshatch schemes, Johns was able to allude to the perspectival space in Munch's painting. At this point, having worked almost exclusively with the crosshatch motif for a decade, Johns might have asked himself if it was possible to develop a pictorial space—something that he had rejected through his career—in which he could layer something other than the crosshatches. And, to follow the implications of echoing Munch's painting with his own disavowal of the self, he must have wondered, was it possible to make a self-portrait in which he is not seen? How could he extend his preoccupation with the body's material progress in time, and with the mind's acknowledgment of that changing state, to an even more palpable level of specificity?

CHAPTER 8
NOTES

1. Mark Rosenthal, *Jasper Johns: Work since 1974*, exh. cat. (New York: Thames and Hudson, with the Philadelphia Museum of Art, 1988): "Many more layers and varieties of gestural crosshatching and brushstrokes animate the encaustic surface of *Weeping Women* (1975)" (p. 27); and "Johns says that no system of markmaking is present in his work" (p. 105). See also *Jasper Johns: Writings, Sketchbooks, Notes, Interviews*, ed. Kirk Varnedoe, comp. Christel Hollevoets (New York, Museum of Modern Art, 1997), pp. 40, 41, 43, and 45, where schematic sketches and writing are reproduced.

2. Johns saw it in the atelier of Aldo Crommelynk, who worked extensively with Picasso in the 1950s and '60s and editioned many of his prints.

3. In addition to Picasso's print, Johns might have been familiar with his 1937 painting *Weeping Woman* (Tate Gallery, London), which the English artist Roland Penrose bought from the artist. As Penrose pointed out, the work's palette of bright colors—red, blue, green, and yellow—is "totally unassociated with grief." Roland Penrose, *Scrap Book* (London: Thames and Hudson, 1981), n.p.; quoted in Judi Freeman, *Picasso and the Weeping Women, The Years of Marie Thérèse Walter and Dora Marr*, exh. cat. (Los Angeles County Museum of Art, 1994), p. 117.

4. Jasper Johns, "Sketchbook Notes," *Art and Literature* (Lausanne) 4 (Spring 1965); repr. in *Jasper Johns: Writings* (note 1), pp. 37, 59.

5. Hans Richter, *Dada Art and Anti-Art* (London: Thames and Hudson, 1966), p. 89.

6. Penrose (note 3); quoted in Freeman (note 3).

7. Ajit Mookerjee, *Tantra Art: Its Philosophy and Physics* (New Dehli: Rupa and Co., 1994), p. 30. See also idem, *Tantra Asan: A Way to Self-Realization* (New York: Ravi Kumar, 1971); and idem, *The Tantric Way: Art, Science, Ritual* (New York: New York Graphic Society, 1977).

8. Mookerjee, *Tantra Art*, (note 7), p. 30.

9. The other two *Between the Clock and the Bed* paintings are from 1981 and 1982–83. See Demosthène Davvetas, "Jasper Johns et sa famille d'objets," *Art Press* (Paris) 80 (Apr. 1984); repr. in *Jasper Johns: Writings* (note 1), p. 218.

DD: *Are the three paintings in the show titled* Between the Clock and the Bed *a homage to the work of [Edvard] Munch?*
JJ: *Yes, they are a reference to the work of Munch. One of my friends sent me a postcard. I liked it. A series of thoughts followed.*

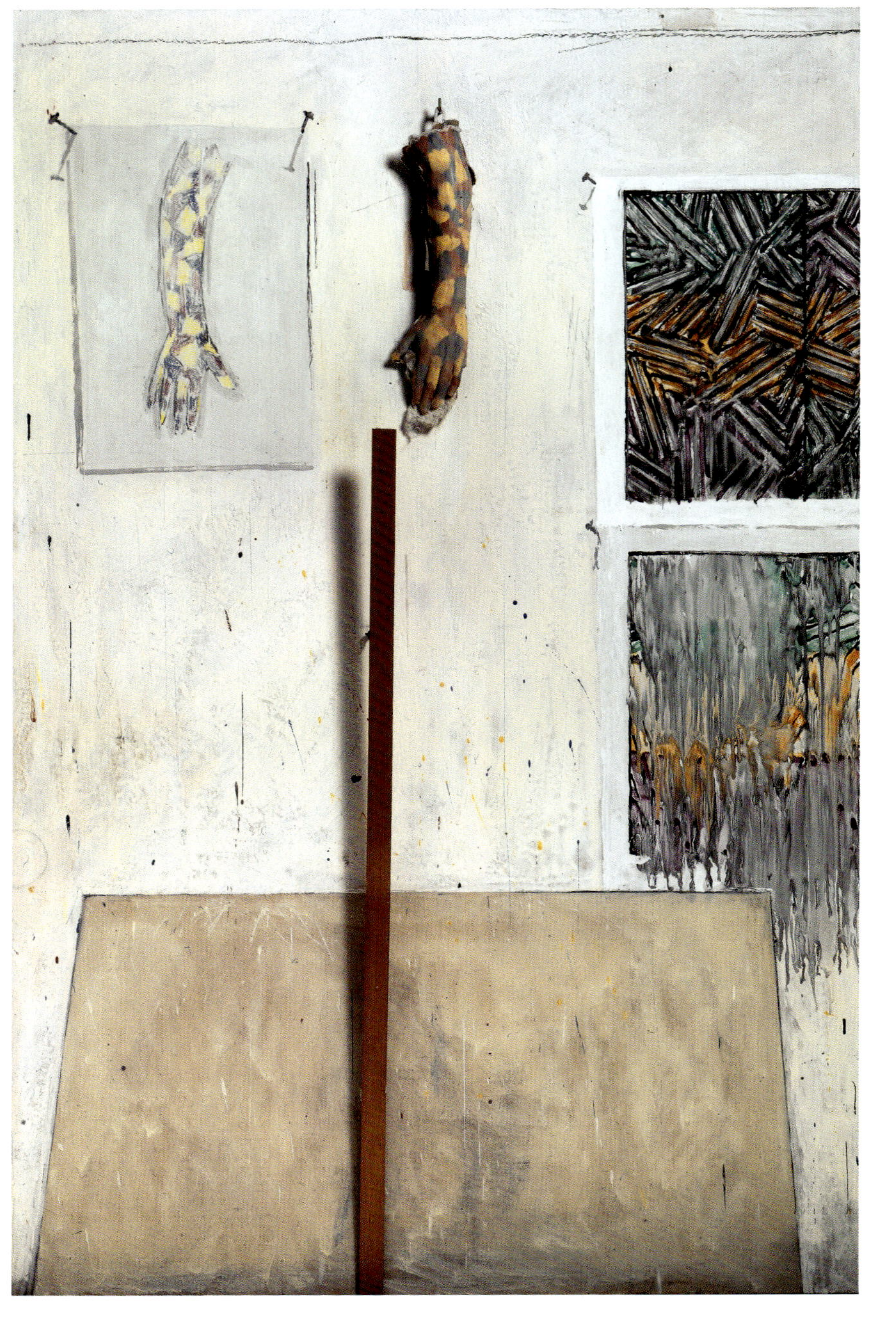

fig. IX: 1 **Jasper Johns** *IN THE STUDIO* 1982
Encaustic and collage on canvas with objects 72 x 48 x 4 in. (182.9 x 121.9 x 10.2 cm)
Collection the artist

Chapter 9

I.

Johns's 1982 painting *In the Studio* (fig. IX: 1)
marks a sharp departure from the crosshatch paintings
that had preoccupied the artist for a decade.

It is an expansive, analytic response to the implications regarding spatiality that confronted Johns in the first two *Between the Clock and the Bed* paintings (see fig. VIII: 6), which he had completed the previous year. As we have seen, these works both mirror themselves and allude to Munch's *Self-Portrait between the Clock and the Bed* (fig. VIII: 7), in which perspectival space plays a crucial role. Johns had found a new challenge: Could he reflect real things in a real space?

The question is not without repercussions. For Johns to introduce depth into his work at this point would have seemed like nothing less than a complete reversal, which in many ways it was. He had begun at the very forefront of painters who took subject matter into the realm of abstraction by incorporating ready-mades, but, as many who championed his early work pointed out, he not only rejected perspective and spatiality, but he also was the first artist to conflate ready-mades and flatness, which, as history bears out, paved the way for Pop Art. Johns's new direction was an answer to questions his recent explorations had made him ask, as well as a refusal to conform to expectations raised by his own early, and indeed seminal, work.

Johns's career is marked by a persistent need to declare freedom from all external agendas, including those that canonize him, while remaining true to his own perceptions and preoccupations. For him, refusing to follow the implications of his own art would be tantamount to surrendering to the outlines of others and to suppressing his insights in favor of those that have been codified by critics and theorists. That would make him into something he had never been: an academic artist. At the same time, Johns seems compelled to acknowledge that his decisions, whatever they are, must arise out of the particular logic that he set in motion in *Flag* (fig. I: 1), when he recognized that figure, ground, and time are inseparable, and that in certain instances appearance and reality do coincide. The effects of time's passage on the individual are as crucial to *Flag* as they are to *In the Studio*. Although manifested in very different ways, in each work the artist constructed his perception of a thing's relationship to reality—in the first, of an image to a surface; in the second, of a form to a place in which things exist—and how this gathering of stuff is rooted in reality.

In the Studio incorporates a wooden strip that has been hinged to the bottom-left center of the painting and tilts out, protruding noticeably into our space. This element mirrors the leaning empty canvas that the artist collaged at the bottom center of the painting. The angle of the trapezoidal canvas is less severe than the triangular table of fruit jutting up like a prow from the bottom of Pablo Picasso's *Demoiselles d'Avignon* (1907) and functions similarly, acknowledging the viewer's physical presence. It is as if the empty canvas is waiting to be mounted on the wall or has just been taken off, replaced by the things that are there. The echoing of the protruding strip occurs throughout the painting. Everything has its physical or visual counterpart. As Johns wrote in "Sketchbook Notes," "(Cézanne?—Each object reflecting the other.)"[1] In the case of *In the Studio*, the physical and pictorial both reflect each other and form an attachment. As with his two *Painted Bronze* sculptures (figs. III: 4, 5), the moment of the painting is between the after and the before.

Above the strip and to the right, Johns used a hook to affix a lifelike, mottled cast of a child's arm to the work's surface. The hook occupies the horizontal midpoint of the painting, near the top edge. Just to the left of the cast, the artist depicted a drawing of the mottled arm pinned to the wall. To the right of the cast, also pinned to the wall, are images of two small, related crosshatch paintings, one directly above the other. The space between the central hook and the edges of the drawing, and of the two paintings, feels exactly equal, establishing in the composition a sense of symmetry that the strip offsets. Both crosshatch paintings are incomplete; their right sides are cut off by the actual painting's physical edge. This suggests that we are in the room and that our point of view prevents us from taking it all in.

Although the crosshatches of the composition's paintings resemble those in *Between the Clock and the Bed*, they are different in color and structure, which is to say they are unique in Johns's oeuvre. In effect, these images are fragments that represent original paintings that we do not know. In each, the two leftmost panels comprise three stacked rectangles dominated by a single color: they are, from top to bottom, green, orange, and purple. In the adjacent and only partially visible panels, the colors are in inverse order: purple, orange, and green. That they are evidently only parts of a whole suggests that one panel of each work exists solely in the world of the painting, while the others exist in both art and life. While the topmost panel is intact, the bottom one is in a state of decomposition, with rivulets of wax running together as they stream down the melted painting. This pairing of a perfect, tactile articulation of the crosshatched surface and a melted one recalls the pairing that occurs in the *Corpse and Mirror* paintings (1974 and 1974–75), and the transformation that is intrinsic to time's passing.

Johns's juxtaposition of the cast of an arm and the drawing of it does not derive from Surrealism, with its practice of combining incommensurables or of picturing the "logic" of dreams. Rather, Johns's preoccupation signals his belief in an underlying perceptual connection between them that involves at least one of the following actions: mirroring, repetition, shifting, and physical transformation. The drawing of the arm becomes the cast arm and vice versa. The two pinned paintings mirror themselves, each other, and time's passing, with the top one achieving this duplication pictorially, and the bottom one doing it materially. Nor should we regard Johns's use of mirroring and shifting as some elaborate trick. Rather, he employed these devices to help reveal a thing's intractable bond with reality and change.

In the cast and in the drawing of it, Johns underscored the equation that he had made previously between flesh and encaustic. Both arms are covered with red, yellow, and blue splotches that fit together like a jigsaw puzzle. By applying the primary colors to the arms' skin, the artist used the figure/ground bond to make his equation explicit. Just as with *Flag*, *In the Studio* is Johns's analogue for the body caught in time. The melting painting hanging nearby is palpable evidence that both encaustic (and flesh) are vulnerable to changes in the environment, and that dissolution is inherent and inescapable. By allowing the empty trapezoidal canvas and the paintings to extend beyond the work's edges, the artist shifted them into our space, much as he did with the tilting strip. We are part of the world that *In the Studio* inhabits, and we too are subject to the reality it both mirrors and defines.

The crosshatch paintings within the painting allowed Johns to register the ravaging effects of reality. At the same time, the space of his studio, as well as its wall—to which things have been attached—calls across time to Munch's studio and to the paintings mounted on its wall. The melting surface of *In the Studio* is factual—the result of heat applied to it—and declarative. The unused, but by no means pristine, canvas that Johns affixed to the painting is firmly anchored by the left, right, and bottom edges of the largely white studio wall, on which little drips of paint are spattered; on the lower-left side, there is an impression, made by a tin can, which is truncated by the painting's edge. Along with the melting painting and soiled canvas, the wall is itself subject to time and reveals its effects. Johns generated a visual tension between the verticality of the painting (the tilting strip and hanging cast, which, in being subject to gravity, confirm their communality) and the horizontality of the ground, which is a slice of an expanded painterly experience.

In *Painted Bronze (Savarin can with brushes)* (fig. III: 5), the dirty paintbrushes frozen in place become memento mori, in that their real-life counterparts would, poetically speaking, remain in their turpentine-filled coffee can forever once the artist was no longer able to clean up for himself. In Johns's painting of a part of a studio wall, with a section of an unused canvas visible at the bottom, he depicted his own inevitable absence (capturing the moment he can no longer attend to his existence), with time continuing to change and break all things down. Completed more than two decades apart, these two works, a painted sculpture and a partially unpainted painting, embody two different manifestations of time's disintegrating effects. Rather than an isolated, aestheticized thing or moment, the used coffee can and dirty studio wall reveal the link between the momentary and the eternal, the single instant and infinite time.

II.

Perilous Night (fig. IX: 2) chronicles a further step in Johns's passage from one kind of painting to another; it is a work of both departure and arrival.

In order to document this journey, the artist introduced a new motif, derived from the two knights in the Resurrection panel of Matthias Grünewald's *Isenheim Altarpiece* (c. 1512–16). According to the artist, he first made tracings of figures in Grünewald's masterwork in the summer of 1980, after he received a portfolio of reproductions from Wolfgang Wittrock, a dealer in modern drawings.[2] He later traveled to Colmar, France, to see the altarpiece. On the left side of *Perilous Night*, divided compositionally into two adjacent rectangles so that it resembles a diptych, Johns used a magenta outline to delineate the two startled knights on the left. On the right, he included a number of two- and three-dimensional objects. Johns would return to this compositional structure in the two paintings entitled *Racing Thoughts* (figs. IX: 3, 4) and the cycle of paintings known as *The Seasons* (figs. X: 8–11). Johns's primary goal from the early 1980s into the mid-1990s was to bear witness to the effects of time and the anxieties it raises. It is no accident that he used such titles as *Perilous Night* and *Racing Thoughts*.

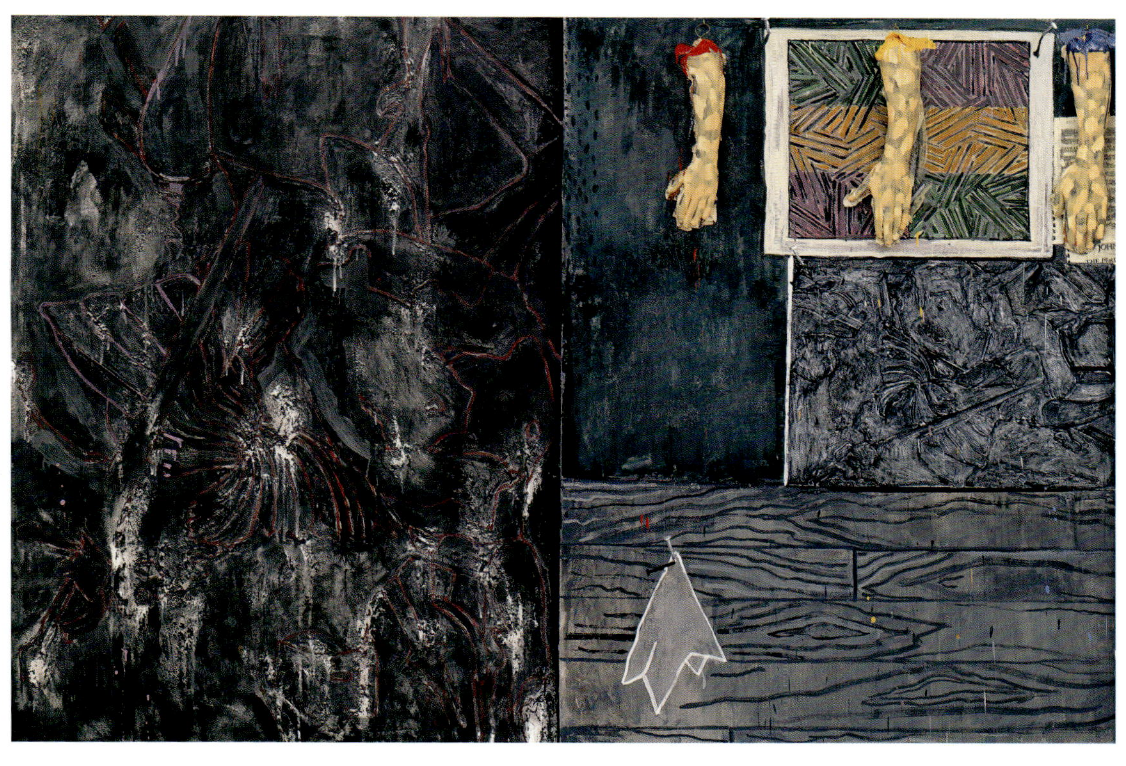

Jasper Johns *PERILOUS NIGHT* 1982 fig. IX: 2
Encaustic on canvas with objects 67 x 96 x 5 in. (170.2 x 243.8 x 12.7 cm)
National Gallery of Art, Washington, D.C. Robert and Jane Meyerhoff Collection

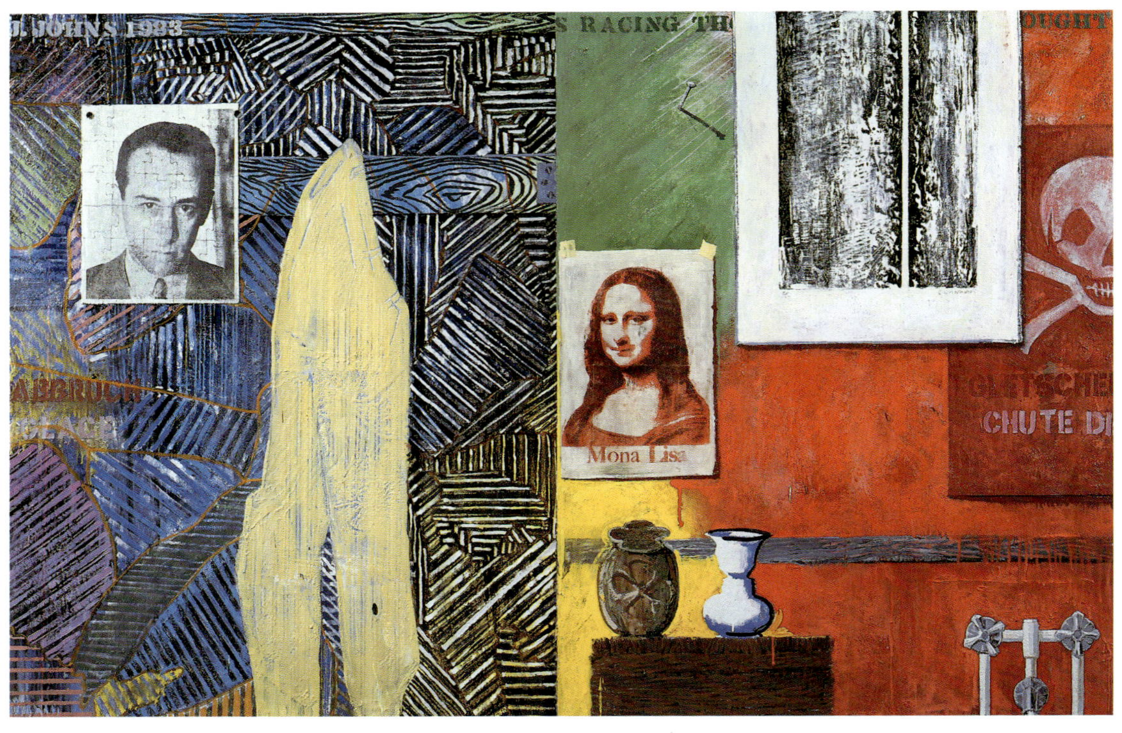

fig. IX: 3 **Jasper Johns** *RACING THOUGHTS* 1983
Encaustic and collage on canvas 48 x 75 1/8 in. (121.9 x 190.8 cm)
Whitney Museum of American Art, New York. Purchased with funds from the Burroughs Welcome Purchase Fund; Leo Castelli; the Wilfred P. and Rose J. Cohen Purchase Fund; the Julia B. Engel Purchase Fund; the Equitable Life Assurance Society of the United States Purchase Fund; the Sondra and Charles Gilman Jr. Foundation Inc.; S. Sidney Kahn; the Lauder Foundation, Leonard and Evelyn Lauder Fund; the Sara Roby Foundation; and the Painting and Sculpture Committee

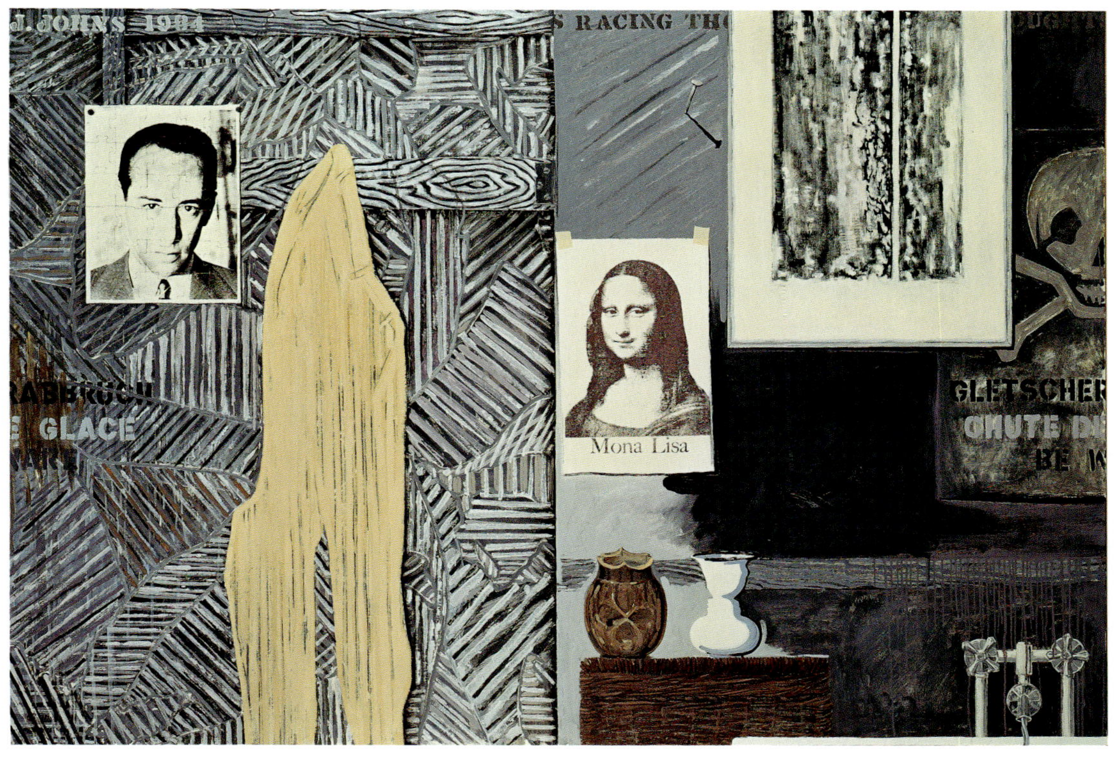

Jasper Johns *RACING THOUGHTS* 1984

Oil on canvas 50 x 75 in. (127 x 190.5 cm)

Collection Robert and Jane Meyerhoff

fig. IX: 4

The knights in the lower-left foreground of the Resurrection panel of Grünewald's altarpiece have been startled awake by Christ's ascension from his tomb, but their helmets and visors have slipped down over their eyes so that they are unable to witness the miracle. Thus cut off from their surroundings, each is trapped in his own world. The startled figures recall the arm extending up in *Land's End* (fig. V: 1), at once resisting and succumbing. That they are both *uncomprehending* recalls the remark Johns made in his "Sketchbook Notes": "The watchman leaves his job & takes away no information." The magenta outline turns the two knights into a single, awkward, splayed figure falling headlong into a field of black. The watchman, who has been startled but sees nothing, is the artist's motif for birth and for the unthinking body over which none of us have control. It is on the right side of the painting that the artist registered the conscious, thinking self, or what he called the "spy" who "stations himself to observe the watchman."[3]

By rotating the magenta-outlined shape ninety degrees, Johns made it point downward, as well as extended it beyond the painting's top edge. The figural form seems to rise, sink back, and finally descend. And by cropping the outline, Johns conveyed the figure's intrinsic discomfort; he does not fit anywhere, even though he plunges toward both the ground of the painting and the one on which we stand. In reheating the encaustic surface in places, so that the black began to drip, Johns created a second kind of descent, echoing the falling outline and suggesting that the body will one day sink even deeper into the ground in which it is already embedded.

The painting's title is the same as an early piece of music by John Cage; indeed, Johns included a silkscreened version of the title page and sheets of the score as a collage element on the painting's right side. The title also refers to "The Star Spangled Banner" ("Whose broad stripes and bright stars through the perilous fight/ O'er the ramparts we watched were so gallantly streaming"); and to the knights who have been stirred awake by Christ's departure from the tomb. *Perilous Night*—or perilous knight—is a homophonic pun that alerts the viewer to the inextricable bond of figure (knight) and ground (night), as well as to the vulnerability of the body to time. Linguistically, the title joins figure (knight), ground (black encaustic), and time (night) in a complex entity that underscores the inseparability of the magenta outline and the black field. The reality at the core of these connections is a perilous condition. They are "united states" that have started to merge. As I see it, the conflation of figure, ground, and event recalls Johns's dream of painting a flag nearly thirty years earlier. While *Perilous Night*'s reference to the national anthem evokes *Flag*, this is just one of the links between the two paintings. Like the knights, Johns was awakened by a revelation, but, in contrast to them, he was not oblivious to it, for his vision from the dream became *Flag*.

The title *Perilous Night* may link the painting to *Flag*, but it also suggests the artist's uncertainty about what will happen to his motifs if they are taken into a new territory, one defined by spatiality. The peril of this night (or passage) is that it registers the artist's decision to move from a compressed, flattened space (the painting's left side) to a perspectival space (the painting's right side). Here Johns chronicled three different possibilities: real things, sculptural forms, and illusion. On the top, he combined actual objects (Cage's score and the strip of wood that extends from top to bottom along the right edge) with three lifelike casts of hands and arms, and a painting—a close simulation of the faux-crosshatched work at the top right of *In the Studio*—depicted as pinned to the wall. In the middle, a gray version of Grünewald's knights, now correctly oriented, is nailed to the wall. And in the bottom section, he painted a gray or sooty wall, articulating the grain of its wood boards clearly, almost cartoonishly. Nailed to it is the image of a gray handkerchief with a white border (the nail, like others in the painting, casts an exaggerated, heavy black shadow). By securing the handkerchief to the horizontal wooden planks, Johns deconstructed his flag motif. Most likely derived from Pablo Picasso's etching of a weeping woman (fig. VIII: 2), the handkerchief approximates, and even perhaps parodies, the location of the flag's canton, and the planks' wavy grains evoke the ripples of a flag fluttering in the wind at night. The combination of the wooden wall and handkerchief is the one pictorial allusion that Johns has ever made to the American flag since his early painting; it suggests that he was waving farewell to making a painting and a thing be synonymous, as in *Flag*, as well as surrendering to the depiction of things in a shallow, layered space.

The questions raised by the mirroring Johns deployed in his *Between the Clock and the Bed* cycle brought him here. In those paintings, however, he remained faithful to his conceptual framework, working with an abstract motif made of parallel lines. The transformation that occurs between the left and the right side suggests the possibility that Johns recognized that, to be true to his art and its implications, he had to establish a perspectival space that could mirror real things caught in time, something he had never done before. Is it all that surprising that a state of foreboding, precariousness, interruption, and decline resonates throughout this dark, nighttime painting? The stars of Johns's flag have fallen out of the sky in *Perilous Night*. There is no dream to remember now, and no miracle to witness. Time's passing and his own work have brought the artist to a place of disturbing exposure, but, to his credit, he meticulously recorded the journey in his art. The sagging handkerchief registers farewell and surrender, which is one way to understand our passage through time. There was no going back, no evidence of regret, no passion recollected in tranquillity. He would do what his art demanded of him.

It is instructive to examine the right side's components carefully. Each of the three mottled arm casts, placed equidistant from one another, is attached to a hook with thin wire. Each cast is slightly different in length, suggesting that the molds were taken of the same person at different times. A primary color—red, yellow, blue—spills over the top of each arm and down, like gushing blood—a startling conjunction that expands upon the artist's equation of encaustic with flesh. The arms are stumplike bodies literally covered by and filled with color, the venerable stuff of art. Reversing the knights, who fall into the paint, here the paint falls out of and onto the arms. Whereas, on the left side, Johns asyndetically joined figure and ground, the sculptural arms on the right conflate flesh and paint.

The title page and part of the score of Cage's *Perilous Night* are almost completely hidden under the cast in the top-right corner. Because the title page is cut off at the painting's physical edge, the score is attributed to "John C," which can be read homophonically, with

"C" as "see." We have to look closely at the narrow space between the wooden slat and the painting's edge to find the "C / see." It has to be spied out.

In this upper section of the painting, as noted earlier, the artist combined actual objects and pictorialism, while pulling off the difficult task of establishing a material bond between them. He also incorporated three-dimensional objects into the ordinarily two-dimensional figure/ground relationship: by bisecting the crosshatch painting, the middle arm cast becomes an interruption, a barrier, and a figure. The picture within the picture comprises three crosshatched, stacked rectangles, painted, from top to bottom, green, orange, and magenta. To the right of the arm, in the same painting, the palette of the stacked rectangles is reversed: magenta at the top, orange in the middle, and green at the bottom, which repeats the structure of the crosshatch painting in the top-right corner of *In the Studio*. In this context, however, the inversion echoes the falling figure of the knights on the composition's left half; the sculptural arm bisecting the painting also can be said to be falling into the painting (paint), an interpretation that reaffirms the bond between figure and ground. The change that takes place in the crosshatch painting is complete and irreversible.

The gray of the knights—whose forms Johns rotated back, as we have seen, to their correct position—brings the figures and surrounding field into an even closer proximity than in the magenta and black half of the painting. The different measures of experience that Johns examines in this painting connect it to *According to What* (fig. VI: 2), where he also chronicled various materialist ways of arriving at literal facts. As is usual with the artist, the continuity he sought to uphold in *Perilous Night* is the one that binds us to reality.

In *Flag* Johns had found ways to unite the states of dreaming and waking, as well as to collapse together figure, ground, and time. In *Perilous Night*, he juxtaposed a compressed space on the left with a visually and physically layered space on the right. An artist who has spent much of his career joining, affixing, and layering one thing with or against another, Johns, as should be apparent by now, recognized in *Flag* that he was uniting distinct but bonded states in order to reflect a true relationship to reality. And here, in a painting started years after *Flag*, the artist once again joined separate but distinct states by establishing a continuum between them.

In *Perilous Night*, Johns in effect entered deeper into a perilous territory (pictorial space) fraught with obstacles and pitfalls, not the least of which is a spatiality declared obsolete by theoreticians and critics and therefore of little use to a radical artist. Another problem he faced was how and what to mirror, since his literalism requires that the space in his paintings refer to something actual. Whereas, in *Flag*, Johns arrived at a physically layered space, on the right-hand side of *Perilous Night* he literally layered the painting with physical objects, collage, and illusions. But that compressed pictorial field must also include the viewer, so that it not only exists in, but also connects to, the present. *Perilous Night* both *is* a wall and *mirrors* a wall to which flat and round things have been attached. By including the waking, though blinded, knights—distant relatives of the person who dreamed he saw himself painting the American flag—Johns dared himself to, as he put it, "drop the reserve."[4] Would the trace of autobiography in this painting become more visible in the ones to follow? As always, this question is connected to a formal issue: Would a proliferation of personal references tempt Johns to succumb to the pictorial aspect of illusionism that he had resisted since *4 the News* (fig. VI: 3), when he first cited the American trompe l'oeil master John F. Peto?

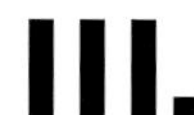

Johns completed at least a dozen paintings
between 1983 and 1988
in which he made specific reference to a room
in the house in upstate New York
where he lived at the time.

Because he had rejected spatiality and was praised for the innovative way he elevated familiar things into the realm of abstraction, a number of observers, as noted previously, felt that the artist had betrayed himself when he began exploring layered, perspectival space. What many (and this includes some of the artist's earlier supporters) saw as his full withdrawal from abstraction was further complicated by his use of seemingly autobiographical motifs, albeit in ways that were perceived as guarded and aloof.[5] Yet again these readings are tied to an external narrative and are ultimately reductive. The paintings are neither a retreat nor autobiographical, at least in the simple sense that autobiography is usually understood. They do not reveal anything about Johns's private life that we do not already know, nor do they encode or hide something about him that we suspect. They are not about the artist as an "I," but as a thing, a state we all share.

Two of these paintings Johns titled *Racing Thoughts*. The earlier one (fig. IX: 3) is executed in encaustic, largely in primary and secondary colors, with discrete passages in ocher, brown, black, gray, and white. The later one (fig. IX: 4), in oil, is far more monochromatic, with patches of ocher, brown, and bluish violet. Otherwise, the paintings are compositionally identical. Both depict a room with a bath, its rim and faucet visible in the lower-right corner; it is a place where one sits in water, naked and normally alone.

The location of the tub, in which is it easy to imagine ourselves, thereby placing us inside the pictorial space, turns the painting into a depiction of both the artist and his audience. The motivating theme behind the two paintings shares something with *Painted Bronze (Savarin can with brushes)* and the Map paintings (see fig. IV: 2), works in which a solid form is immersed in or surrounded by liquid. This sense of engulfment, and the likelihood that it will only get deeper, is a source of the artist's understandable anxiety and the paintings' title, *Racing Thoughts*. In them, the idea that Johns constructed, mirrored, and investigated is the split perception that occurs when we sit or lie in a tub, entirely submerged but for our head.

Like *Perilous Night*, *Racing Thoughts* is divided into two equal parts, with the left pertaining to the unthinking body and the right to the conscious mind. The difference is

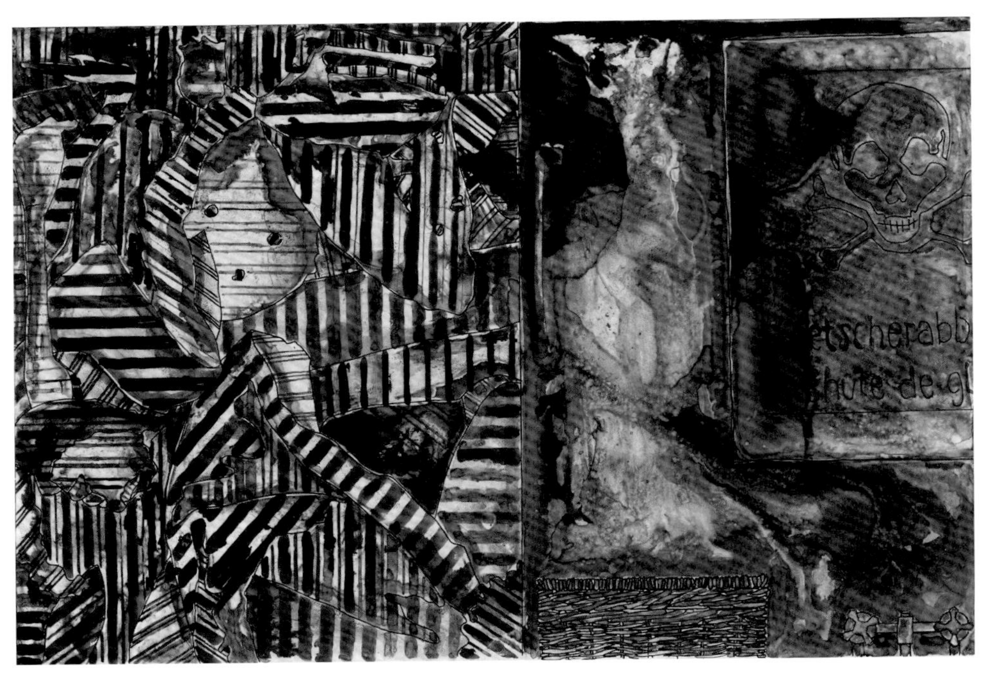

fig. IX: 5 **Jasper Johns** *UNTITLED* 1983
Ink on synthetic polymer sheet 24 3/4 x 36 1/4 in. (63 x 92.1 cm)
The Museum of Modern Art, New York. Gift of the Lauder Foundation

that instead of the conceptual split of *Perilous Night*, each section of *Racing Thoughts* roughly corresponds to portions of the artist's rustic bathroom. In an interview, Johns said, "Every image or object in *Racing Thoughts* was from something in the studio or the house."[5] One senses that Johns's progression, from his earlier mirroring of Munch's self-portrait to the perspectival paintings that followed, would lead to the challenge of mirroring an actual situation. Johns's site and the things in it all exist, but the way he structured them is fictive, something he purposefully made up. If, as early observers concluded, Johns lifted a familiar image (the flag) into the realm of abstraction, here he elevated things he owned into the realm of speculation.

The left half of the painting ostensibly depicts a rustic wooden door with two horizontal wooden boards: a narrow strip across the top, and a wider one about a quarter of the way down. Over the lower board hang a jigsaw-puzzle portrait of Leo Castelli, who was Johns's dealer at the time, and a pair of tan corduroy pants. On a simple level, then, the left side of the work depicts a door with two items suspended from it. A closer look discloses that this is and is not the case, a conundrum not unlike the experience of *Flag* and both *Painted Bronze* pieces.

Johns used a wood-grain pattern to define the two horizontal bands as boards, as well as to distinguish them from the rest of the door, which is made up of interlocking, puzzlelike sections, all composed of hatching. In addition, he depicted a hinge at the right end of the wider board, directly adjacent to the wall occupying the painting's right half. The hinge tells us that this is a door and that it is closed, giving the bather privacy. Some of the interlocking sections share an orange outline, which crosses over the horizontal boards, even as the wood changes from door to cross brace and back to door. The orange outline makes the door into a figure/ground problem in which cross brace and door are united, even as they remain distinct. By now, we know that the issue of figure/ground is not solely a formal one, and that something else is going on.

The puzzle pieces composing the portrait of Castelli, which has been thumbtacked to the door, echo the irregular contours of the interlocking parts. This visual echo suggests that puzzle and door are linked, with Castelli's portrait being the one clearly visible thing. Here it is important to know that Johns executed an ink drawing on plastic, *Untitled* (fig. IX: 5), which points to *Racing Thoughts*. The right half of the drawing contains some of the same motifs as the painting, while the left features a figure composed of interlocking sections of linear patterns. In the drawing, figure and ground have fused into a complex but discernible image.

We will learn from examining two later paintings, *The Bath* and *Untitled* (both 1988), in Chapter Ten that the figure I suggest is embedded in the door/ground of *Racing Thoughts* is the wretched, boil-covered victim of Saint Anthony's fire, who is sprawled across the bottom-left corner of the Temptation of Saint Anthony panel of Grünewald's *Isenheim Altarpiece*. Common in the Middle Ages, Saint Anthony's fire is a disease caused by poisoning from a fungus (ergot) that grows on ryegrass and contaminates the rye flour used to make bread. People contract the disease by eating what they need to survive; in turn, the disease begins to eat them—an irony certainly not lost on Johns. Ergot contains a chemical, lysergic acid diethylamide (LSD is chemically related to ergot), that drives sufferers insane and causes gangrene in the hands and feet due to the constriction of the blood supply to the extremities. One literally begins to rot away.

Half in protest and half in resignation, Grünewald's dejected figure raises his left arm, which ends in a withered stump. His lower body has morphed into that of a demon, complete with boil-covered legs and webbed feet. By portraying the lower extremities of the feverish figure in this way, Grünewald re-created the state of hallucination that afflicted those wracked by the poisoning; as their fingers, toes, hands, and feet dropped off, victims believed that they were being burned at the stake or that the fires of hell were inside their bodies and working their way to the surface.

If, in *Racing Thoughts*, the feverish figure is present, he remains buried in the wooden door or ground and is not disclosed. Something is there, although we do not know what it is, nor do we need to. If we get too hung up on Johns's iconography, I think we miss his point, which is the figure/ground relationship and the metaphysical connotations of that bond. Johns's possible joining of the figure above (Castelli) and figure below (Grünewald's feverish, incurable victim) both deepens and broadens the implications the artist first discerned when he made the magenta outline of the knights in *Perilous Night*. First, the artist had now found a way to extend his conception of the figure/ground relationship to a common event, in this instance, someone sitting in a tub of water. Second, while he had used other familiar objects in the past, such as a coffee can full of dirty paintbrushes and a map of the United States, to explore the bond between form and formlessness, in *Racing Thoughts* he added the ultimate indeterminate element, the viewer's body. We imaginatively project ourselves into the painting, sitting or lying in the tub, and stare at the wall, which mirrors our solitary existence. Third, the site of the painting—Johns's bathroom, fictively reconstructed—enabled him to chronicle an array of insights, borne of an intimate familiarity with the objects depicted, into the bond between form and dissolution.

Behind the tub's front rim is a wicker laundry hamper on which rest two pots, one commemorating the Silver Jubilee of England's Queen Elizabeth II and Prince Philip, and the other made by the eccentric late-nineteenth/early-twentieth-century ceramicist George Ohr, who has been called the United States' first art potter.[7] As in *In the Studio* and *Perilous Night*, such pairing and echoing is repeated throughout *Racing Thoughts*. The hamper continues an idea that Johns explored in *Painted Bronze* (*Savarin can with brushes*) and *Fool's House* (fig. VII: 4): one sign of life is the ability to clean up after oneself. One day, however, the brushes will not be wiped off, the broom will no longer tidy up, the dirty cup will go unwashed, and the hamper will remain full of soiled laundry.

Cleanliness is also the function of a bath. The spigot is on, and water (encaustic) pours into the tub. The faucet and the cruciform ribs of its two flanking handles are echoed by the indented impression visible on the Ohr pot; each handle could fit inside the piece's hollow. This suggests a sexual connection, particularly since the Ohr pot rests directly beneath a poster of the *Mona Lisa* that is taped to the wall. There is even a Tantric allusion, with the genital faucet and cruciform handles located partly beneath a Swiss highway sign bearing the image of a skull and crossbones. In his *Tantric Detail* paintings (see fig. VIII: 4, 5), the artist directly explored the conjunction of sex and death, of beginnings and endings, but here he constructed the view out of disparate objects—a highway warning sign, a faucet, the *Mona Lisa*, and an Ohr pot. One senses that the artist is now seeing (spying on) things differently.

Racing Thoughts is neither a hermetic assembly of iconographic details nor an eccentric collection of objects Johns happened to have in his house and studio. Each inclusion is deliberate, based on his vision of reality as a continuum in which the material world is both caught and undergoing change. Having spent a decade schematically structuring the placement of his crosshatches, he brought this thinking to bear in the paintings he did between 1982 and 1995, where the focus was a room, place, wall: a layered space. The meaning that each thing accrues is determined by what it is, where it is placed, and the different ways it reflects something else. *Racing Thoughts* is in effect a hall of mirrors in which each reflection embodies another view of our bond with reality and reveals the corrosive effects of time.

In *4 the News* (fig. VI: 3), which the reader will recall alludes to a composition by the trompe l'oeil painter John F. Peto (fig. VI: 4), and works that followed, Johns was relatively literal in his use of things; to that degree, he resisted the illusionism that is a central characteristic of "fool-the-eye" painting. In *Racing Thoughts*, he undertook the demands of this manner because, as I see it, his process had led him to the realm of things seen in perspectival space. In this sense, the artist also had to "drop the reserve" about making art that "reminded [him] of someone else's work—an idea, a gesture, paint quality I would try to get rid of it. But now it would not faze me in the least."[8]

Johns stenciled the words "RACING THOUGHTS" in capital letters along the top of the painting's right half. Partly because of the placement on the wall of an image of a framed lithograph by Barnett Newman, *Untitled* (1961), the stenciling is interrupted, reading as "S RACING THO," with most of the "O" cut off by the left side of the print. The "O" reappears on the other side of the print, continuing "THOUGHTS" as "OUGHTS," although the final "S" disappears off the painting's right edge, only to appear alone at the left of the painting's right half. Thus we read: "S RACING TH OUGHT." The arrangement of letters suggests that the right side of the painting could be curled to meet the left side, creating a cylinder to reunite "THOUGHTS." Below and partially covered by the print is the Swiss highway sign. Its German and French phrases are cropped by the painting's right edge, but reappear in the mirrored area on of the painting's left side. They translate as "Beware of falling ice." Thus *Racing Thoughts* can be understood as a cylinder within a cylinder, with the right side tightly curled on the very inside, attached at the bisection's seam to the outside cylinder, made from the left side. This configuration suggests that there is a public figure (Leo Castelli) who is falling apart (puzzle) and a fragmented, interior figure made up of a male (Prince Philip's profile), females (the *Mona Lisa*, Queen Elizabeth's profile), and bodies caught in time (skull and crossbones and faucet). The outer and inner are connected but separate, as is everything else in the painting.

In addition to being the view from the bathtub, the painting redefines the self-portrait by conveying the personality of the artist as an individual with an exterior life (the Castelli puzzle, the corduroy pants) and an inescapable interior (the body made up of fragments). The right side (the *Mona Lisa* and skull and crossbones), which can be identified with Johns's spy, as well as the tighter, more deeply hidden cylinder, is studying the left side, that of his watchman, who interfaces with the real world. If we accept that the larger, hatched areas might contain, cover, or signal the presence of Grünewald's tormented, boil-covered figure, subsumed in the door, ground, and paint, we must consider that Johns placed Castelli's head over it. At the same time, there is something slyly wicked about Johns's tacking a portrait of his dealer to the door. Was the artist casting Castelli as a "watchman [who] leaves his job & takes away no information"?[9] The jigsaw-puzzle portrait, itself comprising multiple pieces, hangs on a door made of interlocking sections. Both embody a state of fragility; they are destined to fall apart. This state of dissolution is echoed in the translation of the warning "Beware of falling ice." Johns may have been alluding to an anecdote that Jean Cocteau related about Pablo Picasso. The latter was amazed that, when people bathe, they do not dissolve like sugar cubes. Not surprisingly, Johns found this story about Picasso and dissolution appealing.[10] There is an additional aspect to the warning emblazoned on the far right of Johns's bathroom wall. In another "Sketchbook Note," he wrote, "Beware of the body & the mind. Avoid a polar situation."[11] The opposites that the artist told himself to avoid are embodied in the highway sign, which warns of falling ice. By splitting the stenciled warning, so that the rest of the word (German) and phrase (French) are continued on the left side, extending in from the edge, Johns emphasized his belief that mind and body, however distinct, are deeply connected. By aligning in a figural arrangement the sign warning of ice and the faucet from which hot water is pouring, the artist acknowledged that he must consider both in material terms, that the mind is also a thing. Encaustic is vulnerable to extremes of cold and heat, and Johns has not privileged one aspect of it over the other. Both the highway sign and the faucet are in front of a red wall, with rivulets of red running over the horizontal wooden board dividing the sign from the tub. The melting or decomposing ground (or reality) has begun to join the skull (or mind) to the body.

In counterpoint to the wooden board dividing the pairing of the sign and faucet and, to a lesser extent, the poster of the *Mona Lisa* and the Ohr pot, is the Newman print, which is divided down the middle by his signature "zip." Cropped by the painting's top edge, the print extends down between the poster and sign. While the Newman covers some of the sign, the skull and crossbones remain in full view. Both the actual and the implied divisions made by the wooden board and the print encourage us to see with our mind's eye and recognize that the entire right side has been divided into interlocking rectangles that include both figure (poster, sign, print, basket) and ground (red, yellow, and green wall).

The other object that Johns placed between the two vertical configurations of the *Mona Lisa* and Ohr pot, and the sign and faucets, is a white ceramic pot made to commemorate the twenty-fifth wedding anniversary of England's rulers. The pot is notable for its articulation of a Rubin's figure, a negative-/positive-space motif that combines two facing profiles, with the area between them resembling a vase. In this case, the queen's profile is on the right and her consort's is on the left. Johns first incorporated a Rubin's figure in his lithograph *Cups 4 Picasso* (fig. X: 1). The dynamic created by the positive/negative relationship of profiles and pot evokes Johns's spy and watchman, as do the skull and crossbones of the highway sign, which serve as a notice in two ways: they are a warning to motorists and a symbol of mortality. The mind (the profiles) must monitor the body's progress (the vase) in time. At the same time, recalling Chuang Tzu's dream of the butterfly and what he called "the transformation of things" (see Chapter One), and the artist's preoccupation with the figure/ground relationship, here figure and ground are inseparable, as well as capable of shifting (being transformed) from profiles to pot and back.

This brings us back to "OUGHT," the letters that appear to the right of the Newman print and above the skull and crossbones. The homophone of "OUGHT" is "aught," or zero. Dirt, decomposition, death, cleanliness, and the sexual drive are all acknowledged beneath a word that means responsibility but that also suggests nothingness, the two poles of our existence. Grünewald's diseased figure may signal our ultimate fate, but this should not deter us from engaging reality with open eyes. Thus *Racing Thoughts* seems to suggest that even though Johns is destined to end up as nothing ("0"), he ought to be responsible for everything in the painting (including the empty spaces), which is a reaffirmation of his commitment to truthfully examining the individual's relationship to reality. This is Johns's definition of the artist's role.

CHAPTER 9
NOTES

1. See Jasper Johns, "Sketchbook Notes," *Art and Literature* (Lausanne) 4 (Spring 1965); repr. in *Jasper Johns: Writings, Sketchbooks, Notes, Interviews*, ed. Kirk Varnedoe, comp. Christel Hollevoets (New York: Museum of Modern Art, 1997), pp. 37, 59.

2. Kirk Varnedoe, *Jasper Johns: A Retrospective*, exh. cat., with an essay by Roberta Bernstein (New York: Museum of Modern Art, 1996), pp. 303–04, which states (p. 303) that the artist received the portfolio from Wittrock in the summer of 1980.

3. *Jasper Johns: Writings* (note 1), pp. 37, 59–60.

4. Quoted in April Bernard and Mimi Thompson, "Johns on ...," *Vanity Fair* 47, 2 (Feb. 1984), p. 65; repr. in *Jasper Johns: Writings* (note 1), p. 217.

5. Peter Schjeldahl, "String Theory," *New Yorker*, May 30, 2005, pp. 96–97. "His best pieces (including above all, for me, his maps of the United States, which are lavished with inexhaustible eruptions of inspired gesture and piquant color) bring maximum emotional energy to bear on subjects of minimum personal significance; and they keep his cleverness busy making crucial structural decisions; his worst pieces are about the artist himself, and teem with gratuitous bright ideas."

Michael Kimmelman, "Sifting among the Icons for the Key to Johns," *New York Times*, Oct. 18, 1996, pp. C1, C32. "But there was also a generosity and accessibility to that early work, his famous reticence aside. On the other hand, the art since 1982 seems less decipherable, more crabbed and even sanctimonious, although Mr. Johns says he is opening himself up, dropping his reticence. He wants it both ways: encouraging you to translate his encoded images, like hieroglyphs, but then refusing to make them cohere interestingly."

6. Quoted in Bernard and Thompson (note 4).

7. Mark Rosenthal, *Jasper Johns: Work since 1974*, exh. cat. (New York and London: Thames and Hudson, in association with the Philadelphia Museum of Art, 1988), p. 85.

8. Quoted in Bernard and Thompson (note 4).

9. *Jasper Johns: Writings* (note 1).

10. Johns related the anecdote to me sometime in the 1980s.

11. *Jasper Johns: Writings* (note 1), pp. 34, 56.

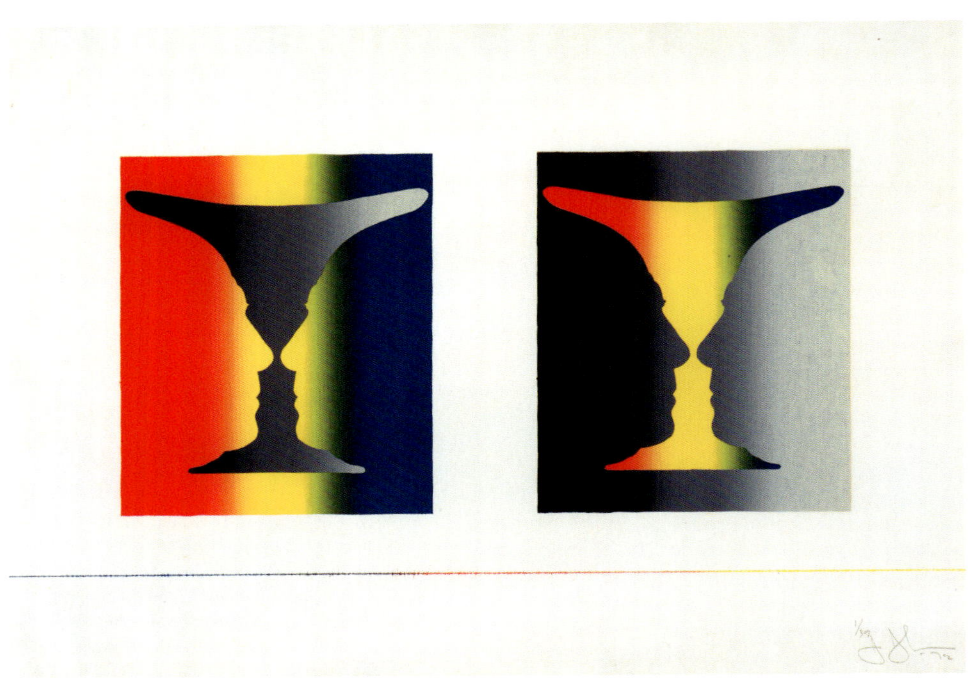

fig. X: 1 **Jasper Johns** *CUPS 4 PICASSO* 1972
Lithograph 22 1/2 x 32 1/4 in. (57 x 82 cm)

Chapter 10

I.

The objects Johns included in his two *Racing Thoughts* (figs. IX: 3, 4) were not just things found around his house but also motifs that suggest or represent elements of the art of Leonardo, Peto, Ohr, Newman, and, in a less visible way, Grünewald.

In addition, it is likely that the site and the perspective were inspired in part by Jean Cocteau's anecdote about Pablo Picasso (see Chapter Nine). While Picasso is only an oblique presence here, Johns's interest in this artist was hardly new, as we have already seen in the discussion in Chapter Seven of the relationship of Johns's *Weeping Women* (fig. VIII: 1) to Picasso's 1937 etching *Weeping Woman* (fig. VIII: 2). Johns saw his first actual Picasso in 1949 and "thought it was the ugliest thing [he'd] ever seen."[1] His first visual reference to the Spanish artist occurred in two lithographs, *Cups 4 Picasso* (fig. X: 1) and *Cups 2 Picasso* (1973), which he produced in response to a request for a contribution to a portfolio that honored the artist on his ninetieth birthday. In the prints, Johns employed the Rubin's-figure device (see Chapter Nine) so that two profiles of Picasso face each other, the space between them forming a goblet. Johns's interest in the device is another manifestation of his preoccupation with the interaction of figure and ground. In a handful of Picasso's paintings, all of them dating to after 1936—the year that Picasso started his most celebrated composition, *Guernica*—Johns would find another way to investigate the dynamic nature of this relationship.

The first motif derived from Picasso to enter Johns's work was inspired by a portrait, *Woman in Straw Hat* (fig. X: 2). Johns saw a reproduction of the painting in the book *Picasso's Picassos* by David Douglas Duncan, which documents the artist's personal collection of his own work.[2] These objects had been never before been published, a fact that would have caught Johns's attention. Picasso painted *Woman in Straw Hat* just before he began working on *Guernica* and his many etchings of a weeping, inconsolable woman. It depicts a head that is at once a sculpture and a flowerpot resting on a pedestal. Picasso distorted the head so that the eyes, which look in opposite directions, are embedded in breastlike forms and orifices. The curlicue mouth can also be read as female genitalia. Head and body have been compressed into a single, disfigured entity.

One could say that Picasso's portrait is the visual opposite of the Rubin's figure that Johns used in *Cups 4 Picasso, Racing Thoughts*, and other paintings that he did in 1983 and 1984. In *Cups 4 Picasso*, the facing profiles (head) and goblet (body) are at once distinct and inseparable, while in Picasso's painting, head and body have been squashed into a sculptural form. In *Untitled (A Dream)* (fig. X: 3), Johns took Picasso's image and, following its implications, distorted it further: "It became extremely poetic, something that conveys many meanings at once. While looking at it, it interested me that Picasso had constructed a face with features on the outer edge. I started thinking in that direction, and it led me to use the rectangle of the paper as a face and attaching features to it."[3] Elsewhere, he said, "I was working with Picasso's *Straw Hat with Blue Leaves* [*Woman in Straw Hat*]. He extended the woman's features to the outer edge of her face. I got the idea to push the features to the outer edge of the canvas, the canvas with the features attached to it."[4]

The extreme distortion that Johns performed on Picasso's already contorted image transformed head and canvas into a single entity. The face is now rectangular and utterly flattened. One eye is stuck in the top-left corner, and the other peeps out from the lower-right edge. In a reversal of Picasso's figure, in which the eyes look outward in opposite directions, in Johns's version they turn inward. A pair of cartoonlike lips (also resembling mountain peaks) sit along the bottom edge, near the right side, while the nostrils' stylized curlicue floats above and to the left of the mouth. Johns's conflation of the head/face with the canvas extends the connection he has long made between flesh and encaustic. It also restates in a simplified form the interrelationship of body, wall, and painting that he explored in *Perilous Night* (fig. IX: 2). Starting with an untitled drawing in pastel and graphite (1984; collection the artist), Johns returned to this image for more than a decade in paintings, drawings, and prints.

According to Johns, he associated the rectangular face with the "first images or forms of a child"[5] or what could be called infantile impressions. Johns also acknowledged that one inspiration for his distortion of the Picasso was a drawing that he had seen in an issue of *Scientific American* while he was in the army, but that he could not remember in detail. In 1991, after he had already used the motif of the rectangular face numerous times, he looked up the drawing. He found it in a 1952 article by Bruno Bettelheim about a schizophrenic girl who had lost her parents. The article reproduced a number of the girl's

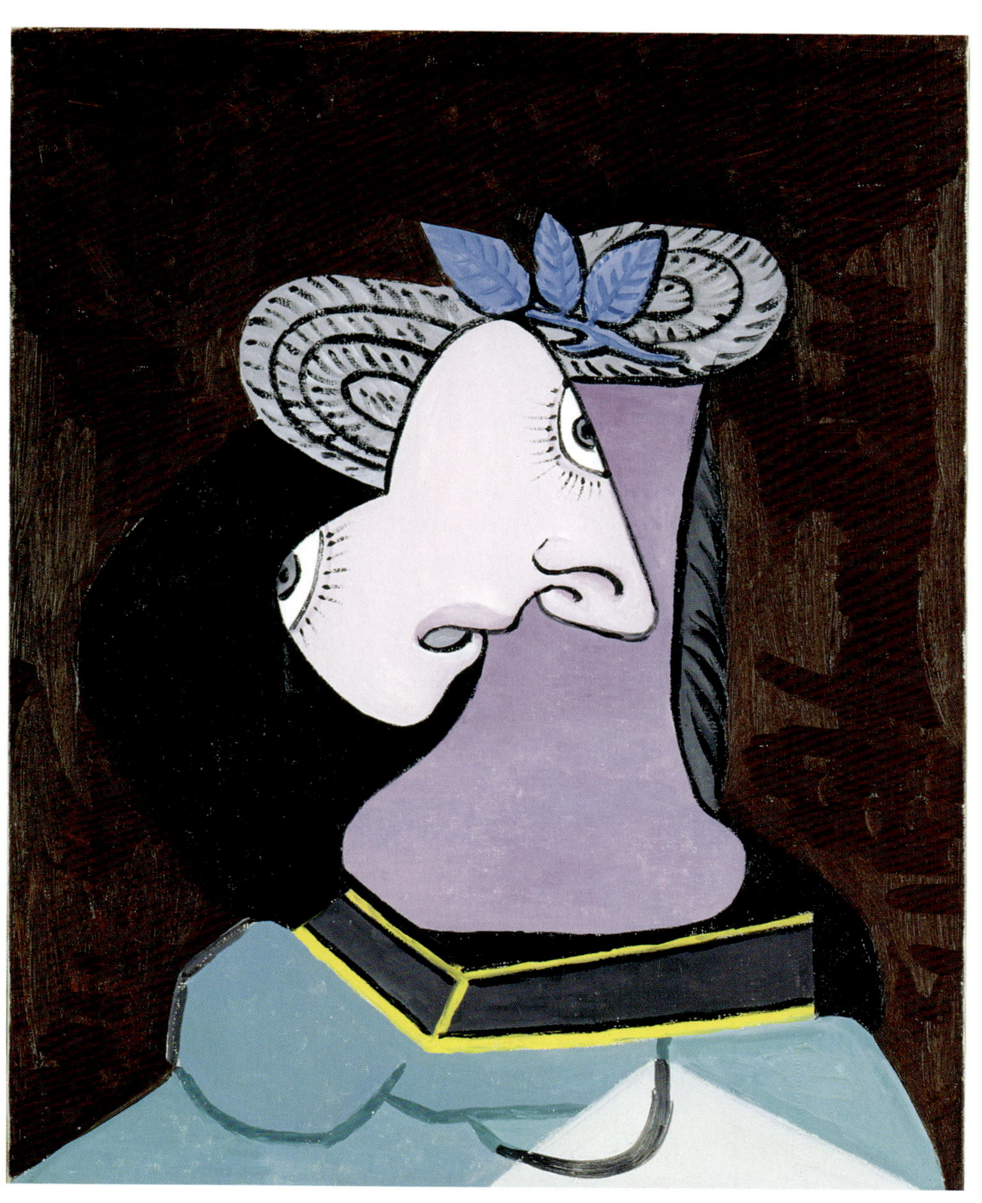

Pablo Picasso *WOMAN IN STRAW HAT* 1936
Oil on canvas 24 x 19 3/4 in. (61 x 50 cm)
Musée Picasso, Paris

fig. X: 2

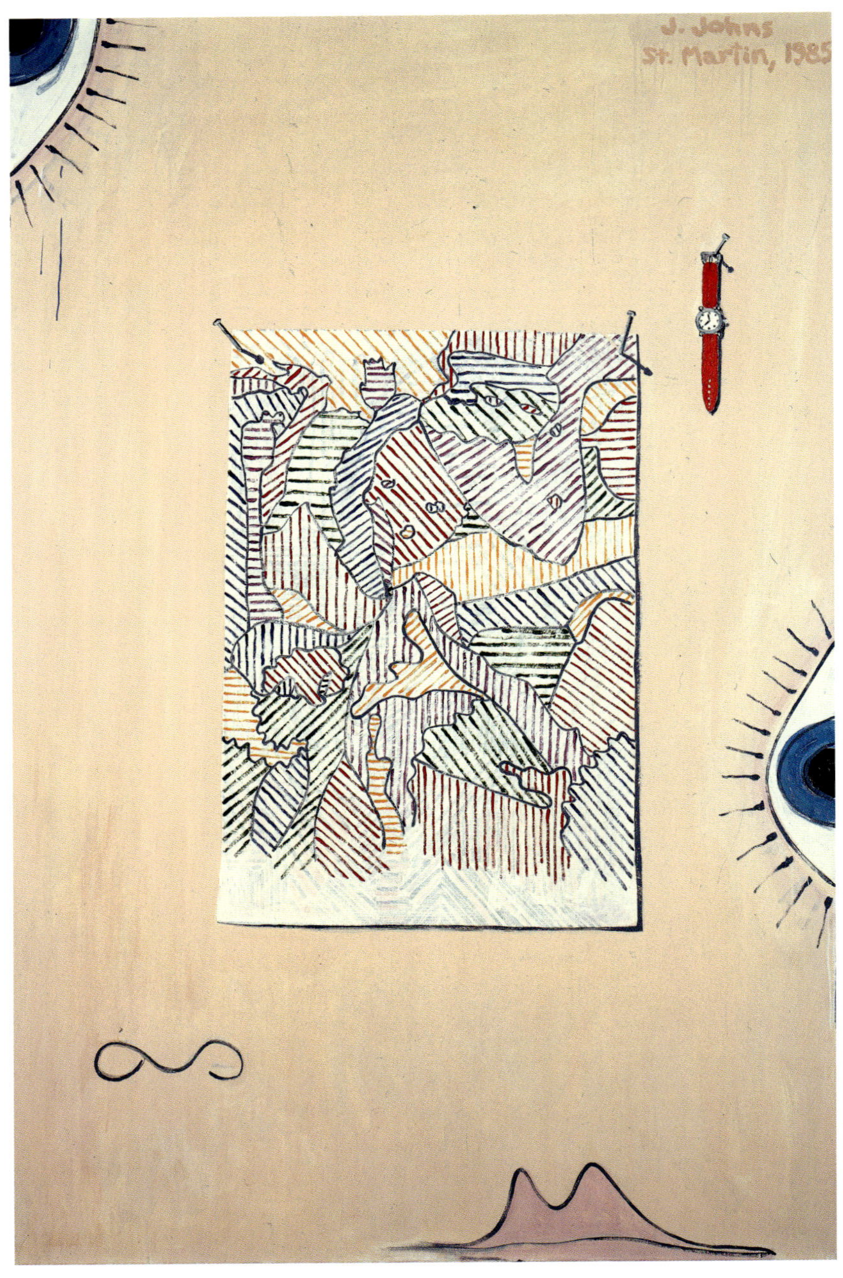

fig. X: 3 **Jasper Johns** *UNTITLED (A Dream)* 1985
Oil on canvas 75 x 50 in. (190.5 x 127 cm)
Collection Robert and Jane Meyerhoff

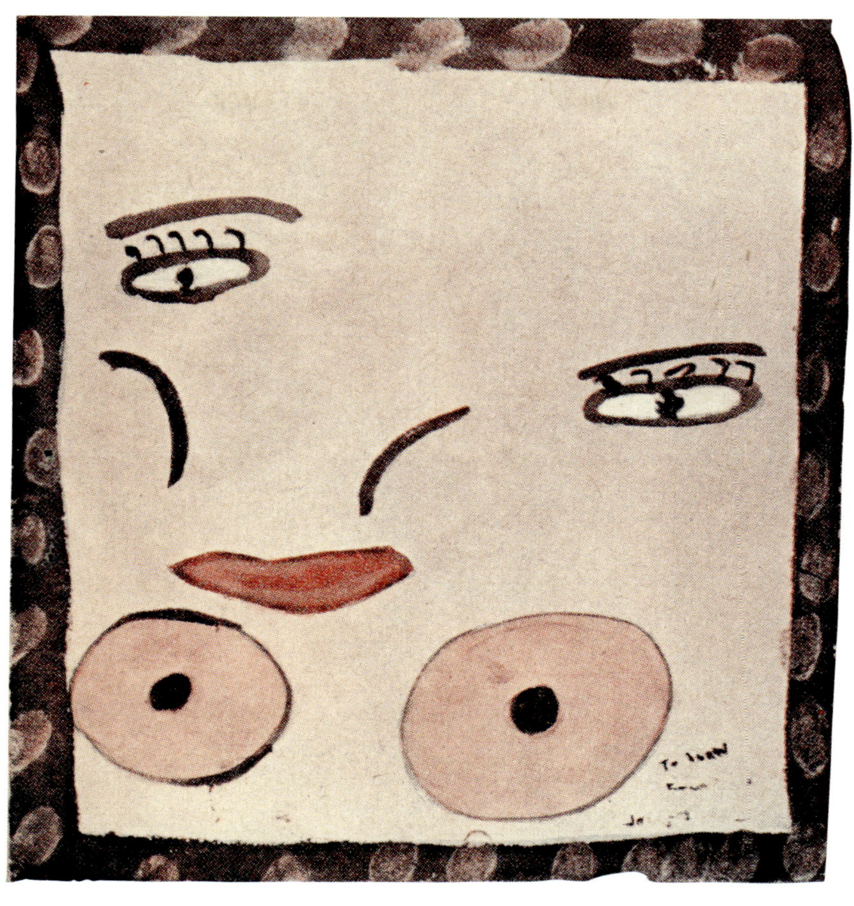

Anonymous (schizophrenic child)

fig. X: 4

THE BABY DRINKING THE MOTHER'S MILK FROM THE BREAST

From Bruno Bettelheim, "Schizophrenic Art: A Case Study," *Scientific American* 186, 4 (Apr. 1952), pp. 30–34

drawings, along with a text detailing her progress. Bettelheim had titled the one that had stood out for Johns *The Baby Drinking the Mother's Milk from the Breast* (fig. X: 4); the patient had made it long before she was able to reintegrate her personality. It bears a remarkable resemblance to Johns's versions of Picasso's portrait. In several subsequent paintings, the artist juxtaposed the drawing from the Bettelheim article with the face it had inspired. In the first of these works (*Untitled* [1991]), he also interspersed the letters of his name with those of Bettelheim. Moreover, Johns reversed half of the letters so that one set faces the other.

In *Untitled (A Dream)*, Johns utilized the expanse of flesh in the middle of the rectangular face as a ground upon which to depict a drawing of the boil-covered wretch from Matthias Grünewald's *Isenheim Altarpiece* (c. 1512–16) rendered into an interlocked assembly of hatch-marked shapes. Unlike the figure that seems to be embedded in the wooden door of *Racing Thoughts*, here we can more easily discern a body, with one leg and its web-toed foot delineated upside down in the upper-right corner. Two nails hold up the drawing, with the one on the right piercing the web-toed foot, holding it upside down. As the nails literally make clear, the link between the observing mind and the unconscious body is a source of suffering that cannot be gotten rid of. In addition, the artist nailed a red wristwatch to the face. There is no escaping the many indignities that we have to endure, with time being one of them.

By equating face and canvas and by combining hatch marks and interlocking shapes in a drawing of a drawing, Johns fused figure and ground twice. The three nails (the same number used to hang Christ from the Cross) remind us of the effects of gravity and of the vulnerability of flesh. So too there is pain in spying rather than in looking, in seeking to be self-aware and to understand reality. *Untitled (A Dream)* unites inside and outside so that neither applies: the eyes look in, but a drawing is nailed to the face. This conundrum denies interiority, psychological or otherwise. In fact, this amalgamation returns to perceptual questions that have haunted the artist since he made *Flag* (fig. I: 1); does the dream take place inside the mind/body or is the individual caught inside the dream? What is the nature of their bond? In this case, the dream is quite different from the one in which Johns saw himself painting the American flag. While the inverted, falling figure from Grünewald's altarpiece, which is contiguous with the ground, embodies the artist's painful awareness of time and its consequences, it also evokes a common occurrence in dreams, the feeling that one is falling. The pinned drawing and watch also underscore that we are all subject to gravity and are being pulled downward.

In *Untitled* (fig. X: 5), Johns depicted, in an almost cartoonish parody of trompe l'oeil, three pieces of cloth nailed to a painting/wall that again articulates Grünewald's fatally afflicted figure, this time in interlocking sections of gray, brown (cadaver-like colors), and orange. On each distinctly hued cloth, he inscribed an image: his rectangular head/face, Picasso's distorted head, and an optically ambiguous head after a motif created in the early twentieth century by W. E. Hill that flips visually between a young woman's and an old woman's profile.[6] Optically, from left to right, blue (eyes looking inward) and red (eyes looking outward), when mixed, equal violet (old woman/young woman looking both

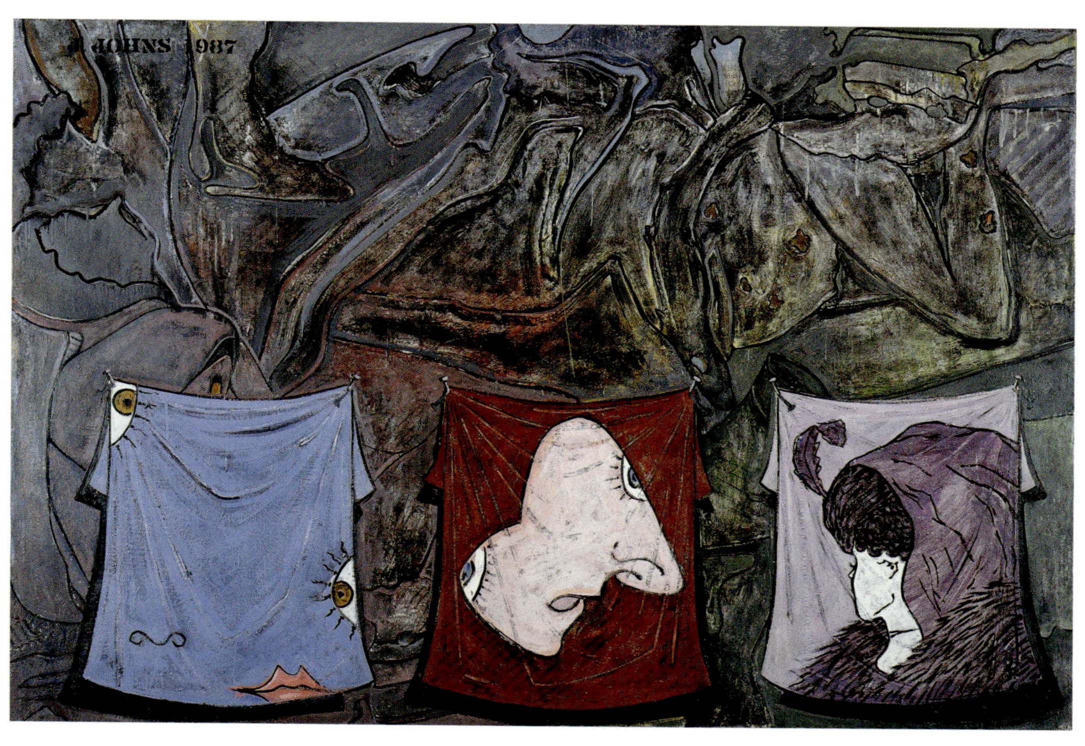

Jasper Johns *UNTITLED* 1987
Encaustic and collage on canvas 50 x 75 in. (127 x 190.5 cm)
Collection Robert and Jane Meyerhoff

fig. X: 5

INTERNATIONAL NEWS SPOTLIGHT

JAN KRUGIER

Expressions of the Soul

Jan Krugier has become one of the world's leading dealers and has exhibited some of the century's great artists. At home in Geneva, Krugier talks about his life and reminisces about his relationships with everyone from Giacometti to Picasso

Violently distorted, a lone fragmented figure crouches on a stark black background, his painted contours cut by strokes of midnight blue—the essence of isolation, nihilism, futility. "This is a very beautiful work, the kind of work I call a 'to be or not to be' painting," says Jan Krugier, gesturing toward the dark Francis Bacon portrait that hangs in the entrance hall of his Geneva home.

Elegant, distinguished, with a shock of white hair and piercing blue eyes, Krugier leans on a cane as he welcomes his visitor. Founder of one of the world's most important modern-art galleries, based in Geneva and New York, the 69-year-old embodies the tradition of the noble dealer. Over the last four decades, he has shown great artists from the 19th and 20th centuries—Courbet, Degas, Delacroix, Géricault, Ingres, Balthus, Beckmann, De Chirico, Ernst, Klee, Léger, Morandi. And he has created thematic exhibitions, such as "The Presence of Ingres," "Victor Hugo and the Romantic Vision," and "The Predominance of Cézanne," that have explored the affinities between works of different periods. He has also become closely associated with Pablo Picasso, as the exclusive dealer for the collection of the artist's granddaughter Marina Picasso.

But despite his success and the respect that surrounds him, one senses an uneasiness, and Krugier sometimes seems to almost tremble with inner torment. His attraction to work like the Bacon, with its haunted, existential quality, comes as no surprise, linked as it is to a life of enormous suffering and the witnessing of the century's gravest atrocities.

Krugier speaks haltingly and with great difficulty of his own past. A Polish-born Jew, he was still a boy when World War II broke out. In 1942, when he was 14, Krugier and his family were arrested and deported to the concentration camps. The rest of his family was murdered, but miraculously Krugier himself managed to survive—twice he escaped the work camps, and the third time he ended up in Auschwitz-Birkenau and then Buna. He survived the death march and was sent to Mittelbau-Dora and then to Bergen-Belsen, from which he was liberated in 1945. Krugier talks about those years with tremendous hesitation, calling them "terrible, just terrible," but is constantly reminded of their sorrows, stamped upon him like the number he wears on his forearm.

During the war, he recounts, a patrician Swiss family close to his own searched desperately for Krugier and his relatives. At war's end, when they discovered that only young Jan had survived, the Swiss family adopted him. An aspiring artist, Krugier wished to pursue a painting career and studied at the Kunstgewerbeschule in Zurich, where he was a pupil of Johannes Itten, one of the founders of the Bauhaus.

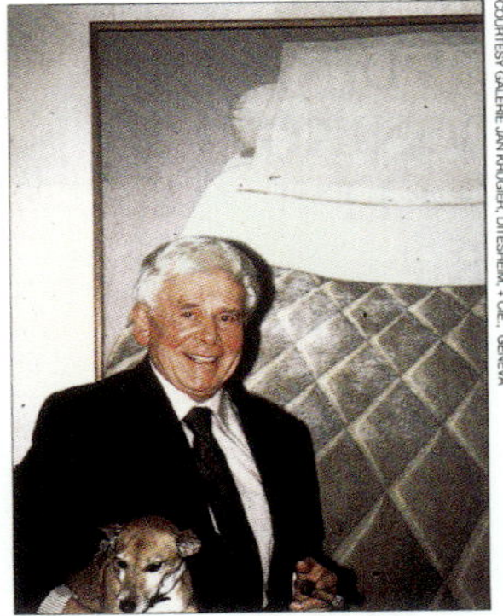

COURTESY GALERIE JAN KRUGIER, DITESHEIM + CIE., GENEVA

Jan Krugier, dealer and obsessive collector.

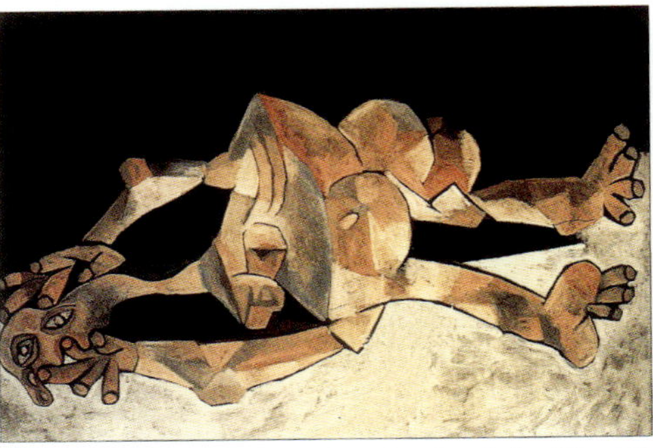

***Reclining Nude*, a 1938 work by Pablo Picasso from the collection of his granddaughter Marina. Krugier has had a long relationship with the artist's family.**

fig. X: 6 **Pablo Picasso** *RECLINING NUDE* 1938
As reproduced in *ARTnews* vol. 87, 4 (Apr. 1998), p. 82

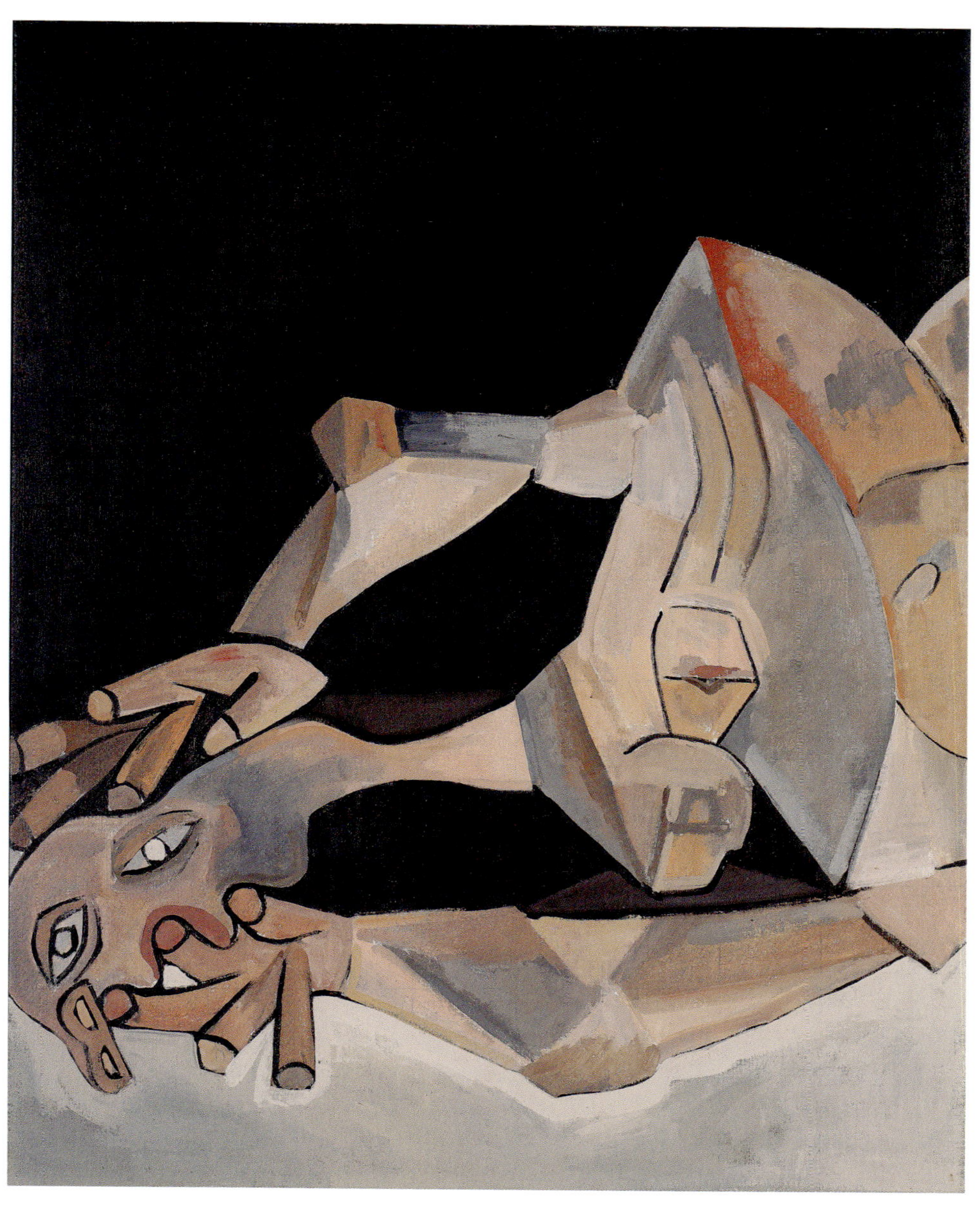

Jasper Johns *AFTER PICASSO* 1998
Oil on canvas 34 1/2 x 28 1/2 in. (87.6 x 72.4 cm)
Collection the artist

fig. X: 7

backward and forward).[7] With his representations of looking, Johns chronicled the individual's relationship to reality and time; looking inward or remembering, looking out at the world, and looking back and forth in time. In "Sketchbook Notes," Johns wrote, "The spy must remember & must remember himself and his remembering."[8]

After distorting Picasso's contorted head/body in the mid-1980s and continuing to work with different motifs derived from him for more than a decade, Johns set out in the late 1990s to do something more direct: copy him. The source for *After Picasso* (fig. X: 7) is a small reproduction of *Reclining Nude* (fig. X: 6) that appeared in *ARTnews* in April 1988. Interestingly, the artist chose not to see the original until after he completed his own painting.[9] Without knowing the dimensions of Picasso's canvas, he selected one almost exactly the same height as *Reclining Nude* but considerably smaller in width, because he did not plan to include the lower torso or legs, preferring to focus on the woman's head and upper torso.

Picasso painted *Reclining Figure* in the aftermath of the Fascist attack on the Catalonian city of Guernica; the prone, twisted body represents one of the many victims that he pictured as the Spanish Civil War morphed into World War II. It may be pure coincidence, or another example of Johns's associative powers, that *Reclining Nude* recalls another Picasso painting, also titled *Reclining Nude* (1942), a work Johns would have known well, as it was in the collection of New Yorkers Victor and Sally Ganz, who were longtime collectors and friends of his. Done in Paris during World War II, the painting shows Picasso's lover Dora Maar naked on a mattress in a bare room, her fists clenched and her legs awkwardly crossed. Perhaps Johns's memory of the Ganz's Picasso clued him in—either subliminally or consciously—to the fact that *ARTnews* had inadvertently reproduced the 1938 Picasso upside down. Given his long preoccupation with falling and reversal, I suspect that Johns might have realized that there was something amiss with the reproduction. Nonetheless, the small, wrongly oriented, and badly cropped reproduction spoke directly to him.

In Picasso's painting, the woman lies on the ground, but in Johns's iteration she is on what could be a bed, her fingers in her mouth; she appears at once elderly and infantile. I think what inspired Johns to do the painting is the helplessness of her supine, face down position and of her age, whether old or young. That cojoining of young and old is also intrinsic to Hill's optically ambiguous image, mentioned above. Along with the painting, Johns did three drawings. In two of them, *After Picasso* and *Study after Picasso* (both from 1998 and in graphite; collection the artist), Johns focused on the fingers and mouth. In the latter, he reduced the head and fingertips to a curving shape and circles. Three of the circles rest comfortably in the cavities along the bottom edge of the head/form, recalling Johns's above-cited interest in the "first images or forms of a child." The finger in the mouth evokes an infant, while the prone figure facing down conveys someone dying. The indivisible bond between beginning and ending is a theme that Johns previous explored in *Tantric Detail* paintings (see fig. VIII: 4, 5), and would subsequently explore in *Catenary (Henri Monnier)* (fig. XI: 4). It is also worth noting that Johns made his upside-down Picasso after he had responded to a reproduction of the artist's *Fall of Icarus* (1958),[10] a large mural that UNESCO commissioned for its Paris headquarters, by incorporating Picasso's stick figure of the falling Icarus into *Mirror's Edge* (1992) and *Mirror's Edge 2* (1993). In addition, in both *Untitled* (1992–94) and *Untitled* (1992–95), Johns inverted Picasso's Icarus so that he is rising rather than falling. He may have intended the rising figure to suggest that art is one way we try to counter gravity, even as we must succumb to it.

In 1985 Johns completed *Summer* (fig. X: 9), a painting that is related compositionally to *Perilous Night* and *Racing Thoughts*. As in these canvases, the left side of *Summer* has to do with the unthinking body, or watchman, while the right side concerns the individual's consciousness, or spy. Two works by Picasso influenced *Summer* and the three paintings—*Winter*, *Fall*, and *Spring* (figs. X: 11, 10, 8)—that followed it. Thematically related, this cycle of four paintings is known collectively as *The Seasons*. As with *Woman in Straw Hat*, both of these sources came from *Picasso's Picassos*. The first is *The Minotaur Moves His House* (1936), in which a minotaur pulls a cart loaded with a painting, a horse giving birth, and a ladder all roped together. From this composition, Johns borrowed the ladder and rope, as well as the stars and wagon wheel, which assume the same form as the black semicircle in his much-earlier *Periscope (Hart Crane)* (fig. V: 5). He also filled up the four paintings with things, as if each canvas were a cart. The second source is *The Shadow* (1953), in which Picasso depicted a room with a voluptuous nude lying on a bed. A shadow, presumably the artist's, rises from the bottom edge as if he were entering the room. The positioning of the shadow and of its tapered form suggest that the viewer could also be casting it, and that anyone who looks into this interior is an intruder. Connecting this painting to *The Minotaur Moves His House* is the image of an archaic sculpture of a horse pulling a cart, sitting in the upper-left-hand corner, presumably on a shelf.

Unlike his earlier explorations of the modernist master, in which Johns either distorted motifs or preserved them, in *The Seasons* he replaced Picasso's shadow with his own and filled the minotaur's cart with his stuff. In each of the four paintings, Johns depicted his shadow merging with a wall, alluding to a wall or walk on his property.[11] Each shadow leans slightly to the left and merges with its surroundings. Other motifs running through *The Seasons* include a black semicircle containing a directional arrow, an arm, and a handprint, all derived from *Periscope (Hart Crane)*; a triangle, square, and circle that most likely refer to the art of Paul Cézanne; classic symbols from Japanese art; various George Ohr pots; and Rubin's figures. For each season, Johns positioned the arm and handprint at a different angle to refer to the cycle of time, both passing and infinite.

Johns incorporated mirroring to establish continuity across the series. In each cart, he planted a spy: in *Summer*, a poster of the *Mona Lisa*; in *Fall*, an outlined profile of Marcel Duchamp; in *Winter*, the white contour of a snowman; and in *Spring*, the Silver Jubilee pot, a Rubin's profile/vase, along with a similar device, Ludwig Wittgenstein's outline drawing of an animal that can be seen as a duck or a rabbit. Each of these faces/heads observes (spies on) the shadow (watchman) as he sinks deeper and deeper into the ground.

Structurally, *Summer* and *Winter* are divided vertically into equal rectangles, with the shadow on the left in the former and on the right in the latter. *Fall* and *Spring* display

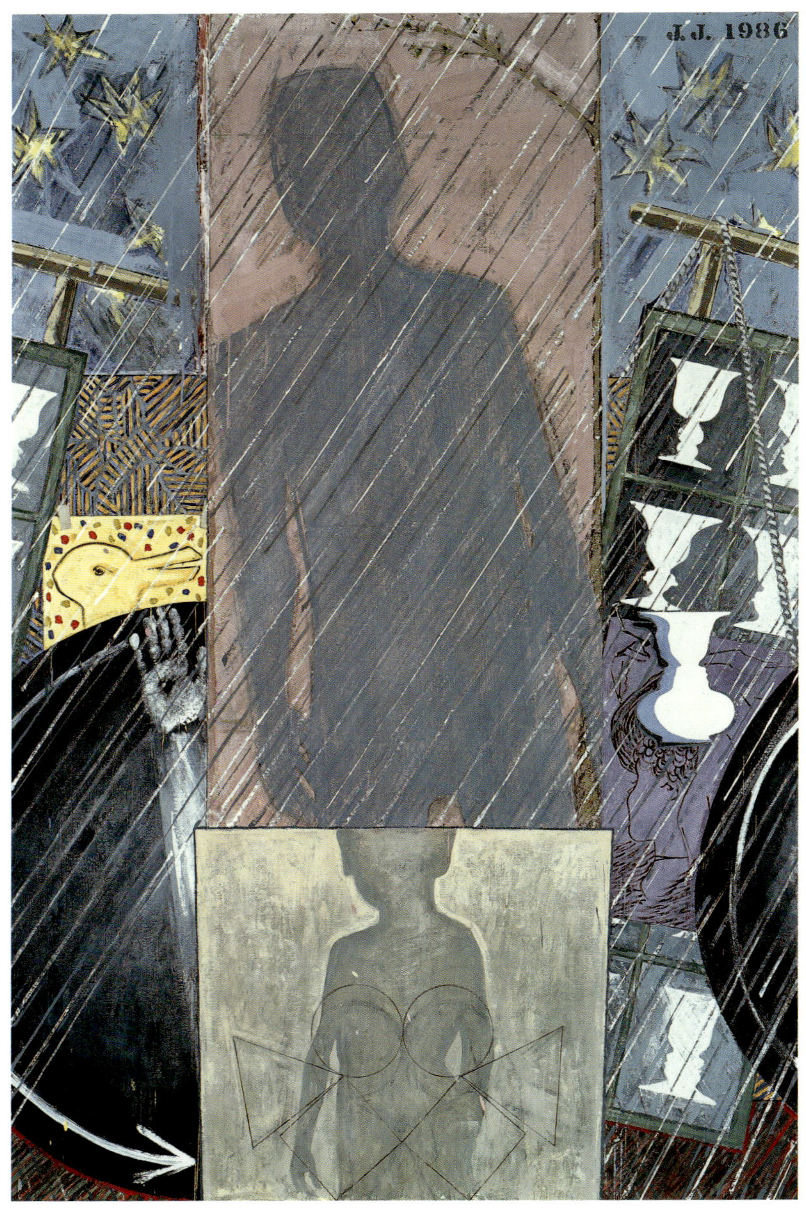

fig. X: 8 **Jasper Johns** *SPRING* 1986
Encaustic on canvas 75 x 50 in. (190.5 x 127 cm)
Collection Robert and Jane Meyerhof

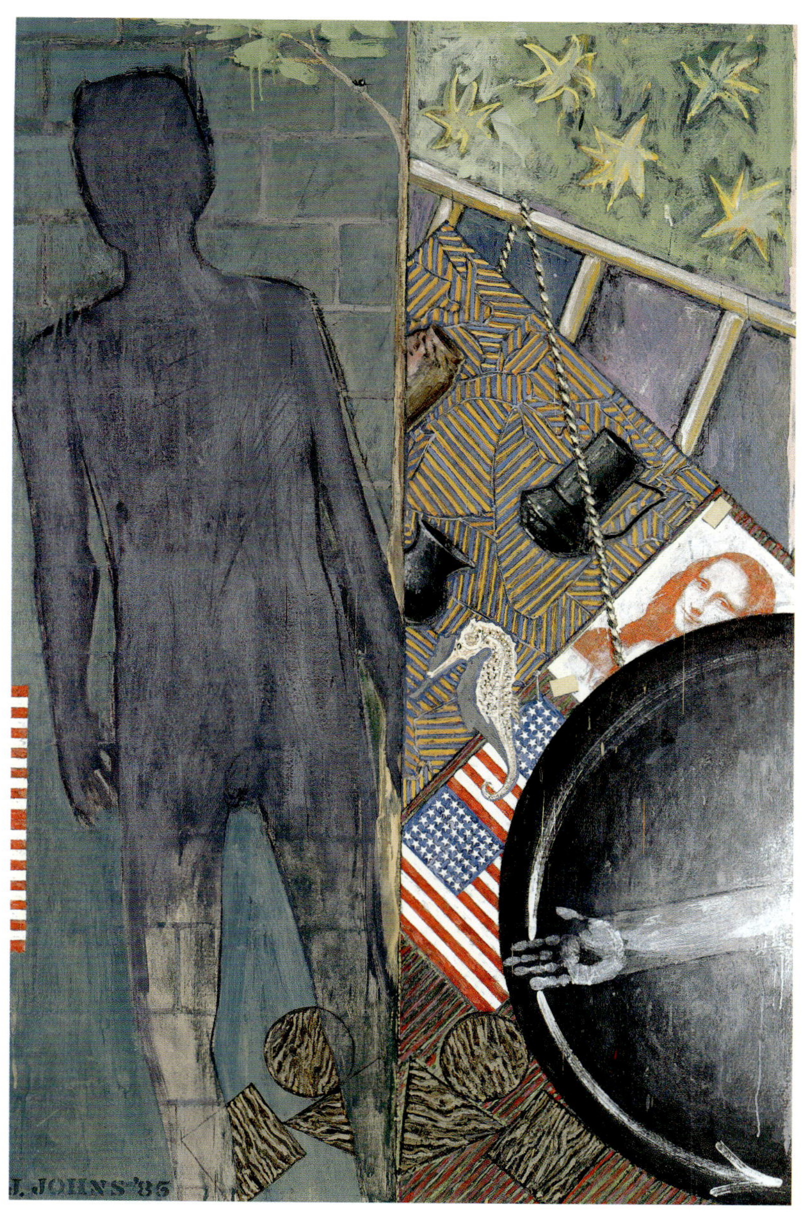

Jasper Johns *SUMMER* 1985

Encaustic on canvas 75 x 50 in. (190.5 x 127 cm)

The Museum of Modern Art, New York. Gift of Philip Johnson

fig. X: 9

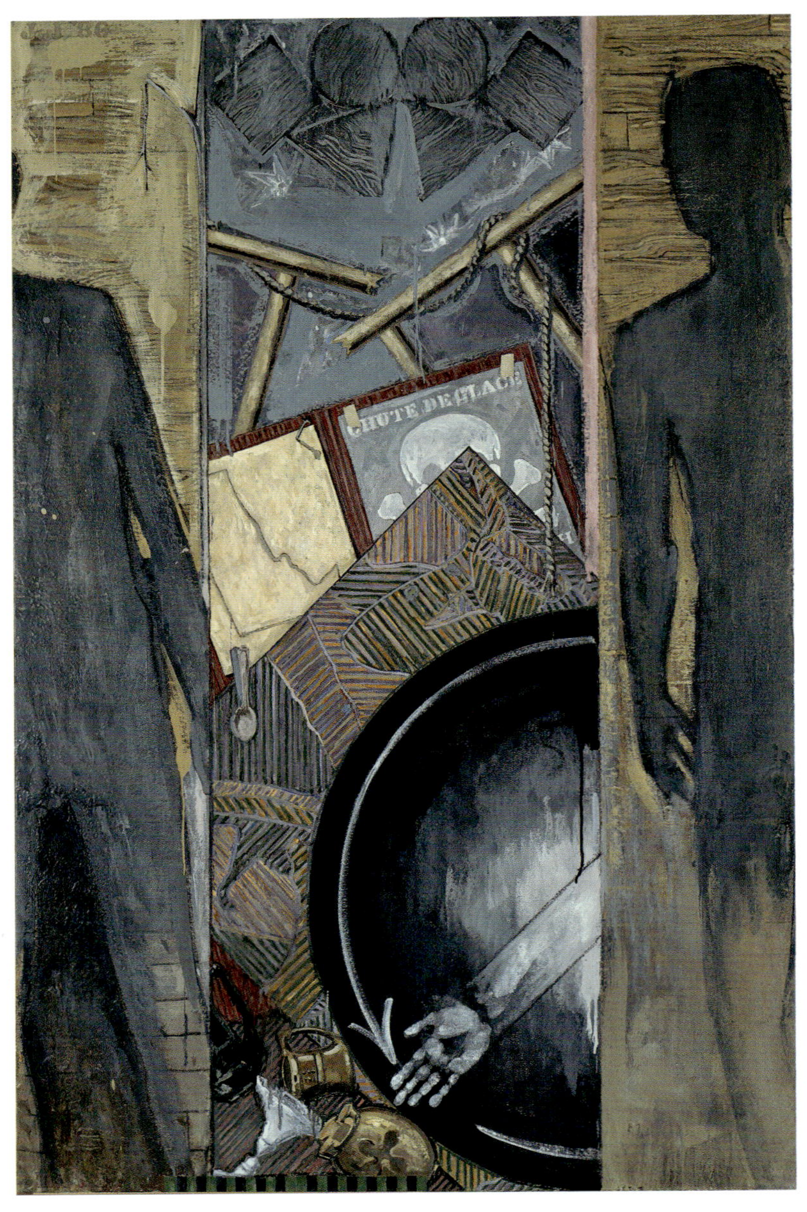

fig. X: 10 **Jasper Johns** *FALL* 1986
Encaustic on canvas 75 x 50 in. (190.5 x 127 cm)
Collection the artist

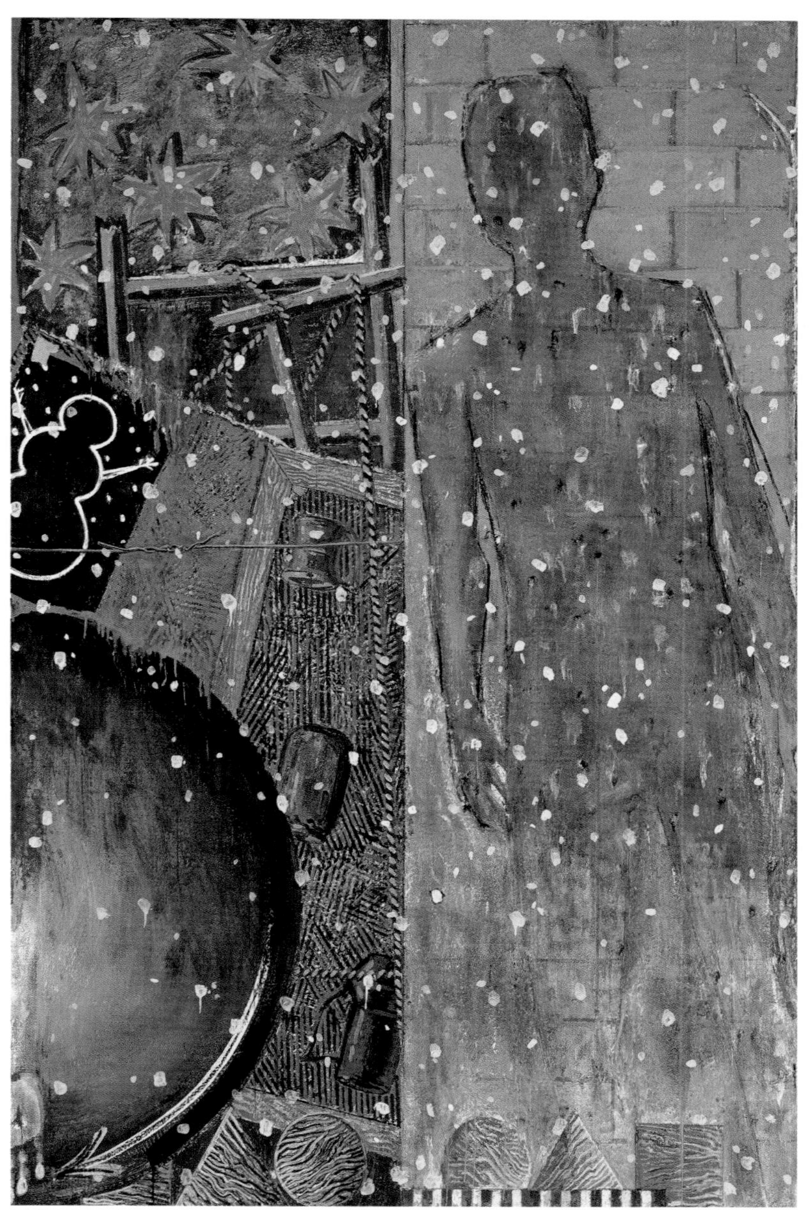

fig. X: 11

Jasper Johns *WINTER* 1986
Encaustic on canvas 75 x 50 in. (190.5 x 127 cm)
Private collection

three vertical divisions: a wide midsection flanked by two narrower rectangles of equal width. In *Fall* the shadow is split, with one part appearing at the left and the other on the opposite side. In *Spring* the shadow fills the middle rectangle, above a light-ocher, nearly square section on which Johns painted the shadow of a young boy, overlaid by a reversed pairing of two linear designs composed of a circle, triangle, and square. The geometric forms resemble butterfly wings, as if to suggest that the shadow of the boy will molt into that of the man. In *Summer*, *Fall*, and *Winter*, these same geometric forms, more loosely attached or entirely separated, are rendered in faux wood grain. In *Summer* and *Winter*, they are arranged symmetrically at the bottom of each painting, suggesting that if the paintings were folded in half down the middle, they would be aligned. Body and mind are distinct but indivisible.

By tracing his own shadow, Johns used the literal in service of the metaphysical. The individual's conscious and unconscious interactions with reality are once again the primary line of inquiry that Johns took in *The Seasons*. The motifs in the cart are emblems of the conscious looking required of the spy, while the featureless and partially submerged shadow is that of the watchman. The body moves in and through the world, while the mind can imagine an *elsewhere*. For Johns, however, the mind must observe the body, must recognize its passage in time, and must exist in the present, even as it looks back and forth.

It rains in *Spring* and snows in *Winter*. A hummingbird nests in a tree and a seahorse floats in *Summer*; the mind is aware that the water (or dissolution) is rising. In the mostly tan *Fall*, a broken tree branch dangles. The attributes of each season are transitory: whatever pleasures they give will, like the things themselves, pass into oblivion. And yet, despite this painful realization, Johns's vision of reality is neither tragic nor self-pitying. The seahorse, duck/rabbit, and childlike drawing of the snowman obviate any sense of the doom we might wish project onto the paintings. The artist's intention is to offer testimony on the effects of time, to observe the process with clinical detachment, and to neither shrink back in horror nor call attention to himself. For Johns the ideal artist is someone who does not avert his eyes.

During the period in which these and other paintings influenced by Picasso were in process, Johns heard a story that, while unsubstantiated, had an impact on him. The artist Paul Brach told him that when Picasso first saw a painting by Willem de Kooning, he pronounced it, with delight, to be a "melted Picasso."[12] Given Johns's use of encaustic, and the various paintings in which he melted the wax to signal the corrosive effects of time, it is not surprising that Johns would put this anecdote to use in two paintings, *The Bath* (1988) and *Untitled* (fig. X: 12), the last paintings Johns has done to date on the subject of the individual immersed in a bathtub. To my mind, they are the most unsettling treatments of this subject, largely because of the way in which they incorporate the wretched figure from the *Isenheim Altarpiece*. In *Racing Thoughts*, Johns combined a crosshatch pattern, faux wood grain, and an orange outline in ways that suggest, I believe, the presence of a figure emmeshed in the wooden planks of the door; in *Untitled* (fig. X: 5), he had painted three cloths attached to a wall, a surface into which he had embedded the figure and used a palette of close values to mute its contorted features. In other words, we can see in these two works a progression of emergence; the figure literally rises into the realm of visibility and becomes contiguous with the picture plane. In addition, for all of Johns's gyrations, Grünewald's featureless victim and his own shadow do have something in common: both are at once anonymous and specific, which is what we are in the face of time.

In *The Bath*, Johns rotated Grünewald's despondent figure so that his cowled head is positioned in the upper center of the pale-blue "I" shape, which can also be read as a wall. Because the head is directly above them, the faucet and handles of the bathtub become the afflicted figure's genitalia. White dots mark the upper half of the blue field, evoking the boils detailed in the original. "Taped" over the figure are two unequal rectangles, each of which features part of the head/body form in Picasso's *Woman in Straw Hat*. In splitting the Picasso into sections and moving them to the edges, Johns seems to have reenacted what the Spanish artist had done in his painting, which was to push the eyes to the edges of his figural form. However, the section on the right edge of Johns's work contains both of the outward-looking eyes, as if they are now gazing toward the future. It is also worth noting that Johns placed the larger, left-hand portion of Picasso's painting on the right side of his composition and the smaller, right-hand portion on the left. Yet the inversion feels correct: our eyes tell us one thing, while our mind tells us another.

In *The Bath* and *Untitled*, Johns's renderings of Grünewald's hopeless, suffering figure and of Picasso's disturbing head underscore their close morphological similarity. With his prominent nose and forehead, the afflicted figure's profile resembles that of Picasso's distorted woman; the shape of his cowl also echoes that of her violet hat. What are we to make of these similarities? Are they simply resonances that Johns was keen enough to notice? Or, by connecting a diseased figure (contorted from within) with a distorted figure (manipulated from without), what did he mean us to understand? Johns recognizes that time affects us both externally and internally. While the body is not conscious of itself, the mind is cognizant of exterior circumstances, of time and change, including what affects the body. In effect, the body resembles *Flag*, which, with its unstable materials, has literally rotted on the inside.

At the same time, Johns expressed an unsparing, wicked humor by applying heat to the painting's surface, melting the two Picasso-related sections. On one hand, he reified Brach's anecdote. On the other, his application of real heat also literalized the commonplace reality of taking a bath, which makes the immersed body hot and the head sweat. And, he seems to have transferred the disease that is destroying Grünewald's victim to Picasso's woman. A painting that appears to be tightly composed—structured along horizontal and vertical lines—nonetheless throbs and comes undone in its contact with heat.

Once we realize that the head is taped above the figure, which is immersed in blue encaustic (water), we also recognize that the scene could be an aerial view; we are looking down at someone who is slowly sinking. The edge of the tub, which presumably extends into our physical space, is centered along the bottom edge. This suggests that we have stood up in the tub, while the framing of the layered space infers that we are looking down. On the left side of *The Bath*, a wooden wall stands flush with the blue

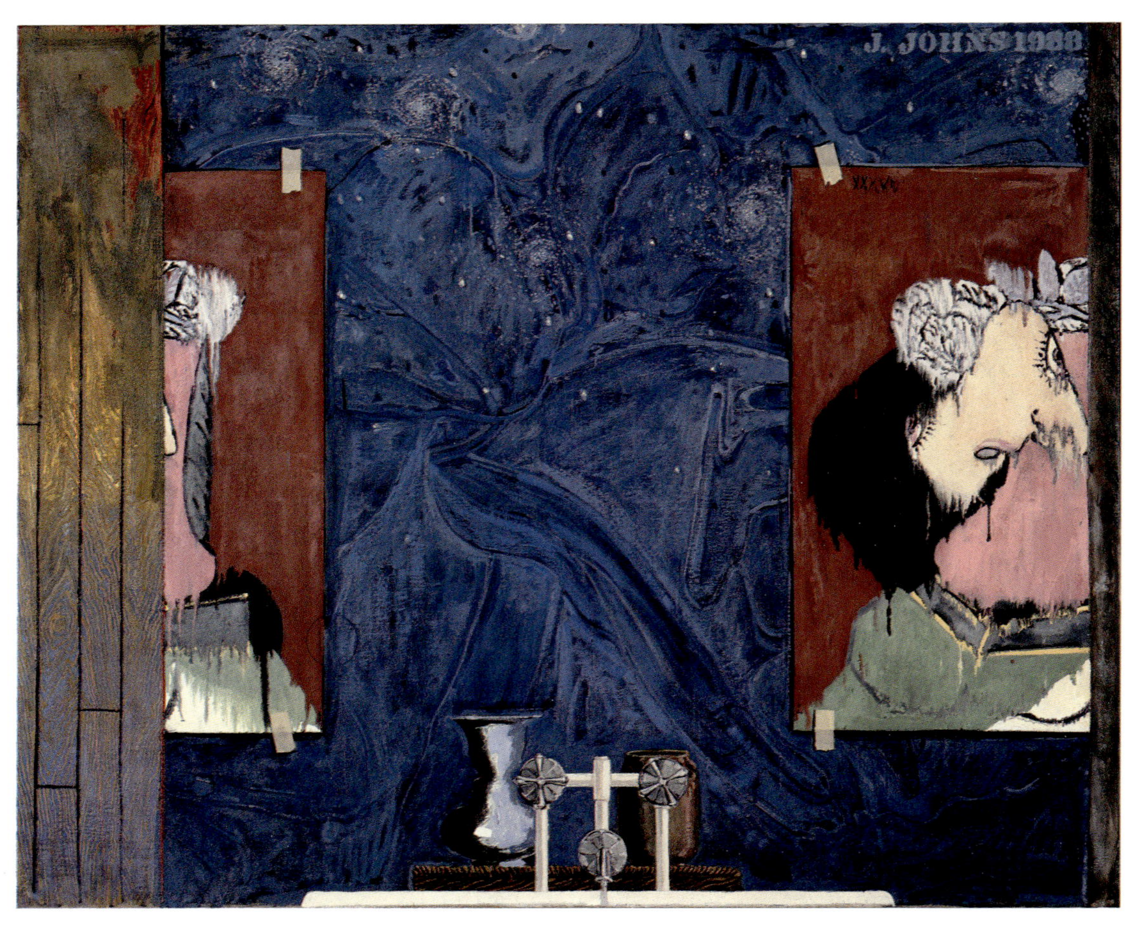

fig. X: 12 **Jasper Johns** *UNTITLED* 1988
Encaustic on canvas 48 1/4 x 60 1/4 in. (122.6 x 153 cm)
Collection Joel and Anne Ehrenkranz

expanse, and a narrow wooden strip is flush with it on the right. The abutting of the taped Picasso along the edges of the wooden wall and strip hint at the likelihood that blue encaustic (water) is very close to spilling over. The boards of the leftmost wall could be a floor. It is as if, in *The Bath*, Johns submerged the outline of a figure in a shallow, squarish opening (a box) filled with water. In *Untitled* the galaxies swirling in the upper part of the blue, near the area of the fevered figure's head, bring the rotting body and distant stars together, as does the Silver Jubilee pot with its Rubin's figure, uniting figure and ground.

This joining recalls the opening line of "The Snow Man" by Wallace Stevens: "One must have a mind of winter / To regard the frost and boughs / Of the pine-trees crusted with snow." The poem ends: "For the listener, who listens in the snow, / And, nothing himself, beholds / Nothing that is not there and the nothing that is."[13] We may be able to think, but that does not mean that our brains are more than matter. Daoists believe that the individual on the path to enlightenment will see that the Milky Way and the body are interchangeable, that each is made of the same substance. We may be staring down into our grave, but the view is neither singular nor horrifying. The transitory (the body) and the infinite (the galaxies) are inseparable and discrete.

CHAPTER 10 NOTES

1. Quoted in Kirk Varnedoe, *Jasper Johns: A Retrospective*, exh. cat., with an essay by Roberta Bernstein (New York: Museum of Modern Art, 1996), p. 120.

2. David Douglas Duncan, *Picasso's Picassos* (New York: Harper and Bros., 1961). p 113.

3. Quoted in Michael Crichton, *Jasper Johns*, rev. ed. (New York: Harry N. Abrams, 1994), p. 70.

4. Quoted in Robert Saltonstall Mattison, *Masterworks in the Robert and Jane Meyerhoff Collection: Jasper Johns, Ellsworth Kelly, Frank Stella* (New York: Hudson Hills Press, 1995), p. 36.

5. Quoted in Amei Wallach, "Jasper Johns: On Target," *Elle* (Nov. 8, 1988), p. 154.

6. W. E. Hill's illustration first appeared in the English satiric magazine *Puck* 78 (Nov. 6, 1915), with the caption "My wife and my mother in law / they are both in this picture—find them." The image was reproduced in the 1960s and '70s in a number of books on the psychology of perception, where Johns most likely first saw it.

7. In a later work, *Untitled* (1991), Johns depicted inward-looking eyes in a horizontal format, which, along with the lips that resemble mountains, in the lower right, suggests that the image is both a landscape and a body. On a red ground, he painted Picasso's head (in green) and Hill's double image. Each head/face looks in a different direction: Johns's looks in, Picasso's looks out, and the Hill image looks both forward and back.

8. By moving from a compressed space to a perspectival one, the artist seems to have gained greater access to his own life, its things and memories. In *Montez Singing* (1989), he included a schematic drawing of a red sailboat beneath a sunset. Montez Johns was the artist's step-grandmother, and he remembered her playing the piano and singing "Red Sails in the Sunset." See Carter B. Horseley, in Sotheby's, New York, *Contemporary Art from the Douglas S. Cramer Collection*, sale cat. (Nov. 14, 2001), lot 14. See also Roberta Bernstein, "Seeing a Thing Can Sometimes Trigger the Mind to Make Another Thing," in Kirk Varnedoe, *Jasper Johns: A Retrospective*, exh. cat. (New York: Museum of Modern Art, 1996), p. 66.

9. Michael Fitzgerald, *Picasso and American Art*, exh. cat., with a chronology by Julia May Boddewyn (New York: Whitney Museum of American Art, in association with Yale University Press, New Haven and London, 2006), p. 299.

10. Bernstein (note 8). Johns told Roberta Bernstein that he saw the work reproduced in Arianna Stassinopolous Huffington, *Picasso: Creator and Destroyer* (New York: Simon and Schuster, 1988), p. 80.

11. Fitzgerald (note 9), p. 301.

12. Ibid., p. 293.

13. *The Collected Poems of Wallace Stevens* (New York: Alfred A. Knopf, 1957), p. 10.

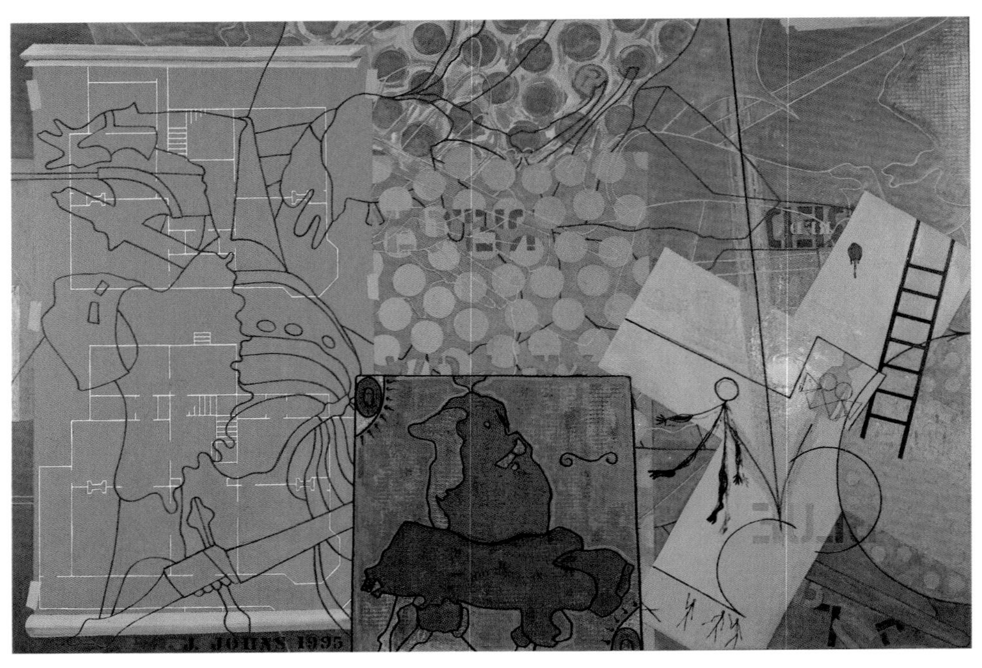

Jasper Johns *UNTITLED* 1992–1995

fig. XI: 1 Oil on canvas 78 x 118 in. (198.1 x 299.7 cm)

The Museum of Modern Art, New York Promised gift of Agnes Gund

Chapter 11

I.

Between 1997 and 2003, Johns finished nineteen paintings collectively known as the Catenaries.

In the catalogue published on the occasion of an exhibition of these paintings at Matthew Marks Gallery, New York, Scott Rothkopf began his essay, "Suspended Animation," with this paragraph:

> Jasper Johns's paintings had grown too full. The pictures that closed his 1996 retrospective at the Museum of Modern Art in New York were jam-packed with signs of Johns's life and art—and signs of the intricate relationship between them. *Untitled*, 1992–95, ... for example, alone contained a blueprint of his grandfather's house, "taped" trompe l'oeil style to the picture's surface; a schematic rendering of a Grünewald soldier from the Isenheim altarpiece; the notoriously inscrutable "green angel"; a ladder, a boy's shadow, and other elements from Johns's "Seasons" cycle, themselves often borrowed from previous works; an arrow and circles and stenciled letters; and a swirling galaxy small enough to suggest just how expansive this painted universe was. With its compositional and conceptual density, *Untitled* represented a grand summa of more than a decade's worth of work that had preceded it. And then Johns wiped the slate clean.[1]

Even Johns's admirers had been vexed by the two most recent paintings, both untitled, to appear in his retrospective at the Museum of Modern Art, New York, ten years earlier (1992–94 and fig. XI: 1).[2] The reason is clear. Known for nearly thirty years for making art using familiar things (flags, targets, ale cans, maps, and so forth) and a neutral, abstract vocabulary (flagstones and crosshatches), Johns seemed to change horses in the early 1980s by introducing into his work a wide range of motifs derived from art history and other sources, all of which suggested that he had become an iconographic painter. The problem, of course, was that no one could satisfactorily decode Johns's iconography and so, in many cases, continued to read his work either as art about art or as encoded autobiography. Johns's response to these widespread interpretations was, as Rothkopf characterized it, the "notoriously inscrutable" *Green Angel* (1990), a painting whose sources the artist has adamantly refused to reveal. For some, this was further proof that Johns was playing games with his viewers, deliberately trying to prevent understanding of his work.[3]

While identifying the origins of Johns's motifs may enhance our appreciation of what he does, it is certainly not required. Is it necessary to know that the source for his 1993 paintings *After Holbein* (fig. XI: 2) and *After Hans Holbein* (1993) is a 1541 drawing of a young nobleman holding a pet by the German artist (fig. XI: 3)? Would it help to be aware that there is some dispute as to whether the animal is a lemur or a marmoset, and that Johns once had marmosets? Is it important to note that marmosets are monkeys from Brazil and thus a New World animal, while the nocturnal lemurs are evolutionary predecessors of simians and not technically monkeys, or that they are from Madagascar, and therefore an Old World animal? And what are we to make of Johns's painting *Bushbaby* (2003), whose title is another name for a lemur? Is it about this nocturnal creature?

Once we try to read Johns's work iconographically, we inevitably become lost. This was true even when his motifs were familiar things, and is only more so now. But, as *Green Angel* makes clear, Johns does not want our relationship to his works to be confined to their iconography. The motifs are not symbols to be decoded, but, as Johns wrote in his "Sketchbook Notes," "things" placed in "a continuity of some sort ..." where there are no boundaries between "the space" and "the objects."[4] Even though they are dissimilar, the four profiles forming the two cups in the lithograph *Cups 4 Picasso* (fig. X: 1), as well as the ground, are reversed, but there is no boundary; they are always joined to one another and becoming one another. And these reversals might recall to us Chuang Tzu's dream of being a butterfly (see Chapter One), and the recognition that tranformation is unavoidable. For Johns it seems that the "continuity" is reality, a realm of invariable change and transformation. Nothing is fixed or permanent. From the beginning, he has used "things" to try to register this understanding of material existence, to embody, as the artist put it, his "sense of life."

After Holbein is at once a highly specific and a featureless portrait; in that regard, it is related to the startled knight in *Perilous Night* (fig. IX: 2), the artist's shadow in *The Seasons* (figs. X: 8–11) and the fevered figure in *The Bath* (1988) and *Untitled* (fig. X: 12). Exposure to sunlight has faded Holbein's drawing so that the boy's face is now ghostlike, which Johns reflected in his use of pale gray and white in *After Holbein*. In addition, two small sections of the sixteenth-century paper have been torn away, one in the middle of the top edge and the other in the middle of the right side. Johns inventoried both tears in his paintings.

In *After Holbein*, the artist used the contours of the portrait as a template that delineates a half-length view of the sitter in Tudor-era clothing, complete with a plumed hat. He cradles a round-faced creature with large ears and a long tail. The hat plume and the sitter's face and proper right hand are articulated in a gray and white wood grain pattern, which extends to the creature's face and tail, as well to as the upper-left background. The wood pattern, including knotholes, runs vertically like a paneled wall; its clearly defined planks remind us of the door in both *Racing Thoughts* (fig. IX: 3, 4) and the wooden wall in *The Bath* and *Untitled*. The gray areas of the painting are patterned with vertical rows of tiny, black, spermlike dots. In some places, the wood grain pattern peeks through the gray, and there are places where gray areas and the wood grain have melted.

Formally, *After Holbein* is an unstable figure/ground painting in which the two elements keep reversing, and we have to keep untangling them. If the face and the wall are the same, which is the figure and which is the ground? And if the brim of the hat and the area adjacent to it are both gray and marked by the spermlike dots, which is the figure and which is the ground? Johns further complicated the figure/ground relationship by melting the encaustic in different areas, so that the wood grain drips into the gray area, and the gray area drips into the wood grain. The melting encaustic also underscores the physicality of what we are looking at; it is a thing and an image, rather than a purely ocular presence. By collapsing the ground with the figure's face, hand, and arm, as well as the animal, Johns conveyed an anonymous portrait forming before our eyes, or, conversely, disappearing into the wood grain. We arrive and depart, living between the *after* (birth) and the *before* (death). Meanwhile, the spermlike dots evoke a moment further back in time, to the instant before conception, while the wood grain (or ground) evokes time beyond our demise, and our absence from it. Johns presented this duality in a straightforward, highly considered manner, treating it as a condition we all inhabit. There is nothing morbid or indulgent about the portrait. If anything, the painting exhibits gentle humor, tenderness, and pathos, for the sitter is imprisoned in paint, with the vertical wooden boards suggesting prison bars. Equally compelling is the relationship between the boy and his pet; the former holds the latter gently and protectively; but, ultimately, of course, we cannot shield ourselves or others from mortality.

As Rothkopf pointed out, *Untitled* (1992–85) contains an image of Matthias Grünewald's soldier. In fact, this form, which at first seems stretched across the entire length of the painting, actually combines two inverted figures, one (outlined in black) at the left, and the other (in a light bluish gray) at the right. Where the two images overlap, toward the middle and right side, the resulting figure seems to be both tangled up in himself and falling. Rising from the center of the painting's bottom edge is the Picasso-derived face/rectangle. Its eyes look toward the "green angel"—the dark, amorphous outlined shapes that extend both vertically and horizontally across the composition's mid-section. The configuration of the two forms within the rectangle, with a dark-umber, horizontal mass superimposed over vertical shapes in ocher and sienna, evokes someone holding either

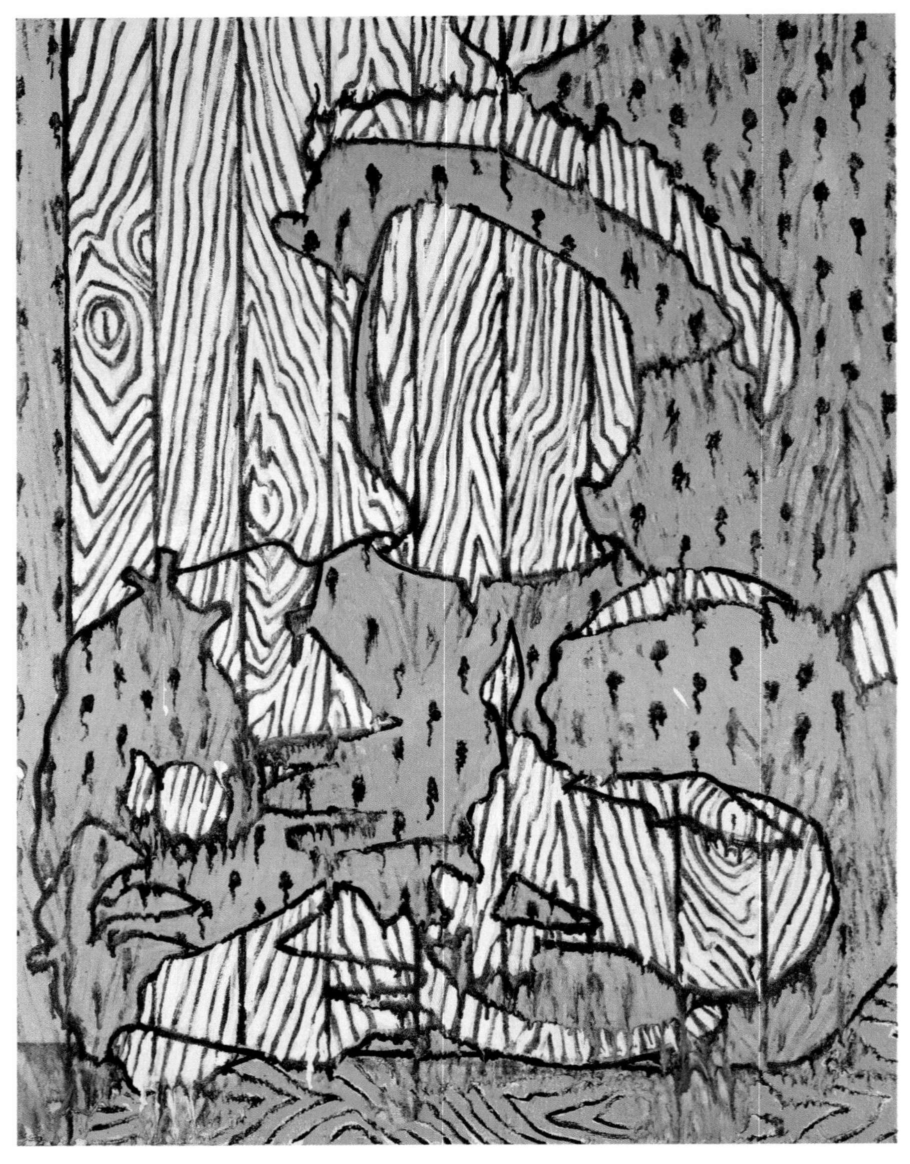

fig. XI: 2 **Jasper Johns** *AFTER HOLBEIN* 1993
Encaustic on canvas 32 9/16 x 25 5/8 in. (82.7 x 65.1 cm)
Private collection

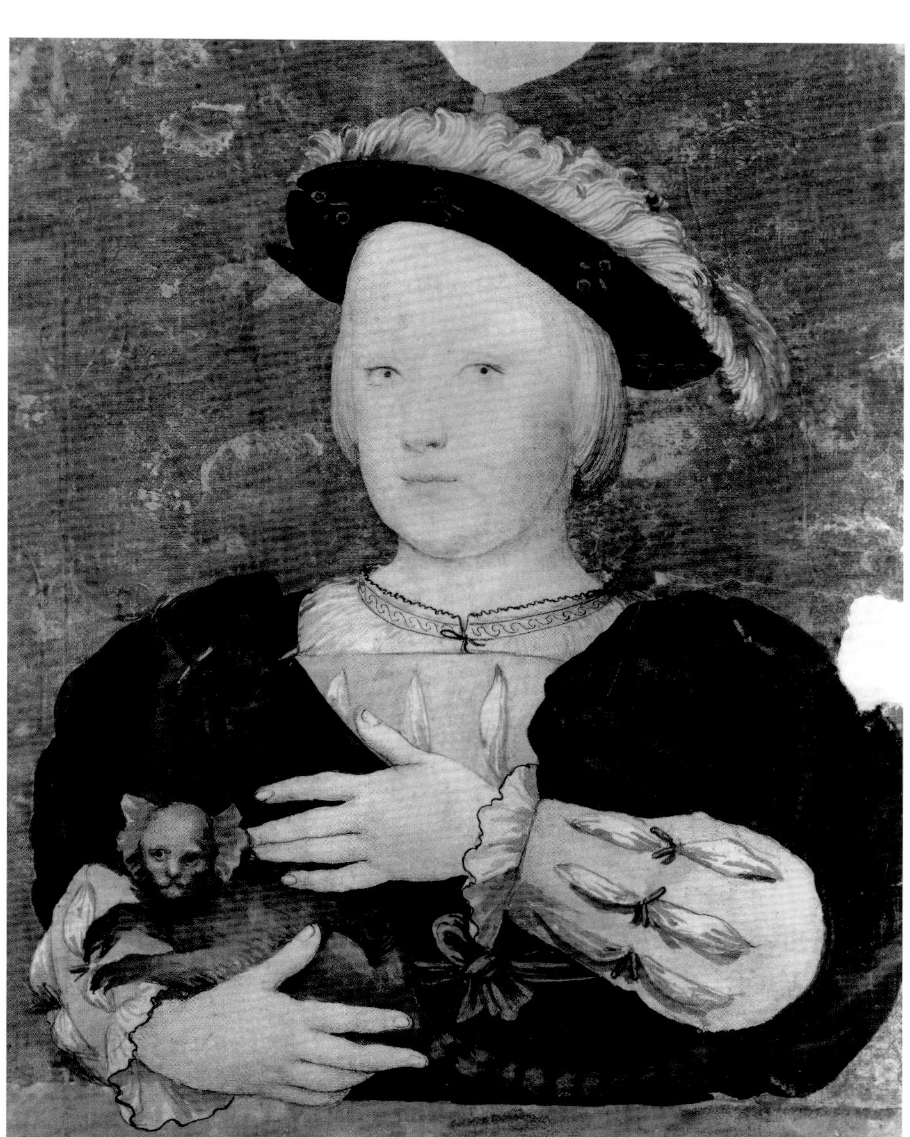

Hans Holbein the Younger *PORTRAIT OF A YOUNG MAN HOLDING A LEMUR* 1541–42 fig. XI: 3
Chalk and watercolor on paper 15 3/4 x 12 1/16 in. (40 x 30.7 cm)
Öffentliche Kunstsammlung Basel, Kunstmuseum

an infant or a corpse. To the left of the face/rectangle, and below the black contours of the "falling knight," is, as Rothkopf pointed out, "a blueprint of [Johns's] grandfather's house, 'taped' trompe l'oeil style to the picture's surface." The blueprint's top and bottom edges are rolled up or folded over, suggesting that their placement (and by extension the view) is temporary. The inverted knight is falling "into" the map. On the right side, an arrow descends nearly to the bottom edge; Picasso's Icarus (see Chapter Ten), inverted, now ascends. A diagonally tilting, crosslike form includes a small, schematic rendering of the shadow of a boy in *Spring* (fig. X: 8), complete with geometric wings; a ladder, which also appears in the three other works that compose *The Seasons* (figs. X: 9–11), is rendered in black; and the stenciled letters (spelling "RED" and "BLUE"), painted in shades of gray, are reversed and/or fall off the lower-right corner of the canvas. At its most basic, *Untitled* is a painting about falling and rising, memory and anticipation, looking backward and forward and inward and outward, confronting reality and its things. Amid all this, Icarus may be rising, but he is eventually doomed to fall. We are all Icarus.

II.

Contrary to what Rothkopf concluded, Johns did not wipe "the slate clean" in his nineteen Catenary paintings.

Rather, he did something radical, and expanded the figure/ground relationship to physically engage the viewer. The "continuity" Johns wrote about in "Sketchbook Notes" now includes us. It is possible that he had initially explored this in *In the Studio* (fig. IX: 1) and *Racing Thoughts*, which contain things that presumably extend into our space. This inclusion of the viewer is particularly evident in *Catenary (Henri Monnier)* (fig. XI: 4), where we become the figure looking at a figure spying on a couple making love behind a four-panel screen. Our view is interrupted by the screen and by the string suspended from outward-tilting wooden slats attached to the painting's right and left sides. Here Johns seems to have been wondering whether we are looking or spying. In turn, we may well ask: How are these actions connected, and how are they distinct from each other? Unable to easily answer these questions, we might feel compelled to consider our own relationship to the painting. In doing so, we look at ourselves looking; we spy on ourselves.

The painting's title cites Henri Monnier, a little-known but once-popular nineteenth-century satiric illustrator whose work Johns saw reprinted in the *Times Literary Supplement*.[5] The Monnier illustration that Johns incorporated into his painting depicts the anonymous voyeur with an erection, its shadow visible on one of the screen's panels. The voyeur (standing for the spy) is alone with his desire; he is spying on two bodies (standing for the watchman) in a moment of sexual gratification. At the same time, we cannot see back to the moment of our conception, much less the moments leading up to

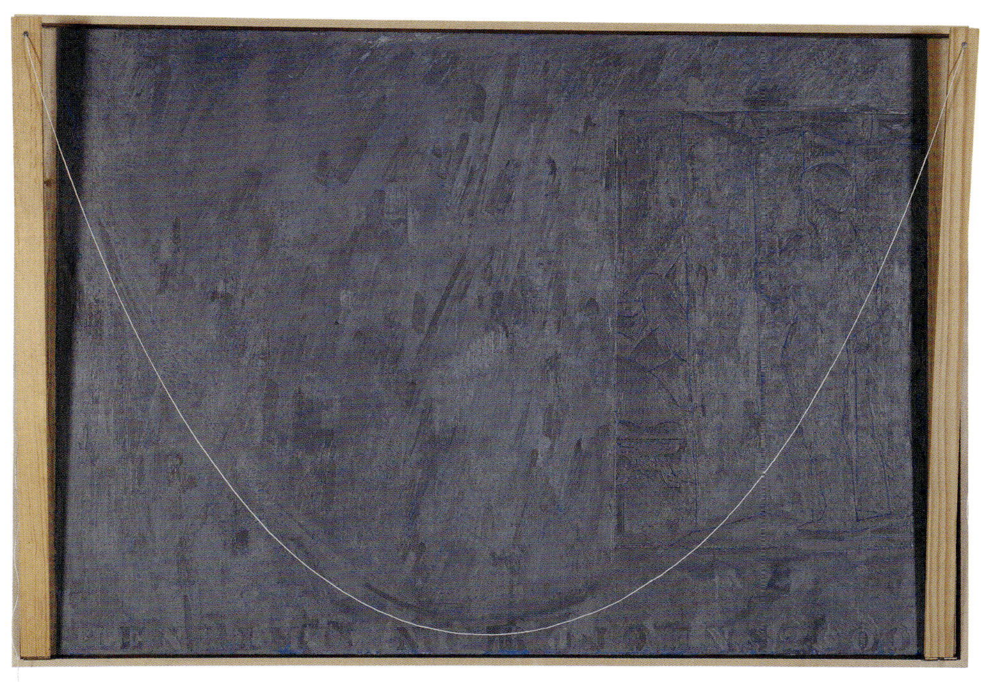

Jasper Johns *CATENARY (Henri Monnier)* 2000 fig. XI: 4
Encaustic on canvas with objects 28 1/8 x 42 1/8 x 3 1/2 in. (71 x 107 x 9 cm)
Private collection

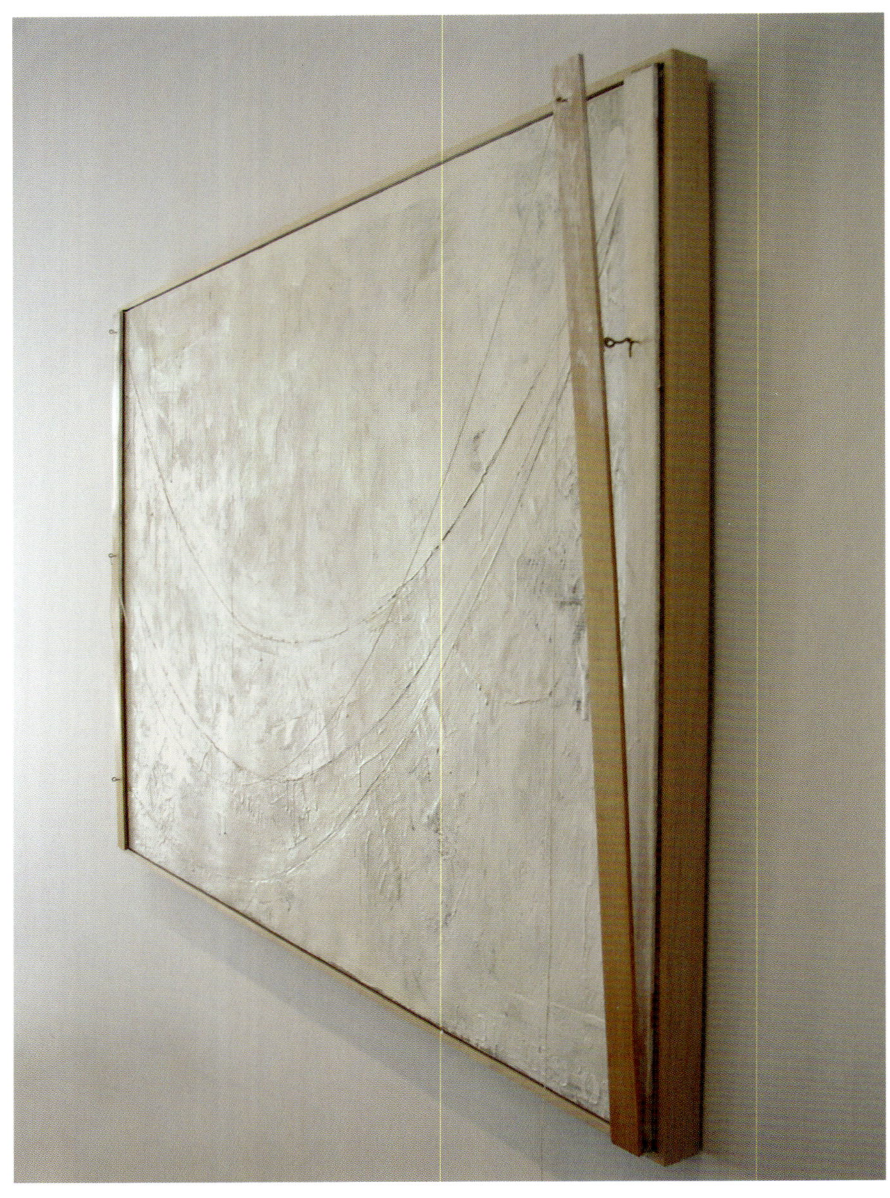

fig. XI: 5 **Jasper Johns** *UNTITLED* (side view showing Catenary structure) 2003
Encaustic on canvas and wood with collage and objects
37 1/2 x 50 1/8 x 4 5/8 in. (95 x 127 x 12 cm)
Private collection

it. And yet those moments are the reason we exist. Much the way he used line to articulate the falling knights in *Perilous Night*, Johns outlined here, in dark blue, the voyeur, screen, and protruding legs of the unseen couple. The scene is contained within a discrete rectangle at the right. Blue is visible along the rectangle's seams, suggesting that there is something beyond even this scene, which is itself about seeing what is happening on the other side. The rectangle has been placed so that its right edge is flush with the faux wooden strip painted beneath the slat extending forward from the bottom-right corner. Strip and slat, with one being a two-dimensional image and the other being palpable, echo each other. The rest of the painting consists of vertical, slightly diagonal, strokes of gray encaustic, with hints of blue peeking through. These falling strokes iterate the catenary's weight. In addition, echoing the arc of the string is a blue line that comes in and out of view; the line is both visual and physical. A second slat extends forward at the composition's left side. Along the bottom edge, the artist stenciled "HENRI MONNIER"; his initials, "JJ"; and "2000," the year he completed the painting. A thin, irregular patch of blue runs along much of the bottom edge, suggesting that Johns started with blue underpainting, to which he applied different tonalities of gray encaustic. The letters and numbers are figures that are inextricable from the ground. The predominance of gray brings the letters and ground into closer proximity; we have to spy everything out. In this largely monochromatic field, there is a subtle, largely downward movement everywhere, from the vertical strokes to the catenary to the tilting slats.

In *Catenary (Henri Monnier)*, Johns continued his inquiry into the figure/ground relationship and the bond between the physical and the visual. In addition, the screen (a layer that limits what is visible) and the seam around the rectangle containing the scene evoke that which can be seen only partially and that which lies far beyond and cannot even be glimpsed. This conjunction of the physical and the visual has been a preoccupation of the artist since his 1955 *Green Target* (fig. I: 2), but in this painting Johns introduced a new element, the catenary, which enabled him to explore this bond from another angle.

The word "catenary" refers to the curve that occurs when a length of rope, string, or chain—of consistent density—is hung between two points. The source for the string, which the artist used in his Catenary paintings, may have been a newspaper photograph of two Rwandan refugees that the artist clipped from the *New York Times*.[6] The standing figure holds an IV bottle, from which a tube runs to the arm of the seated figure. As an image of dependence, the photograph recalls Johns's early drawing *Light Bulb* (fig. III: 1). However, whereas the sculptures stemming from that drawing focused on the bulb, in the Catenary paintings the subject is the connector, which stretches across the painting, creating a slight but noticeable barrier. In *Catenary (Henri Monnier)*, the string hangs down from the two forward-tilting slats attached to each side of the painting (see fig. XI: 4). Affixed near the top of the slat, the arcing string interferes with our ability to see the scene of the voyeur in its entirety. Its placement recalls Johns's line of questions in "Sketchbook Notes": "If the spy is a foreign object, why is the eye not irritated? Is he invisible? When the spy irritates, we try to remove him."[7] On the one hand the catenary is a barrier, and in that regard parallels the screen: each prevents us (voyeur *cum* spy) from seeing everything. On the other hand, by making us aware that we are physically separated from the painting, the catenary underscores the individually distinct but connected existence of sight and the physical body.

At the same time, the string relates to Johns's use of Picasso's *Woman in Straw Hat* in *Untitled (A Dream)* (figs. X: 2, 3). Picasso's painting depicts a form in which mind and body have been joined. Like *Woman in Straw Hat*, the catenary is a thing in which every part is connected and sensitive to external circumstances. Because the catenary is both an obstacle and a signal of the abstract unity of mind and body, it conveys the possibility of a metaphysical threshold. If we were able to exist on the other side, would our minds and bodies be united? The discrete rectangle in *Catenary (Henri Monnier)*, with its suggestion that something else remains to be seen, implies that the answer remains hidden. With a string hovering between the painting's surface and us, the artist further explored the implications of the relationship between *here* and *there*. Also, because of its sensitivity to external circumstances, the catenary opens the painting to the very air of the place it inhabits. Johns has brought time, change, and the viewer into play in a new way.

Historically, it has long been assumed that painting could not open itself up to real time, and that time passing and painting are incommensurable. A painting inhabits an aesthetic zone that is parallel to life, but also separate from it. It is a frozen moment and, in that regard, an illusion. Just as his *Flag* initiated a new way to think about painting, Johns's Catenaries mark another insight: they define change as an essential element of our experience, both visually and physically. In these paintings, Johns juxtaposed stillness (encaustic) and movement (string) as he literally screwed the two together. In addition, both encaustic and string are vulnerable to external circumstances. Gravity is the sole master of the catenary, as it is for us all. The catenary is suspended and affected by its physical circumstances; its interaction with reality will continue even after we are no longer standing in front of the painting.

Near the Lagoon (fig. XI: 6) offers us the chance to further examine what Johns might have meant when he told Richard S. Field, "I think that most art which begins to make a statement fails to make a statement because the methods used are too schematic or artificial. I think that one wants from a painting a sense of life. The final suggestion, the final statement, has to be not a deliberate statement, but a helpless statement. It has to be what you cannot avoid saying, not what you set out to say."[8] The title of the painting refers to a body of water that the artist can see from his house in the Caribbean, and suggests that it is the work's ostensible subject. Johns made it in the studio of that house and, for a time, hung it on the one wall large enough to accommodate it.[9] As I see it, in order for him to avoid making a deliberate statement, he would have had to reject the conventions for depicting water established since the mid-nineteenth century (the seascapes of Gustave Courbet come to mind) because they would be too "schematic or artificial." At the same time, given his philosophical understanding of the proximity and discreteness of the senses, the challenge before him must have been how to make a work that was visual and visceral, ocular and haptic. Encaustic again proved to be the perfect material for Johns's inquiry.

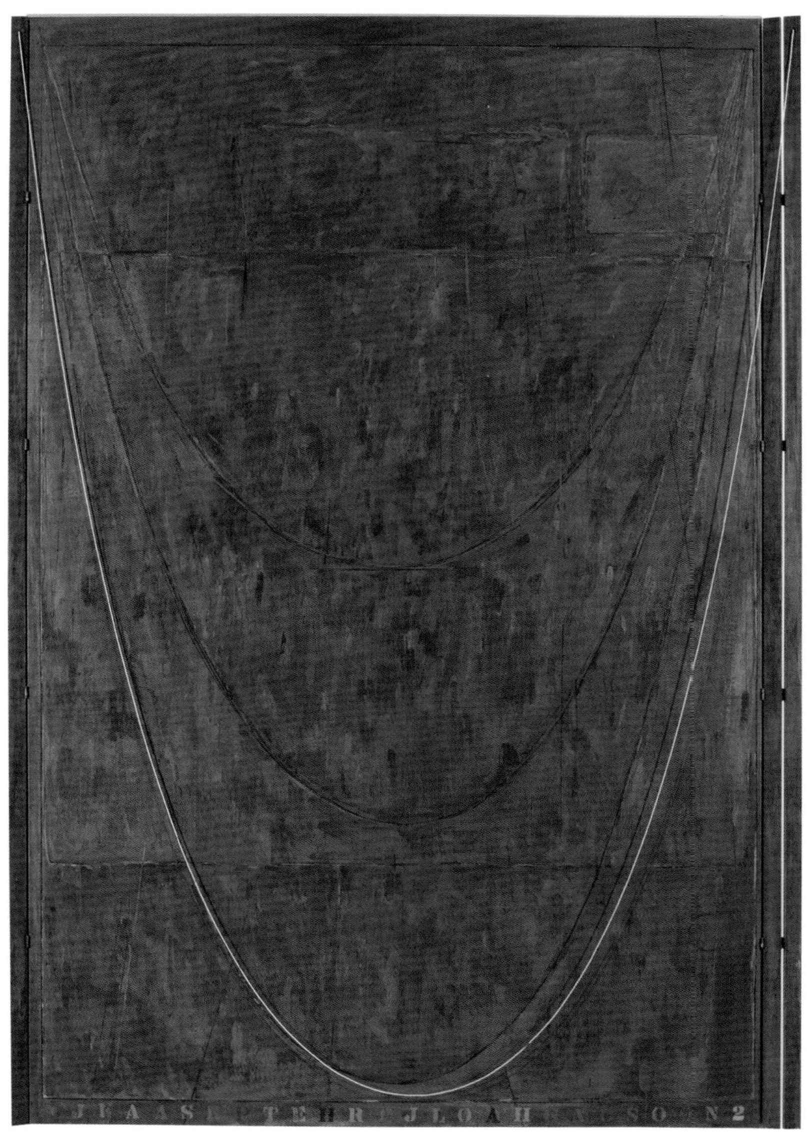

Jasper Johns *NEAR THE LAGOON* 2002–03 fig. XI: 6

Encaustic on canvas and wood with objects 118 7/8 x 78 3/4 x 4 in. (301.9 x 200 x 10.2 cm)
The Art Institute of Chicago. Through prior gift of Muriel Kallis Newman in memory of Albert Hardy Newman

Near the Lagoon is flanked by wooden slats painted more or less the same gray as the monochrome ground. The wooden component on the right side, however, consists of two strips vertically hinged to each other and to the painting's edge. The slats can swing in or fold out, causing the string attached to them to sway. Unlike the tilting slat attached to *In the Studio*, or that attached to *Bridge* (fig. XII: 1), the hinged pieces in *Near the Lagoon* might have been inspired by the painted doors of the *Isenheim Altarpiece*. The double slats on the right disturb the seeming symmetry of the composition, as well as reinforce the perception that the entire painting, not just the string, is not static. This is because the double slats enable the catenary to shift its curve, so that it is not always aligned with the work's central axis. Because the hinged elements suggest that something could be closed over the painting, they call attention to the work's vulnerability to the elements, subtly inflecting the painting's title. It is "near the lagoon" and near dissolution. As in many other works by Johns, something (dissolution) is echoed by something else (catenary).

Johns attached four pieces of linen canvas to the painting's surface. Two are located above a larger one that covers most of the painting; the fourth is found between the largest one and the bottom edge. Johns initially painted the insets and the spaces between them in red, yellow, and blue, with a specific color applied to each inset or space. In a remarkably detailed essay on *Near the Lagoon* and how it was made, conservators Kelly Keegan and Kristin Lister stated that Johns marked a grid of five-inch intervals on the linen support and then used a thread to attach the canvas pieces to it. After unifying the ground and the insets with iron-oxide red, he painted the areas not covered by them iron-oxide yellow. Finally, he applied ultramarine blue to the area outside the rectangle made by the insets and blank spaces.[10]

The thinly applied gray encaustic allows the red underpainting to glow through the mottled surface. Johns intensified the space evoked by the red underpainting with diagonal tan and gray lines that dance ever so lightly over the surface. Johns further complicated the lines by tracing the progressive lowering of the catenary. In order to execute these looping lines, Johns impressed a cord into the encaustic, covered it with encaustic strokes, and then pulled up the cord after the encaustic hardened. This registered the curve as a groove, as well as pulled up some of the underpainting, so that glints of red, yellow, and blue are visible. Shifts between stability and instability on the painting's surface make us think that our eyes are playing tricks on us.

Keegan and Lister pointed out that "Johns engages the surface as a whole, a separate entity from the individual strokes as the skin of the lagoon is separate from the depth below, employing a variety of methods to shape the overall texture and sheen of the work." They continued: "Close inspection of the surface reveals a series of concentric semicircles radiating from the upper left like ripples in a pond...." The authors surmised that in order to offset the "the gloss from reheating" the encaustic, which had to be done in order to seal the painting, Johns used a number of instruments, including one that made a semicircle, to break up the surface.[11] In each of his actions, we sense that the visual and the physical are always connected, and that he is constructing something, rather than trying to make an image.

As in *Flag*, Johns treated *Near the Lagoon* as a thing in which surface and depth are inextricably linked. Both paintings are layered objects that cannot be seen all at once. The difference is that in *Flag*, the artist aimed to make something that resembles the American flag. In *Near the Lagoon*, his goal was not resemblance, although the imprinted, concentric circles and the layering not only convey the lagoon's surface and depth but also the wax's possible interactions with light. It seems to me that in exploring a dream, a scent, falling snow, and a changing body of water, Johns has sought to reconstruct his perception of a moment of transformation. The primary difference between the early paintings and the more recent ones lies in in the evolution of Johns's consciousness of time, and his increasing awareness of death pressing ever closer.

The catenary is the latest manifestation of helplessness in Johns's oeuvre. It belongs to the same family as the arm in *Land's End* (fig. V: 1); the inverted chair and cast in *Watchman* and *According to What* (fig. VI: 1, 2); the tactile, waxen drips in encaustic paintings such as *Weeping Women* (fig. VIII: 1); the rotated knights in *Perilous Night*; and the artist's shadow in *The Seasons*. In *Near the Lagoon*, the catenary hangs down to a point just above a row of stenciled letters and numbers, a mixture of the artist's name, the painting's title, and the date: "N J E A A S R P T E H R E J L O A H G N O S O O N 2." Beginning with the "N," we can, in our mind's eye, disentangle and rearrange the stenciled letters to get "NEAR THE LAGOON JASPER JOHNS 02." In order to disengage the letters, we must textually engage with the painting. By separating the letters of the title, the date, and his name and then placing them so that they alternate with one another, Johns established that the body (the artist) has moved closer to dissolution (lagoon); he has detailed his own passage in time (2002). The letters hover on the brink of chaos, but have not yet fallen into that realm. Still solid, the wax has not yet melted everything together. The proximity of the body to chaos is further inflected by the close but distinct gray tones that Johns used in both the stenciled letters and the surrounding ground. Their palpability reminds us that the body is a thing, not an image or an idea, and that it is always at the mercy of time.

CHAPTER 11
NOTES

1. Scott Rothkopf, "Suspended Animation," in *Jasper Johns Catenary*, exh. cat. (Gøttingen: Steidl Publishers, 2005), p. 5.

2. See for example Michael Kimmelman, "Sifting among the Icons for the Key to Johns," *New York Times* (Oct. 18, 1996), pp. C1, C32.

3. Rothkopf (note 1), p. 6. "The introduction of a Grünewald soldier in *Perilous Night* incited an iconographic truffle hunt on the part of critics eager to decode the new output of an artist whose work had never before seemed to require such decoding. Johns famously grew annoyed with this interpretive quest, and he introduced the unknowable—at least for us—'green angel,' an image whose source he chose to keep obscure. It was as though he wanted us simply to *look*, not to *read*, but even this proved impossible for an audience that had grown accustomed to teasing out obscure points of reference."

4. Jasper Johns, "Sketchbook Notes," *Art and Literature* (Lausanne) 4 (Spring 1965); repr. in *Jasper Johns: Writings, Sketchbooks, Notes, Interviews*, ed. Kirk Varnedoe, comp. Christel Hollevoets (New York: Museum of Modern Art, 1997), pp. 37, 59.

5. Rothkopf (note 1), p. 18 and n. 39.

6. Ibid., p. 8, fig. 10.

7. *Jasper Johns: Writings* (note 4), pp. 37, 60.

8. *www.yale.edu.opa28.n17story4.html*

9. I remember first seeing the painting in the artist's residence in Saint Martin, F.W.I., in the winter of 2005–06.

10. Kelly Keegan and Kristin Lister, "A Shifting Focus: Process and Detail in 'Tennyson' and 'Near the Lagoon,'" in James Rondeau, Douglas Druick, et al., *Jasper Johns: Gray*, exh. cat. (Art Institute of Chicago: 2007), pp. 162–73.

11. Ibid., p. 171.

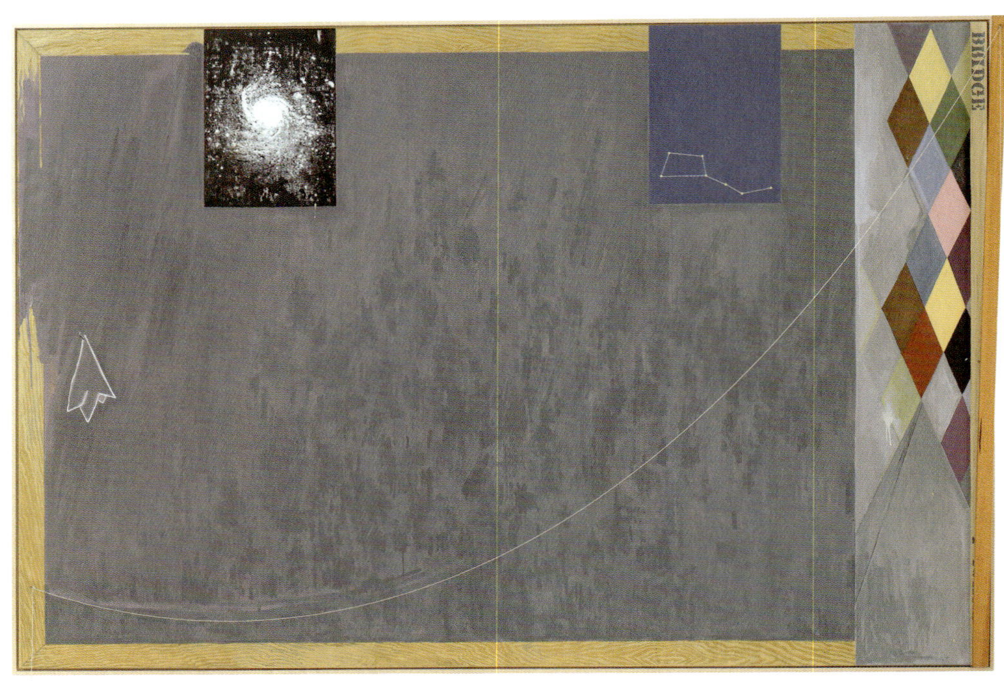

fig. XII: 1 **Jasper Johns** *BRIDGE* 1997
Oil on canvas with objects 78 x 118 x 8 in. (198.1 x 299.7 x 20.3 cm)
San Francisco Museum of Modern Art. Anonymous gift

Chapter 12

I.

One of the recurring elements in the Catenary paintings is a colorful diamond pattern, which runs vertically and is usually flush or nearly so with the canvases' right edges.

Johns included the diamond pattern in his first Catenary, *Bridge* (fig. XII: 1), *Untitled* (1997), *Untitled* (1998), and *Catenary (I Call to the Grave)* (fig. XII: 2). For Scott Rothkopf, the pattern "summons Picasso's harlequin,"[1] but in an interview, Johns stated that, when working on these paintings, he did not have Picasso specifically in mind.[2] This suggests that the artist was thinking more generally of the harlequin, the classic Commedia dell'Arte character who is both a clown and an acrobat. More agile physically than mentally, he is a familiar symbol in literature, art, music, and dance of the solitary, misunderstood artist. For example, Charles Baudelaire described the figure's dualistic nature in his prose poem "Le Vieux Saltimbanque" ("The Old Clown").[3] Johns's interest in the harlequin seems to derive from his own split figure of otherness, the watchman and the spy (see Chapter Six). But I would argue that he does not embrace the Romantic view of the artist as isolated figure, but rather he sees us all as harlequins, solitary beings possessing body (the watchman) and mind (the spy).

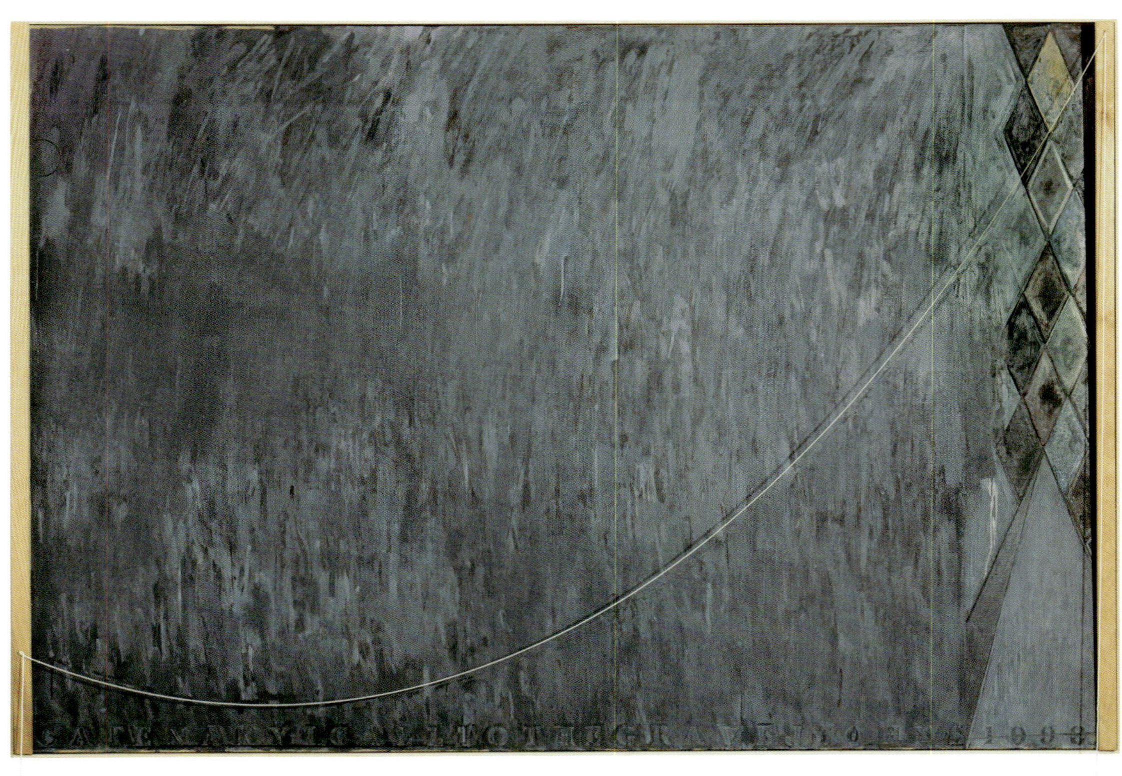

fig. XII: 2 **Jasper Johns** *CATENARY (I Call to the Grave)* 1998
Encaustic on canvas with wood and string 78 x 118 x 8 in. (198.1 x 299.7 x 20.3 cm)
Philadelphia Museum of Art. Purchased with funds contributed by Gisela and Dennis Alter, Keith L. and Katherine Sachs, Frances and Bayard Storey, the Dietrich Foundation, Marguerite and Gerry Lenfest, Mr. and Mrs. Brook Lenfest, Marsha and Jeffrey Perelman, Jane and Leonard Korman, Mr. and Mrs. Berton E. Korman, Mr. and Mrs. William T. Vogt, Dr. and Mrs. Paul Richardson, Mr. and Mrs. George M. Ross, Ella B. Schaap, Eileen and Stephen Matchett, and other donors in honor of the 125th anniversary of the museum, 2001

In the four Catenaries and three subsequent works (see below) that feature a diamond pattern, Johns continued probing his lifelong preoccupations: the figure/ground relationship, the transformation of one thing into another, and living in time. In these interrelated concerns, as I have argued throughout this book, I see the artist examining and contemplating what it means to be a thing both buffeted by and responsive to time. Johns's exploration of these issues led him early on—from at least 1960, the year he made the two sculptures entitled *Painted Bronze* (figs. III: 4, 5)—to an inevitable question: How do we look without flinching at the impending chaos of our inescapable demise? Part of his answer, as his proximity to mortality increases by the day, is that he maintains the same curiosity, humor, and analytic attitude that have characterized his approach since he completed *Flag* (fig. I: 1) over fifty years ago.

Another response can be detected in the title Johns gave his first Catenary, *Bridge*. Moving away from work in which he had juxtaposed similar but not quite identical objects (such as stacked flags, ale cans, numbers, letters of the alphabet), Johns shifted his focus in the Catenaries to the exploration of the bond between seemingly disparate things that were neither actual objects nor depicted ones located within a room or taped to a wall, and between beginnings and endings, especially as they happen across a large expanse of time. It seems to me that in the Catenaries he wanted to achieve a continuity among things separated across time and space, and that the catenary (or string) enabled him to do so. With their gray grounds, as well as the recurring motif of the spiral galaxy, a number of Catenaries evoke a solitary individual at night, looking back at the past as well as forward to the future, and how in that act of remembering and contemplation disparate things are put together. This interest in unlikely associations stems back at least as far as the early 1990s, when the artist made a connection between his adaptation of Picasso's *Woman in Straw Hat* (fig. X: 2) and an illustration Bruno Bettelheim included in an article that Johns had read years earlier (fig. X: 4).

In *Untitled* (1987) (fig. X: 5), Johns had registered three kinds of looking on the three pieces of cloth he depicted nailed to his rendering of the diseased figure in Matthias Grünewald's Temptation of Saint Anthony panel (c. 1512–16). From left to right, they are: looking inward or remembering, looking out at the world, and looking back and forth in time. In eschewing nails in the Catenaries so that the insets along the top of the compositions seem to be deposited within the paintings' monochromatic, gray grounds, Johns seems to have been attempting to bring different kinds of looking into closer propinquity, as well as to mark the progress time has made in bonding figure and ground. This growing unity is reinforced by the curving catenary. While, as noted in Chapter Eleven, it is a barrier, physically and visually interrupting our view of the work, it is also a "bridge" that joins things dispersed across the painting's surface.

On the far right of *Bridge*, flush with its right edge, is a colorful diamond pattern painted to look like an inset. The pattern is contained within a vertical band whose light-gray encaustic ground methodically covers some of the diamonds. A slightly darker gray pyramid rises from the bottom edge; its sharp tip and sloping sides suggest that it is the space between two pant legs that extend beyond the band's edges. In joining the pyramid's lines with the flat lozenge pattern above, Johns indicated the transformation of a three-dimensional form into a two-dimensional design. The joining of pyramid and diamond pattern also suggests an acrobat balancing on a point, which enables us to read the catenary in another way; it is the tightrope the artist must traverse in order to see what is on the other side, as well as what joins him to past and future. To the right of the pattern is a wooden frame on which Johns stenciled the word "BRIDGE." This is mirrored by the repetition of "BRIDGE" stenciled in the reverse direction on the inside surface of the slat extending away from the painting (to which it is attached by a hook and an eyelet). The string curves down from the top of the extending slat to the bottom-left side, where it is attached to a trompe l'oeil wooden board. This board frames three sides of the painting: top, bottom, and left.

In the four Catenary paintings that are horizontal in format and contain the diamond pattern, there is a progressive merging of the containing wooden frame (form) and the gray field (dissolution). This progression continues a preoccupation present in *Painted Bronze (Savarin can with brushes)* (fig. III: 5), the three Map paintings (see fig. IV: 2), *Land's End, Device* and *Periscope (Hart Crane)* (figs. V: 1, 4, 5), and *Untitled* (figs. X: 14, 15); dissolution is gaining the upper hand, and nothing can be done to stop it. In *Bridge*, the gray encaustic ground extends over the painted board on the left, near the top. In *Untitled* (1997), it drips from the bottom edge of the board depicted along the topmost edge, as well as bleeds through the board's grain. The ground (dissolution) has started to rise, soak through, and spill from the porous figure (frame), evoking the moment when they become fully merged. Sand, which the artist mixed into the encaustic, is particularly prominent at the bottom right of *Untitled* (1997), where the dark-gray field abuts the board. Here the rough ground extends over the board's top edge, as well as collects on it like mold or fungus. In *Untitled (Halloween)* (fig. XII: 3), the artist used dark-gray encaustic to cover all three boards, traces of which peek through. In *Catenary (I Call to the Grave)*, there is no trace of any boards in the vigorously applied field of vertical strokes of varying grays, which also cover part of the diamond pattern. Moreover, the diamond pattern is darker, with each colored facet muted by a layer of semi-transparent gray encaustic. In this work, Johns linked the ground with a grave and with dissolution by extending the encaustic over part of the lozenge design. The acrobat is partly subsumed by both dark-gray encaustic and dripping, melting paint. Furthermore, the painting's title, artist's name, and date have been stenciled in different tones of gray along the bottom; executed in encaustic, the letters are now the same as the ground. This is in telling contrast to earlier works, such as *Gray Alphabets* (fig. I: 5), where the letters are made of cut paper, and so many others where they are stenciled over the ground.

In *Bridge* Johns employed the string to both pair and connect
a number of elements: the physical (the extending wooden slat)
with the illusionistic (the trompe l'oeil board);
a glimpse of infinity (the spiral galaxy) with humankind's attempt
to bring order to reality's constantly changing nature
as well as to make vastness more palatable (the Big Dipper
with lines connecting the separate stars); order (the diamond pattern)
with chaos (the gray field); plasticity (the pyramid)
with flatness (the diamond pattern).

II.

The artist made another, subtle link between the attached cloth and the pyramid, in that both are volumetric forms that have largely been compressed and flattened. Recalling Pablo Picasso's etching of a weeping woman biting her handkerchief (see fig. VIII: 2), the intersection in *Bridge* of the board and the gray ground extending over it suggests that the ground will one day consume the cloth, and the surrender will be complete. Other than in a graphite and ink drawing, also called *Bridge* (1997), in subsequent Catenaries the pinned cloth disappears, while the borders of the gray encaustic ground expand. At the same time, as in *Perilous Night*, which marked the artist's transition from layered surface to shallow, layered space, the pinned cloth evokes farewell and surrender, in this case registering Johns's shift from pictorial space to something more compressed.

In the narrow *Untitled* (1998), Johns juxtaposed the lozenge pattern with a fire-breathing dragon, a braid of hair, and Asian-style "frog" buttons, all of which evoke an embroidered Chinese robe. According to the artist, the costume was inspired by a childhood memory of dressing up for Halloween.[4] This association is echoed in *Untitled (Halloween)*, a subsequent painting that also contains these motifs. The costume comprises four distinct rectangles fitted together: above are two sections joined by buttons; below are the other two sections, with the two trouser legs. Both the harlequin pattern and the Chinese robe represent instances when one becomes someone else, when the "I" becomes the Other. In exploring this moment of transformation, Johns expanded upon the instant in the dream of the ancient Chinese poet Chuang Tzu in which he becomes a butterfly (see Chapter One). Dressed up, one can become someone or something else.

By pairing the lozenge pattern (the harlequin as Other) and the Chinese costume (a specific memory), Johns was able to connect a moment of transformation with one that was more autobiographical and, at the same time, culturally widespread. Children worldwide are encouraged to transform themselves through specific rituals, costumes, and play. In this pairing, Johns revealed the diamond pattern to be a metonym for either a bodiless figure or a costumed identity. We see clothing but no body, which recalls the left side of Johns's 1983 *Racing Thoughts* pictures (figs. IX: 3, 4). Those works include a jigsaw puzzle bearing the face of Johns's longtime dealer, Leo Castelli, and a pair of tan pants. As a costumed identity, however, the diamond pattern evokes the poster of the *Mona Lisa* on the right side of *Racing Thoughts*. The difference, which is significant, is that, in the

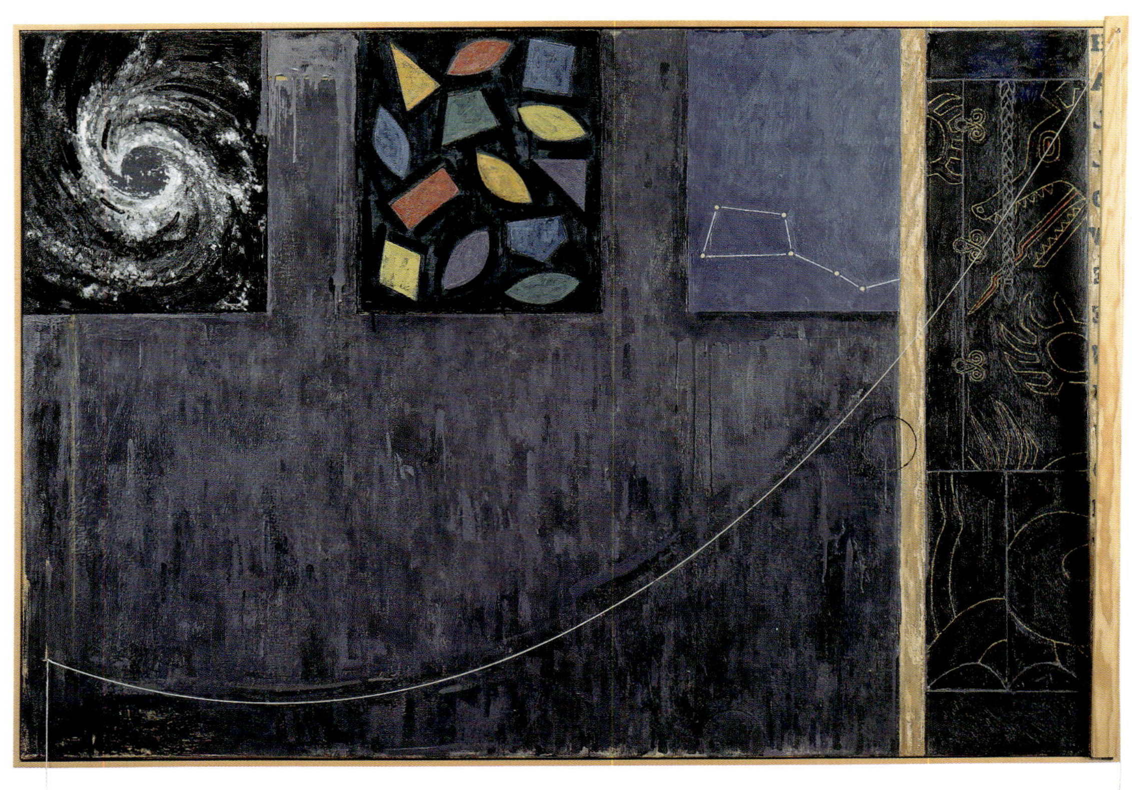

fig. XII: 3 **Jasper Johns** *UNTITLED (Halloween)* 1998
Encaustic on canvas and wood with objects 44 x 66 x 6 in. (111.8 x 167.6 x 15.2 cm)
Collection Marguerite and Robert Hoffman, Dallas

Catenary, the costume (or identity) has become synonymous with the body. Thus, body and mind have moved into closer proximity, a perception reinforced by the looping string, which is a physical indicator of unity.

Although Johns is never explicit about this, it seems to me that he believes that body and mind become synchronized in death; it is the moment when everything begins to fit together. For all the disquiet his pairing of diamond pattern and Chinese costume might create, in *Untitled (Halloween)* a childhood memory seems to have been recollected in relative tranquillity, even though the artist directly acknowledged time's passing by covering three of the four boards framing the gray encaustic field with gray encaustic. The one board left bare is that which separates the Chinese costume on the far right from the gray encaustic field and its three insets, which suggests that the figure is both connected to his memory and observing it from the outside. This dualism brings to mind Johns's watchman and spy, as well as raises a question: Which part of us is involved in remembering? "The spy," as Johns told us in "Sketchbook Notes," "must remember & must remember himself and his remembering."[5] It is the mind (spy) that takes away the information, not the body (watchman).

The insets along the top of the painting are a spiral galaxy on the left; a black rectangle filled with different-colored geometric shapes, including diamonds, rectangles, and triangles, in the middle; and, nearest the Chinese costume, the Big Dipper on the right. All three are manifestations of light, with the one in the middle being Johns's version of a paper lantern that was part of his memory of the Chinese Halloween costume. Extending his exploration of three kinds of looking in *Untitled* (1987), here the artist detailed two sources of light (natural and manmade) and two kinds of patterning (also natural and manmade), and acknowledged a continuum between the finite (lantern) and the infinite (spiral galaxy), and between the solitary individual (the lantern) and the many (the galaxy). Johns's recognition of the bond between the one and the many as being constituted by time's passing can be traced all the way back to the blue canton with white stars in *Flag*. In that painting, the stars, isolated from one another, share a common experience: night. We are all friendless dreamers journeying on our own through the dark. Contrary to what a flag symbolizes, there is no solace.

The inclusion in *Untitled (Halloween)* of an image of the Big Dipper suggests that Johns recognizes that he is part of something larger, even as he remains alone within that constellation of things. The spiral galaxy and the Chinese lantern respectively evoke contemplating infinity and remembering something, and signal the presence in this painting of a realm that is between the *after* and the *before* (see Chapter Three). Covered with gray encaustic, the boards imply that Johns understood the painting to be the Other over which he has some control, the final joining of mind and body. The string that swings down from the slat extending away from the painting (three-dimensional) and over to the gray-encaustic-covered board on the far left (two-dimensional) registers that the transformation from the "I" to the Other, from one kind of material existence to another, is well under way. Developing this investigation further in *Catenary (I Call to the Grave)*, Johns structured this work so that the catenary swings between the tilting slat on the right and the wooden slat on the left. Thus extended outward, the two slats cause the entire painting to become an inset or, as the title suggests, a grave.

III.

In 2003, shortly after he finished the largely white *Untitled* (2003),
the last of the nineteen Catenaries he has made to date,
Johns executed three paintings that incorporate the harlequin pattern:
Bushbaby, *Pyre* (fig. XII: 4), and *Pyre 2*.

In both *Pyre* paintings, Johns located the diamond pattern along the bottom of the canvas. The proportions of the two works are nearly identical to those of *Untitled (Halloween)* and his last Catenary (fig. XI: 6), which suggests that the artist rotated the horizontal format of the earlier paintings until they became vertical. The vertical stacking in the two *Pyres* begins with the diamond pattern at the bottom, above which runs a segmented band containing the letters of the alphabet, and above that a golden field (*Pyre*), and one that is divided symmetrically into black and white (*Pyre 2*).

Both *Pyres* allude explicitly to Picasso's 1915 *Harlequin* (fig. XII: 5), a solemn work made during World War I that depicts a brightly costumed figure whose head is split into a white shape and a black knoblike form (the two parts joined by a toothy, skull-like grin), and a hand that resembles a paw. The knobby form suggests something that has been burned to the bone. With its grinning, misshapen head, Picasso's harlequin recalls Baudelaire's prose poem "The Old Clown," which ends:

> Obsessed with the sight, I looked back, trying to analyze my sudden depression, and I said to myself: "I have just seen the prototype of the old writer who has been the brilliant entertainer of the generation he has outlived, the old poet without friends, family, without children, degraded by poverty and the ingratitude of the public, and to whose booth the fickle world no longer cares to come."[6]

In both Picasso's painting and Baudelaire's poem, the harlequin is a comically grotesque figure who elicits both derision and sympathy. He is the traditional symbol of the doomed artist or poet, the one who remains an outsider, even as he understands what it means to be human. The black, grinning death's head may have inspired Johns to transform Picasso's motifs—the harlequin pattern, the figure's curved belt, the division of his head into black and white shapes—but he eliminated the 1915 canvas's most disturbing elements. Picasso's figure smiles even as mortality overtakes him. By focusing on the geometric design of the harlequin's costume, Johns was able to avoid the obviously tragic aspects of Picasso's work in order to foreground the visual and expressive differences between encaustic and oil.

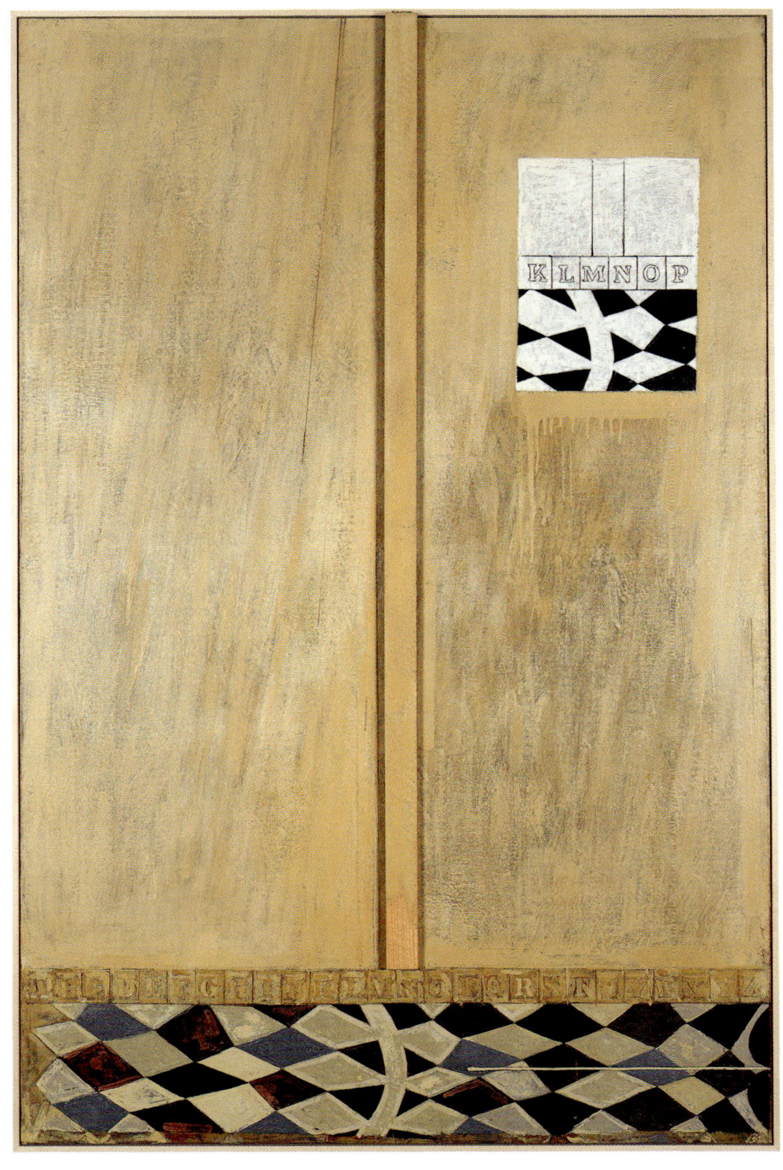

Jasper Johns *PYRE* 2003 fig. XII: 4

Encaustic on canvas and wood with objects 66 1/2 x 44 1/8 x 2 1/8 in. (168 9 x 112 x 5.3 cm)

Private collection

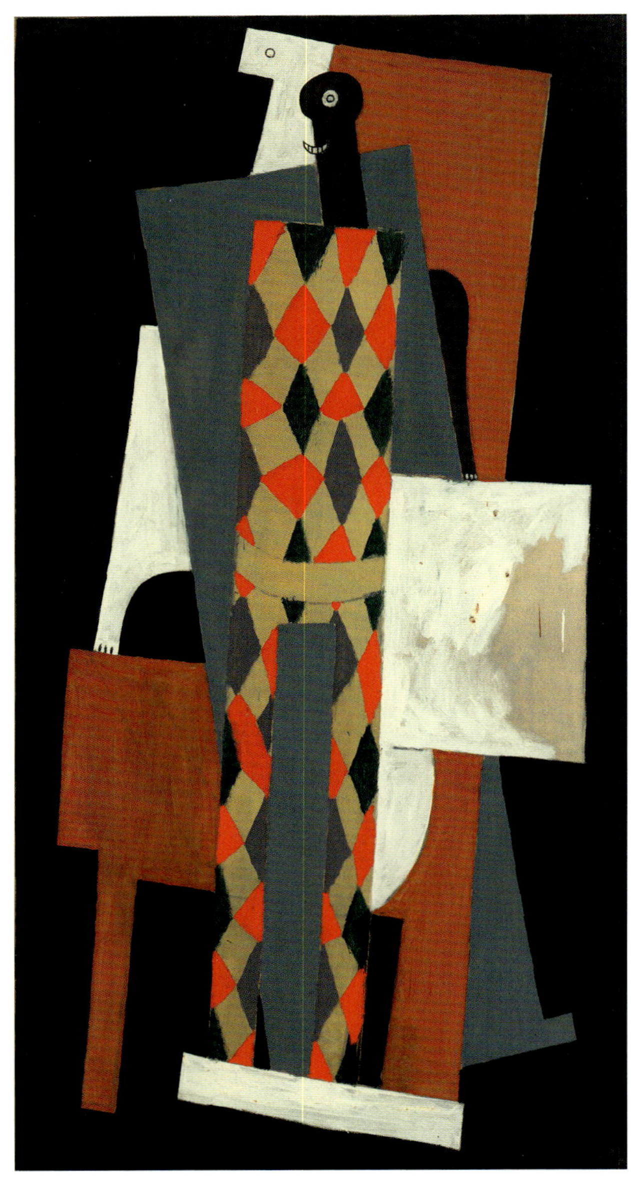

fig. XII: 5 **Pablo Picasso** *HARLEQUIN* 1915
Oil on canvas 72 1/4 x 41 3/8 in. (183.5 x 105.1 cm)
The Museum of Modern Art, New York. Acquired through the Lillie P. Bliss bequest

Pyre was done in encaustic, while *Pyre 2* is in oil. As we know by now, the primary difference between encaustic and oil is that heat is used to seal and set the former, while the latter eventually dries on its own. This material difference suggests why the artist chose to create a golden-yellow field in *Pyre* (evoking the glow of fire) and a mostly black, white, and blue field in *Pyre 2* (conveying the coldness of ash). Derived from the pyramid form with the diamond pattern in the earlier Catenaries, the black triangular shape on the left evokes both a pyramid (sarcophagus) and a bonfire after it has gone out.

In contrast to *The Bath* (1988), where Johns depicted two melting Picassos taped to a wall, he placed the diamond pattern in *Pyre* and *Pyre 2* along the bottom of each composition to suggest a prone body, which, as the works' shared title implies, lies on or before a fire. Picasso also explored this theme in *The Death of Harlequin* (1905–06), but his 1915 painting is far grimmer. In further contrast to both Johns's earlier use of the harlequin pattern and the one in Picasso's painting, the lozenge design in the *Pyres* is more somber in color. It is as if Johns followed through on the implications of the charred-looking head of Picasso's figure. If the two paintings are literally pyres (piles of burning material), then here Johns proposed another understanding of his use of heat, particularly in the encaustic version. At least since *Map*, Johns has concentrated primarily on encaustic's propensity to become liquid. In *Pyre* he focused on the reverse, exploring what would happen if the heat were not removed until the wax burned up.

In *Pyre* and *Pyre 2*, a horizontal row of twenty-six similarly colored rectangles, each of which contains a letter of the alphabet, divides the diamond pattern from the ground above it. Language both separates us from and joins us to reality. The letters are upright in the first painting, while in the second they are rotated to the left so that they are on their sides. Floating above the diamond pattern and row of letters, and to the right of the bifurcating slat, is a pictorial inset (it could also be considered an excerpt), in which a cropped section of the diamond pattern is visible. The cropped section depicts the diamond pattern and the curved belt of Picasso's harlequin, located directly below the middle six letters of the alphabet (K, L, M, N, O, P), which are also included. The shift in placement from the pattern below to part of the pattern above shows that the inset of the figure/pattern and the surrounding ground are totally bonded. The pattern is no longer below, but is now wedded to the ground. Recalling *Flag on Orange Field* (1957), the insets on the upper-right side in the *Pyres* are on the field, as well as partly subsumed by it. Switching to oil in *Pyre 2*, Johns chose a palette of black, white, and blue, which suggests that the fire has subsided, and that the figure has been consumed by the painting (pyre). In this work, Johns not only switched the orientation of the figure, so that its legs extend to the left rather than to the right, but he also placed the band of letters over a depiction of a white slat that seems to move away from the painting. These reversals underscore the perception that the moment of transformation revolves around the instant when all of the elements are composed of the same material and are permanently joined. In death we become our things, which, in Johns's case, are his works of art. Their future is no way guaranteed.

While the evolution of these works over the course of seven years (1997–2003) suggests a narrative, I think that we should resist reaching such a conclusive view. Johns has always been interested in perception, in how we know what we know, rather than in storytelling, and in that regard is not a narrative painter. The coolness with which the artist approaches his loaded subjects conveys his continuing commitment to be a detached but curious observer (spy) who gathers information that the body (watchman) fails to notice.

By removing all of the grotesque features of Picasso's 1915 *Harlequin* or translating them into abstract patterns, Johns extricated the clown/acrobat from its historical context. This stock character is not the artist's alter ego trying to gain our sympathy, but rather a surrogate of Everyman. No longer able to defy gravity, lying prone at the bottom of the painting, Johns's diamond-patterned presence is the most recent manifestation of the implied figures in so many of his earlier works. Beginning with *Flag*, he has dedicated himself to chronicling the journey through time of the solitary individual, and his/her inevitable transformations along the way. In *Pyre* and *Pyre 2*, Johns offered us new insights into that journey, one that has been undertaken by us all.

CHAPTER 12
NOTES

1. Scott Rothkopf, "Suspended Animation," in *Jasper Johns Catenary*, exh. cat. (Gøttingen: Steidl Publishers, 2005), p. 6.

2. Michael Fitzgerald, *Picasso and American Art*, exh. cat., with a chronology by Julia May Boddewyn (New York: Whitney Museum of American Art, in association with Yale University Press, New Haven and London, 2006), p. 315.

3. Charles Baudelaire, *Paris Spleen*, trans. Louise Varèse (New York: New Directions, 1970), p. 25.

4. Gary Garrells, Richard S. Field, and Joachim Pissarro, *Jasper Johns: New Paintings and Works on Paper*, exh. cat. (San Francisco: San Francisco Museum of Modern Art, 1999), pp. 10–12.

5. Jasper Johns, "Sketchbook Notes," *Art and Literature* (Lausanne) 4 (Spring 1965); repr. in *Jasper Johns: Writings, Sketchbooks, Notes, Interviews*, ed. Kirk Varnedoe, comp. Christel Hollevoets (New York: Museum of Modern Art, 1997), pp. 37, 59.

6. Baudelaire (note 3), p. 27.

Index

Photo credits

Photographs of works of art reproduced in this volume have been provided in most cases by the owners or custodians of the works, identified in the captions. Individual works of art appearing herein may be protected by copyright in the United States of America or elsewhere, and may thus not be reproduced in any form without the permission of the copyright owners. The following and/or other photograph credits appear at the request of the artist or the artist's representatives and/or the owners of individual works.

All works by Jasper Johns are © Jasper Johns/Licensed VAGA, New York

All works by Edvard Munch © 2008 The Munch Museum/The Munch-Ellingsen Group/Artist Rights Society (ARS), New York

All works by Pablo Picasso © 2008 Estate of Pablo Picasso/Artist Rights Society (ARS), New York

All works by Frank Stella © 2008 Frank Stella/Artist Rights Society (ARS), New York

All works by Andy Warhol © 2008 The Andy Warhol Foundation for the Visual Arts/Artist Rights Society (ARS), New York

Albright-Knox Gallery, Buffalo: 4, fig. Intro: 1.

© The Andy Warhol Foundation for the Visual Arts, New York: 6, fig. Intro: 2.

Art Institute of Chicago: Photograph by Jamie Stukenberg: 175, fig. XI: 6.

© *ARTnews*, LLC, April 1998: 150, fig. X: 6.

Art Resource, New York: 109, fig. VIII: 2; 119, fig. VIII: 7; 145, fig. X: 2.

Richard Carafelli: 35, fig. II: 2.

Dallas Museum of Art: 68, fig. V: 4.

Fine Art Museums of San Francisco: 85, fig. VI: 4.

Michael Fredericks: 42, fig. III: 1.

Gagosian Gallery, New York: 76, fig. VI: 1.

© Kunstsammlung Nordrhein-Westfalen, Düsseldorf: Photograph by Walter Klein: 84, fig. VI: 3.

Leo Castelli Photo Archives: 129, fig. IX: 4.

Matthew Marks Gallery, New York: 172, fig. XI: 5.

The Menil Collection, Houston: © Hickey-Robertson, 22, fig. I: 5.

© The Museum of Modern Art, New York: 12, fig. I: 1; 15, fig. I: 2; 26, fig. I: 6a; 26, fig. I: 6b, 26, fig. I: 6c; 39, fig. II: 3; 118, fig. VIII: 6; 134, fig. IX: 5; 142, fig. X: 1; 164, fig. XI: 1; 190, fig. XII: 5.

National Gallery of Art, Washington, D.C.: 127, fig. IX: 2.

Offentliche Kunstsammlung Basel: Photograph by Martin Buhler: 169, fig. XI: 3.

The Philadelphia Museum of Art: 32, fig II: 1; 44, fig. III: 3; 47, fig. III: 5; 122, fig. IX: 1. Photograph by Graydon Wood: 182, fig. XII: 2.

Eric Pollitzer: 114, fig. VIII: 4.

© Rheinisches Bildarchiv, Cologne: 46, fig. III, 4; 90, fig. VII: 1; 93, fig. VII: 2; 94, fig. VII: 3.

The Robert Rauschenberg Foundation: Photograph by Jamie Stukenberg, Rockford, Illinois: 52, fig. IV: 1.

San Francisco Museum of Modern Art: Photograph by Ben Blackwell: 180, fig. XII: 1. Photograph by Don Meyer: 62, fig. V: 1.

Smithsonian Institution, Washington, D.C.: 72, fig. V: 5.

Whitney Museum of American Art, New York: 128, fig. IX: 3.

© Dorothy Zeidman: 16, fig. I: 3; 45, fig. III: 3; 67, fig. V: 3; 149, fig. X: 5; 151, fig. X: 7; 154, fig. X: 8; 155, fig. X: 9; 156, fig. X: 10; 157, fig. X: 11; 160, fig. X: 12; 168, fig. XI: 2; 171, fig. XI: 4; 186, fig. XII: 3; 189, fig. XII: 4.

A Thing Among Things: The Art of Jasper Johns by John Yau

Editor: Susan F. Rossen
Production manager: Todd Bradway
Design and typesetting: Anne Galperin

First Edition
Printed and bound in Singapore

Published by:

D.A.P./Distributed Art Publishers, Inc.
155 Sixth Avenue, 2nd Floor
New York, NY 10013

Tel: 212 627 1999
Fax: 212 627 9484
www.artbook.com

ISBN: 978-1-933045-62-7

Library of Congress Cataloging-in-Publication Data

Yau, John, 1950-
A thing among things : the art of Jasper Johns / by John Yau. — 1st ed.
p. cm.
Includes bibliographical references and index.
ISBN 978-1-933045-62-7
1. Johns, Jasper, 1930—-Criticism and interpretation. I. Title.
N6537.J6Y38 2008
759.13—dc22

2008024923